GAY ADVENTURES:
TRUE STORIES OF LUST, LOVE, AND LONELINESS

GAY ADVENTURES:
TRUE STORIES OF LUST, LOVE, AND LONELINESS

Jack Barnhart and Robert A. Schanke, Editors

Illustrations by AnB

Copyright © Jack Barnhart and Robert A. Schanke, 2019

GAY ADVENTURES:
TRUE STORIES OF LUST, LOVE, AND LONELINESS
Illustrations Copyright © AnB, 2019

All Rights Reserved. This book or parts thereof may not be reproduced in any form, stored in any retrieval system, or transmitted in any form by any means—electronic, mechanical, photocopy, recording, or otherwise—without prior written permission of the publisher, except as provided by United States of America copyright.
The right of AnB to be identified as the Illustrator of this Work has been asserted by her in accordance with the Copyright Designs and Patents Act of 1988.

ISBN: 978-0-359-57279-3

Cover Design: AnB

TABLE OF CONTENTS

Introduction   *vii*

1.	Bar, Cinema, T-Room, and Gym	1
2.	Bathhouse	15
3.	Beach, Resort, Park, and Hotel	24
4.	Adult Bookstore	60
5.	Duet	76
6.	First Time	126
7.	Glory Hole	149
8.	Group	156
9.	Married, Divorced	179
10.	Military	205
11.	Student	222
12.	Travel	248

Feedback   *281*

INTRODUCTION

STORYTELLING is on a comeback. Just ask Google. Storytelling festivals now appear at family reunions, libraries, local pubs, even a class at several colleges. It's the "oldest, most reliable form of communication," according to the founder and CEO of Online Newsroom—because it flows more naturally, and because it's real.

The contemporary popularity began in 1988 in Connecticut when enthusiastic storytellers in six locations across the state participated in what they called a Tellabration. The idea quickly caught on so that a mammoth Tellabration now occurs every November in nine countries and in forty states in the US at the same time. Benefits are many, and understandable. Reflecting a sense of community, validating lives and experiences, fostering empathy and pride in one's identity, feeling kinship with others.

Since the cave, men have played "can you top this," and the winner walked away with head held high and reputation boosted. No surprise that storytelling is boldly celebrated by gay men. Maybe women are shy about their escapades, but men love to crow. This is a book of their stories. Imagination can be delicious, especially when boasting about their connections. But unlike most gay anthologies, this is not imagination, not fiction, not fantasy. These stories from hundreds of men are all personal, all true.

For a couple dozen years, I've moderated online a group of scores of gay men, who enjoy swapping erotic photos, websites, and news. Plus, personal stories of their gay discovery and how some have survived, often a challenge in a world that's been slow to understand.

It was October of '17 when I floated the idea to my members that these unique stories needed to be preserved, needed to be passed on. And thus began this project. A variety of ages, walks of life, comfort levels—these stories are all over the charts, from lust, to love, to loneliness. Some have been edited for spelling, punctuation, or grammar, though the original style is intact. Each chapter begins with an original illustration depicting a sample adventure in that chapter.

As we reviewed the stories sent to us, we realized that they fell into twelve distinct situations or locations which are now revealed in our Table of Contents. Taken together, they provide a vivid commentary on what it has been like for gays in America. Particularly in periods when we felt threatened and marginalized, we sought safety and comfort by frequenting bars and cinemas that welcomed gay men and where we might find sexual satisfaction in dark, back rooms. Men's T-rooms and gyms may not have been as immediately promising, but they also were places for us to cruise and to make contacts. For married men who had wives and possibly children, an obvious outlet has been bathhouses, where we could walk the darkened hallways, explore the action in steam rooms, and invite a buddy into an orgy room or a small cubicle—with no names exchanged and no fear of being discovered.

Adult bookstores were another outlet. We could browse the stacks of porn videos and toys, but more brazen was spending a few extra bucks to cruise the small cubicles in the back that consisted of a bench and a TV with porn. Keeping your door ajar meant you were inviting company. Often these little rooms had glory holes in the wall allowing you to peak and poke into the neighboring cubicle and be treated to even more adventure.

Traveling was yet another means of escape from the pressures of the homophobic straight world. We learned how to find gay bars and discos in any big city by heading straight for the warehouse district. Various travel books helped by listing gay-friendly hotels and restaurants. Many privately-owned camps and resorts invited us for special gay-only weekends. Gay cruises were popular. Beaches both in the US and abroad advertised special areas where gays were welcome, usually at a distance from the straight crowd. Sunny and sandy dunes were often busy sites for attitude adjustment.

Several stories feature a recollection of a man's first time with gay sex. It's a typical subject at gay parties, and it seems most gay men remember vividly that first time. Sometimes it was with an experienced person, a relative, a friendly student, and sometimes even with a complete stranger. Whatever the situation, it often brought a mix of excitement and guilt, and would never be forgotten.

Most of us can recall our first time, our exciting adventures when we have traveled, our bold excursions into cinemas and baths and bookstores. Sometimes, these memories are warm and cozy; sometimes ugly and frightening. But they are all real and illustrate what it has been like to be gay in America. Many of the stories in our *Gay Adventures* took place when we were not allowed into the military, not allowed into a same-sex marriage, or when we could lose our job or be evicted—just because we were gay. And although we have achieved many advances in recent years, and we now have the advantage of social media for making contacts, the stigma of our sexuality still exists.

Perhaps more important than the actual stories themselves is the indelible memory the authors have of these stories. Older readers have worn some of these moccasins, and young'uns can see how we have lived, how we have survived, and what might be coming down the pike. In the final section of the book, Feedback, our storytellers have described what it has meant to them to share their stories and what it has meant for them to read the stories of others. We hope you will share their enthusiasm.

In order to contact the editors or the book's illustrator, please send a message to the following email address: weewinkie3@aol.com.

Jack and Bob

BAR, CINEMA T-ROOM, and GYM

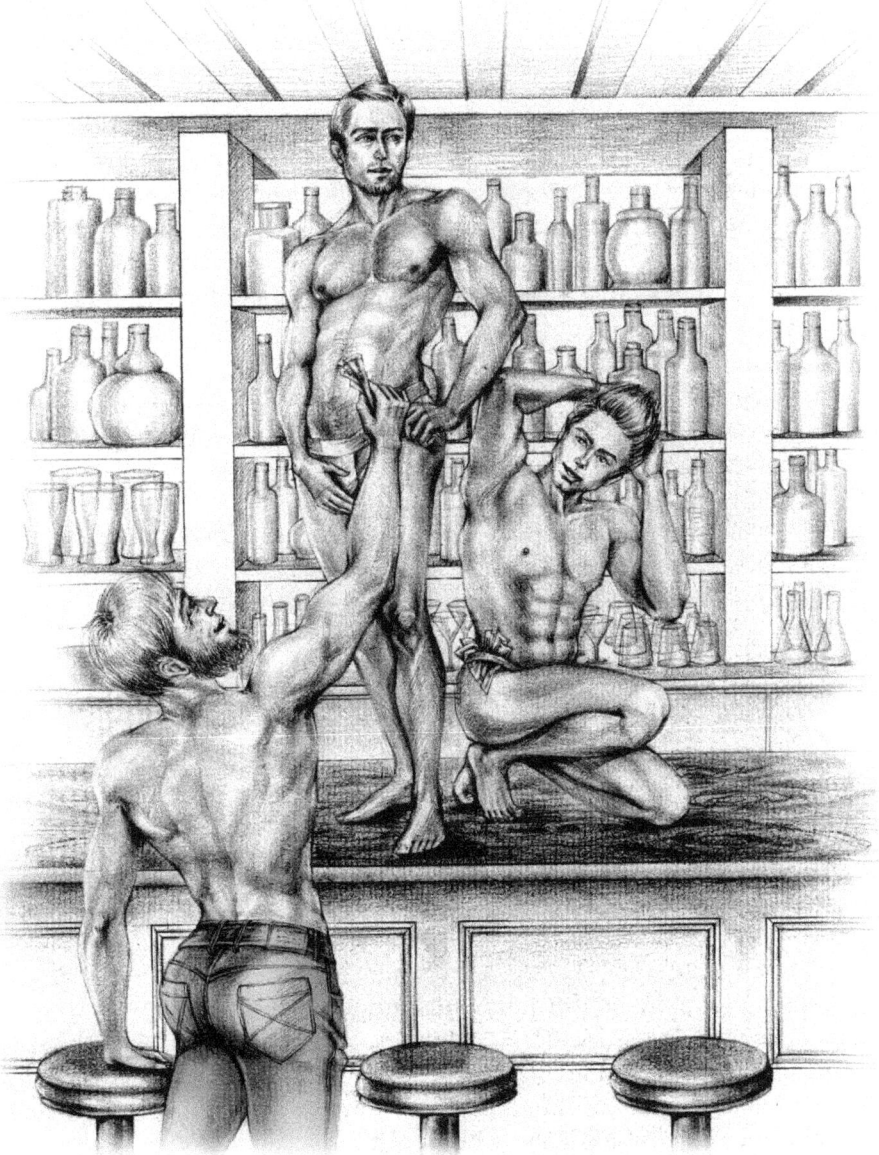

Many years ago, while I was rattling the closet door, I had an assignment in Santa Fe. After I finished my business, I found an adult bookstore that had a local newspaper. So I bought it, and among all the

Bar, Cinema, T-Room, and Gym

personal ads and ads for mail order toys I found an advert for a gay bar. It seems there was only one, or at least that's all that I saw advertised. Since I didn't have to be at the Albuquerque airport until later that night, I thought I'd pay a visit to this gay bar, at least have a drink, and see what they had to offer out-of-town tourists. The adult bookstore wasn't very far from the bar, so I got there in a few minutes.

After I sat in the nearly deserted parking lot for about ten minutes, I finally struck up enough courage to go inside. As soon as I walked in, I realized that I was not dressed for the place. While there were only a few men in the bar, they all had on jeans, a shirt, and a cowboy hat. And there I stood in a business suit. Talk about sticking out like a sore thumb, I was it. Seemingly, each man in the room engaged in making eye contact with me. When I felt that the introductions were over, and I wasn't asked to leave, I went up to the bar and selected a seat about in the middle. As soon as I asked the barkeep for a gin and tonic, I noticed a good-looking man, maybe in his thirties, with a short beard, standing by the juke box with big grin and giving me a nod. I knew I should have ordered a beer.

While sitting there fuming at myself for being such an idiot, this man at the juke box came over with his beer and sat on the stool next to me. He told me his name was Brad and started making small talk about where I was from, what I was doing in Santa Fe, and all that sort of stuff. I don't know why, but he put me at ease, and in few minutes I was asking him the same sort of questions. It turns out that Brad was an art dealer and made his own hours. Today, he felt he needed a break from the routine and came in for a beer. With that, he leaned over and gave me a full, deep kiss. After some unknown time, he broke off the kiss and leaned back. I sat there looking real cool by stammering and stuttering. He asked me if I wanted to continue at his place. All I was able to do was to nod, "Yes." As he got up, I had it together enough to leave a tip for the barkeep, and followed him out.

Naturally, he was driving a truck, and told me he'd wait for me at the parking lot exit. As I'm following him, my heart is thumping wildly and my mouth is as dry as the desert. Pretty soon he pulled into the driveway of this beautiful stucco home. I parked on the street and followed him inside. As soon as we got in and shut the door, he gave me another deep and hard kiss. We were both rubbing our backs and chests as our clothes began to fall off. I don't even remember my coat and tie coming off, but I got his shirt off in no time at all. Damn, he was sexy. Somehow or another we wound up in a bedroom on a bed with clothes coming off pretty damn fast. When we were nude, we took a moment to admire each other's body. We were both in shape by keeping active in a gym, so while neither of us would be ready for a photo shoot, I felt he was hot, hot, hot.

We started kissing again on the bed and somehow manipulated ourselves into a 69 position. Our cocks and balls being nursed drove me to higher senses of joy. I just mirrored what he did to me until I felt I got the gist of it and started sucking his cock and balls with abandon. Then, all of a sudden, Brad stopped sucking and threw my legs up in the air. Oh no—I wasn't getting fucked—no way. Before I could voice my objections, he started tonguing my asshole. This was nothing less than a spiritual experience! I never knew I could feel like this. Talk about climbing the wall. I don't know how I did it, but my feet were walking up the wall. Damn!

After a while we got into a 69 position again, but this time Brad brought some lube. We greased up each other's assholes and got our fingers lubed up. Following Brad's lead, I inserted one finger in his ass and started moving my finger around. Then came the second finger and started hitting the prostate. I wasn't sure where this was going, but it was feeling damn good. Having my cock sucked now with three fingers in my ass, I started feeling like I was about to go over the top. I started making noises and let off Brad's cock long enough to announce that I was cumming. He spit me out long enough to shout, "Me too!"

With that, it only took a few more hits on my prostate to feel something coming straight out of the center of my being that hit my cock with such a force that I literally saw stars. I have no idea how much I shot, but there were jolts and jolts and jolts coming out of my cock into Brad's mouth. Just then, he started to come also with a volume I never imagined. Instinctively, I knew I wanted to swallow his cum but he came so much I couldn't get it all down, and some of it oozed from my mouth.

After sucking on our cocks until they became too sensitive, we turned around and started kissing again. It was strange but wonderful to taste both our cum during this deep kiss and body caressing. We went into his bathroom with an oversized tub and shower where we soaped our bodies in every nook and cranny. We got so hot and bothered that we jerked each other off again. Wow! What a cum. Brad said he needed to get back to the shop, and gave me his card. I still have it in case I ever go back to Santa Fe. I'm pretty sure I'd like Brad to fuck me.

Bar, Cinema, T-Room, and Gym

After the passing of my partner in '99, I took a transfer with my company to San Diego, CA. I lived in Hillcrest, of course, the mini-gay city of Southern California. I lived in a central location with a gay bar, a bath house, and a liquor store, all within walking distance of my apt.

I quickly became a regular at the gay bar. I met a group of guys and, to say the least, we fucked around. I was kinda wild after Ray passed away, I guess trying to fill a void. Anyway, within this group there was this guy named Patrick. We had never messed around, though I really had the hots for him.

Rugged, tall, dark hair, bubble butt. Even though I am a bottom, I can look! Beautiful smile and nice guy. One night, after the bar closed, a bunch of us went to a buddy's house for more beer and talk. I don't remember how we started, but we ended up playing "Truth or Dare."

Kissing, licking nipples, sniffing arm pits. THEN, I was dared to rim Patrick's hole. I was floored and more then eager to do this. Patrick had his pants down in a micro-second. I buried my face between his ass cheeks and began licking his sweet, pink hole. He must have anticipated sex, because he was clean as a whistle. I licked his hole more intensely, grabbing his hips so as to drive my tongue as deep as I could. Then I reached around to hold his now semi-hard cock!

We then realized we were in the middle of a room, with all our friends watching us! We stopped.

But we spent the rest of night taking little looks at each other, a quick smile, a glance. When we stopped for the night, it was obvious that Patrick was going home with me. When we got to my apartment, I walked him into my bedroom, and we undressed each other. I was infatuated with his cock! Thick, great cockhead, decent shaft, well-rounded and full balls. I dropped to my knees. I gave him one of my best blowjobs. He threw his head back as his cock got stiffer, and his cum exploded into my mouth. I slurped and swallowed, trying to get every warm, creamy drop. I'm a bottom, and he knew that when he laid me on the bed, face down, ass in the air, waiting for his pulsing cock. Even though he had just come, he was ready for another round.

He lubed up my hole and guided his cock to my hole. Once his cock was fully embedded in my tight hole, he waited, letting me get used to his girth. Soon he was pumping my hole; we moaned with each stroke. He began to pump me quicker, and he was ready to cum. He pumped two final plunges, and then unloaded another stream of fresh, silky cum.

He pulled out. I rolled him over and slurped the last few drops of cum from his softening cock. Then we slept because, by now, the sun was coming up. We never really dated, though we were fuck buddies. He knew where he would always get a good blowjob and an eager fuck!

It was 1978—I had just turned eighteen, and my parents went out of town to visit relatives for the weekend. Total freedom for a weekend! I decided I wanted to do something naughty, so I grabbed the newspaper, found the movie section, and looked up the address for the porno theater in Greenville—the Flick. The title of the film was *Sex Wish*, starring Harry Reams from *Deep Throat*. It was May, so the weather was hot. I put on a t-shirt and some short shorts—without underwear—socks and tennis shoes and headed to the theater. It was around 6:00 pm when I drove around the parking lot trying to get up my courage. Finally, I parked my Toyota, got out and headed to the entrance.

An old guy barely looked up when I walked in. There was a sign that said "Admission: $10.00". I put a $10 bill on the counter, and he handed me a ticket stub. I walked into the lobby and looked around. The place looked like any other movie theater. I made my way to the entrance to the film. I opened the door and walked in a couple of feet. The place was really dark except for the image on the screen—a blonde girl was sucking a really beautiful cock. My dick got hard immediately. Once my eyes adjusted to the darkness I looked around. There were probably twenty guys spread out in the theater. Most were sitting towards the back, usually alone, except for the back row.

There were two guys sitting next to each other. Both of them had their pants undone and their cocks pulled out. They were stroking each other as they watched the film. I walked past them and took a seat a couple of rows in front of them. Just as I sat down, this guy in the row in front of me turned around, looked me over, and smiled. He was probably in his late twenties with an average build, some beard scruff, and long blond hair. I smiled back and sat down.

By this time, the couple on the screen was fucking; the girl was riding up and down on that big dick. I slowly started rubbing my cock through my shorts. The guy in front of me was obviously stroking his cock through his pants. He looked back again to get my attention. Then he lifted his butt off his seat and pulled his shorts down to his ankles. He was sitting there naked from the waist down. I leaned forward to watch, and he motioned for me to join him. I was scared, but it looked like everybody was there for the same thing. So I moved up a row and sat next to him. I reached over and stroked my cock, and I touched his.

A few minutes later, he had me pull my shorts down. There we were, both naked from the waist down, stroking each other's cocks. It was so hot; I loved feeling so exposed. By then another guy had come into the theater. He saw us, came over, and sat in the row in front of us. Rather than watch the screen, he turned around to watch us. I should have been shy, but I found it a BIG turn-on to be naked in front of these guys and to have someone watch us.

My friend beside me then bent over, put my cock in his mouth, and started sucking me, licking up and down my shaft, then licking my balls. The other guy was watching it all and enjoying it, beating his cock the whole time. Then, my friend got on the floor and lifted my legs. I felt his tongue on my ass, a brand new feeling for me. I moaned out loud! I was in heaven. As he tongued my ass, he grabbed my cock and pumped it. Within a few minutes, I shot my load all over my t-shirt. I came so hard I thought I would pass out.

After I shot, I was embarrassed. I pulled up my shorts, said, "Thanks," as I practically ran out of the theater. I don't know what I was thinking. I guess it was just too much for my young mind to comprehend that I had gotten sucked off in a straight porno theater.

Let's just say I got over being embarrassed and came back the next day and stayed for hours, even stripping completely and fucking one of my new friends while several watched!

Cinema III, upon entry, had video booths to the left and a regular movie screen to the right. I usually went to the booths to get a BJ. Then one evening I decided to go watch a movie. I had never been in a 'regular' movie theater showing porn before—but the old curiosity thing. Upon entering the double doors, I found myself facing a railing with curtains hanging down. You had to turn left to go into the main area of seating. I noticed that there was a slight opening in the curtains right in front of me, so I decided to take a peek in there before entering. I might mention that this was summer, and I had on sweat pants and shorts under them. I pushed the opening up a little bit more to see better and right in front of me were two guys. One on his knees and the other in a seat getting a BJ. I just stood there watching them.

As I stood there watching them, I became aware that another guy had come up behind me, was looking over my shoulder, and also watching. I opened the curtains a little bit more so he could see better. They didn't open much so the guy was standing, basically right behind me and pretty much up against me. I then noticed that I could feel behind me the guy's very ample and hard dick against me. I thought he was enjoying the show as much as I was. Then he reached around me and grabbed my hard cock through my clothes. At first, I thought he just wanted to feel me and maybe rub me a little, but then all at once, he let loose of my dick and pulled my sweats and shorts down and again grabbed my dick before I knew what had happened. He started to stroke me right there. It felt good, so I didn't move away. I let him do that for a bit, while watching the two guys in front of me.

Then I felt the guy behind me move back just a little, but still holding me. I tried to see what he was doing and soon found out without being able to see. He had used his other hand to pull down his own pants. Then he pulled mine lower, and I felt this nice and quite large dick against the crack of my ass. As he was stroking me, he was also rubbing his cock against my ass. Watching the nice BJ in front of me, being jacked by him, and his cock sliding up and down my ass felt really good. Then he was fumbling around a little more and moved back a bit. This time when he pushed against my ass it felt different. He had apparently applied lube of some kind to his dick. I noticed it slid a lot easier. The two guys in front of me kind of turned a bit then—perhaps cramped up or something—and I had to lean a little further to keep watching. As I leaned over more to keep watching, the guy behind me must have thought I wanted something else, and before I could move, his cock was entering my ass.

It was bigger than anything I had had before, so it definitely got my attention, but also, since I was against the railing and bent over, I could do nothing but take it. He did go slowly, but did not stop until it was all in. I was kind of gasping and trying to tell him as quietly as possible, that I didn't really want that, but pinned like I was he just pushed down on me and started to fuck me. Long strokes and it soon felt too darnn good to stop. I was close to cumming anyway and with the added pressure from behind and the show in front of me, I was soon pushing back myself as he came forward into me. I couldn't help it. The guy getting a BJ all at once grunted, and I could tell he was cumming in the other guy's mouth.

This was too much for me. About two minutes later I was cumming, and just a minute or so later the guy behind me was cumming up my ass. He pulled out and was soon gone. It took me a minute or two to recover and pull my pants back up. It was then I found out that there were about four or five guys standing there with their dicks in their hands, jacking off while watching me being fucked. Damn, that was hot, but was the last time I went into the theater part. Great memory I still love to think about.

Back in the day when I was coming out in New York City, I discovered T-Rooms in the Subway. Some were notorious for hot cruising, especially in the evening after work before most men home went to their wives. On one occasion, I met this hot guy in a T-room on the upper West Side around Lincoln Center. I lived near there, so I always got off at that stop. Well, it was a rainy night and no umbrella, so I decided to use the T-room to relieve myself and then eventually cruise.

There were a few guys in there, all rubbing and playing with their cocks. There were two guys going at it with each other in one of the stalls and did not want any company. Also, there were three guys at the urinals, jacking off each other. Well, I was just standing there doing the same thing, and this guy next to me reached over and started rubbing my crotch. He was a little older than me but kind of cute in his own way. So I turned, and we started playing with each other. Then we heard a voice, "OK guys do your business and let's make a move on." Yes, it was a police officer and really not in the mood to make an arrest, but instead get the T-room cleared. So we zipped up fast and left.

Well, this guy met me outside in the upper platform and asked if I lived around here. I said yes! "Can we finish this at your place?" I said sure. Off we went. I lived in a large high-rise building with my grandmother; luckily she was in Florida at the time. When we started walking, he asked where we were going, and I said home. Oh, wow, we live in the same building. Shit! Well, I explained we could still go to my place, and he said why not. His roommate would be home at his. So we went to my place, and since we were soaking wet removed all our clothing and hung them up to dry. While we were doing that there was a lot of groping and touching going on. I was a bit nervous because I had never brought a stranger home before.

Before I knew it, we were sucking face and sucking on each other. My bed was a sofa bed so we opened it up and went at it. He asked me, "Do you rim?" I answered, "What is rimming?" Oh, how his face lit up! He told me to roll over on my stomach and to get on my knees. Well, he showed me what rimming was, and how to do it. I was hooked. I did not want him to stop, and he kept going like it was his last meal to eat my hole. Finally, he had me on my back with my legs up in the air, eating my butt and sucking my cock. I eventually flipped him over and began to rim his ass. He screeched, "For a beginner you sure know your business." That was a great lesson he gave me. We continued playing around with each other's cock and ass for hours, as the rain kept beating down on the windows. We had no place to be or go, so we played for hours.

Finally, his dick was spent and so was he. I made dinner for the two of us, and then we watched TV and played some more. My grandmother was gone for three months, so we had plenty of time every evening and weekends to get together. We decided to play at his apartment, and a few times his roommate would join in. Since it was a studio and everything was open, we had so much fun I wanted to stay in the apartment and never leave. It was a great time to be young, gay, and horny. Eventually, my grandmother's apartment was sold, and I moved away and discovered other T-rooms. But that was my first real T-room extended adventure.

Well, the only story I might have is when I belonged to a gym that was affiliated with our local hospital. Initially, a place for staff and their family to go to exercise and relieve stress but eventually opened to the public. There was even a bar that served cocktails. Anyway, when I joined there was at the same time an influx of muscle men because there was a great weight room. Big muscle hunks, sweating to the iron all day long. Towards the end of the day, a few of the muscle men who had nothing to do but lift gravitated to the locker room. This one guy always chose a locker at the far end of the room from the shower. As soon as he entered the locker room and the door closed behind him, he would strip naked. He would stand in front of his locker, drop his jock into his gym bag, and massage his balls and ass. Then he would pull out a VERY small towel and start the LONG walk to the shower room, I mean SLOWLY because he had to stop at every guy and chat them up, BARE ASS NAKED.

Eventually, he'd make it to the shower room and half the guys there would get boned and turn to face the wall. So he would spend fifteen minutes under the shower with soap suds all around him, spending most of the time on his huge pecs and man-meat. By the time he finished, most of the guys in the shower had gone back to their locker because they knew that the second half of the show was about to start. Muscle Man is the last out of the shower. He goes to a sink and shaves his face, naked. He has to bend down slightly to see himself in the mirror and so his muscle butt is there for all the guys to see—and they all DO see. He takes longer to shave than anyone I ever imagined. Then it's the slow walk back to his locker, way at the opposite end of the room. As he did on the way in twenty-five minutes earlier, he stops by a bunch of the guys to chat, but this time he is semi-boned. He stands by each dude he's talking to, with one leg up on the bench, and his right hand massages his massive left pec, paying attention to his nipple. Frequently, his other hand adjusts his man-meat, slowly, just enough to keep the semi-bone going. I observed this for almost a year as my work schedule allowed me to go to this gym late in the day. I talked to a few guys I got to know, but they did not know if this muscle-god ever "played" with the gym members—sad to say. I think he did it just to show off his muscles and to see how many guys boned in the shower.

Well, that's the only story I have. It's true and I wish I was a member still, but it closed when Lowe's decided it needed to build a store on top of my gym.

I was in my mid-twenties, and Columbus had a Levi leather bar that my future husband and I really enjoyed. I mostly sat and just watched the men go by. One night, what I considered to be one of the hottest men in the place came up and started talking to me. I was very flattered, and surprised that he seemed to find me attractive. He asked if I wanted to walk back into the dance bar. I said, "Sure."

As we walked to the back bar, he was exploring the rip in the back of my 501s. He quickly discovered that he could get a couple of his fingers inside my jeans, and as we walked, he worked his middle finger right up into my hole. He was making me incredibly horny, and I could feel a wet spot forming on the front of my jeans. I was wearing a jock strap, as I remember. He continued to massage my hole, and I continued to get more and more worked up, squirming on his finger as we slowly walked through the bar. I tried to maintain a relaxed expression on my face, but it was getting very difficult. I just wanted to lie down and get fucked!

We stood along the wall, as he continued to finger fuck my hole, smile at me, and whisper hot, dirty talk. He shared that he had a hotel room across the street. He didn't have to ask twice. He took his finger out of me, when we reached the exit, and we were in his room quickly. He literally ripped my Levis off me—I still have them in the bottom of my closet—and I opened his, hooked my thumbs in his chaps, and went to town on his nice, thick, cock. I remember his precum tasted so good.

He grabbed me and pulled me up, throwing me over the bed. He lubed up and was in my loosened hole to the base. He fucked long and hard, and we tried several different positions. I couldn't get enough of his cock. He fucked me until I came, and then he pulled out and blew all over my chest. We played awhile longer, and then both went back to the bar, reeking of sex. I had a difficult time walking, but I felt that fuck for days! Hey, if you are out there, Mike, I'd love a rematch!

I was tapped at my gym to do some testimonial work related to my workouts. Afterwards, the photographer asked me if I was interested in shooting more, and perhaps more graphic. I said yes, being the exhibitionist I am, and loved the process. On my second visit, it was me, the photographer, his lighting apprentice, and his partner. It started off normal enough, but about a quarter of the way through, he wanted me to let go and just be as sexual and erotic as I could possibly be. I made the smart-ass remark that I might need some fluffing, and boy that opened the floodgates. Never had I been the center of so much attention. My photographer put some of his favorite porn on, and it was muscle guys fucking, eating cum, and lots of ass cream pies. I had always loved porn before, but they hooked me bad that time. Today, whenever I shoot, guys eating other guys' cum is a must-have staple and sure keeps me in the mood.

I am a member of a local gym. I usually go in the early afternoons because I work early mornings and want to hit the gym before I get home. There is this one blond, pretty, California guy that is an extreme exhibitionist. He loves to undress when as many as possible are around, and he walks to the showers with towel in hand but NEVER around his waist. Nice cock too—thick, uncut, really meaty—though he may be semi-hard.

Bar, Cinema, T-Room, and Gym

Nice firm, round balls, which I'm sure are filled with warm, creamy cum. Beautiful firm ass cheeks, burly chest, with just the right amount of body hair.

It's an older building, so the showers are four circular water heads, with another four spray heads. Very easy to see your naked buddies, soaping their cocks and balls and caressing their ass cracks. This guy always takes long showers, when the showers are at there fullest. He gets plenty of soap, and then sensually soaps his crack, rolling his balls and soaping his cock with long strokes that always make him semi-hard. Not enough to have his cock stand straight up but it arches forward and looks so damn tasty. After he gets semi-hard he leans back, lathers up his hair, closes his eyes, and with cock protruding out conducts a very sensual shower act.

And drying off is another show. He never dries his feet by raising them up. Instead, he bends down, spreading his ass cheeks, exposing his hole and again "rising" to the occasion. Word is that he has never accepted a sexual invitation nor has he ever been seen partaking in a man-to-man romp.

He may be out of reach, but he sure knows how to sexually motivate our gym crowd. Maybe he's a stripper? DAMN good one too.

I traveled to Las Vegas for a work convention and was staying at Treasure Island Hotel and Casino on The Strip, back in the days when they still had the exciting "Pirate Ship Battle" that took place out in front of the hotel—sadly now replaced by stores. I had decided to take advantage of their gym and spa facilities since it was included in my room fees. Their facilities were great, with a reasonable size gym and decent workout equipment. The attached spa facility was very luxurious, and each person was given a plush terrycloth robe and slippers to pad around in. Some guys watched TV in the main room while I went to shower in the marble showers, all with the hotel's free shampoos and products. There were private massage rooms along a long hall, but a massage had to be booked and paid for in advance, so I skipped that.

Beyond the massage rooms were a large steam room and separate sauna room. Beyond both of those was a large room with two enormous whirlpools and a wet bar where an attendant came in every now and then to serve fruit smoothies. The whirlpool room was empty, so I slipped off my robe and slid naked into one of the whirlpools. Moments later, a handsome, hairy, dark guy came in and did the same but got into the other whirlpool which was about ten feet from mine. He began to talk to me, but I couldn't hear him over the sound of the bubbling water.

He then got up and came over naked to my pool where he scooted over right beside me. After chatting for a few minutes, I learned he was an architect of Greek descent who was from Mexico City. VERY handsome and equally hot. All of a sudden, I felt his thigh against mine under the water and thought it might have been accidental, so I moved my leg away. He moved his closer until we touched again, looked me right in the eye, and said, "You like that?" I grinned my biggest grin and said, "Yeah!" The next moment, he reached over and took hold of my already hard cock and said again, "You like THAT?" And I said again "YEAH!"

At that moment—and I'm not sure if we were being watched—one of the attendants came into the room and said, "Would either of you gentlemen like a smoothie?" We both practically shouted, "NO!" at him, and he hurried off. My new buddy then said, "Want to meet in your room or mine?" I said, "Come back to my room." We both headed out separately, and I thought maybe I had seen the last of him, but he showed up at my room. Since he was leaving the next day, we only had a few hours of mutual fucking and sucking. But it was great, and every time I returned to Las Vegas I hoped to have a similar adventure. While I had others, this was the most fun. If my Greek/Mexican architect buddy reads this, I usually stay at Paris Las Vegas now.

My friend took me to an adult theater in a mid-sized Ohio city. There was some action going on between some of the men in the theater which was showing M-F porn on the screen. I went in and sat down beside a man about fifty who appeared to be a construction supervisor. He whipped out his dick, so I went down on it and sucked him until he blew his load in my mouth. Then he zipped up and left. So I went to the back of the theater, where some men were just standing by the back wall. I got down on my knees and sucked as many cocks as they would feed me and swallowed all the loads. All in all, I probably sucked at least eight cocks, and one of them shot two loads of cum down my throat. It was a great place to suck some straight cock for the afternoon! I have gone back a couple times since then and have yet to be disappointed!

Bar, Cinema, T-Room, and Gym

Years ago there was a bar in Atlanta that was very popular, and it just happened to have a very active backroom. I was there one night when I saw a tall, good-looking, blond hunk that I had the hots for. I had never had the nerve to approach him, however. Well, that night he had his pants around his knees and was in the process of fucking a guy leaning against the back wall. Just about everybody back there in the room had their cocks out, jacking off and hoping for more. I don't know where I got the courage that night, but I went up behind the blond hunk and stuck my cock in his ass. He turned around, smiled at me, and we continued with that three-way fuck. It was totally spur of the moment, but boy was I in hog heaven. That was before AIDS, so of course nobody bothered with condoms back then.

BATHHOUSE

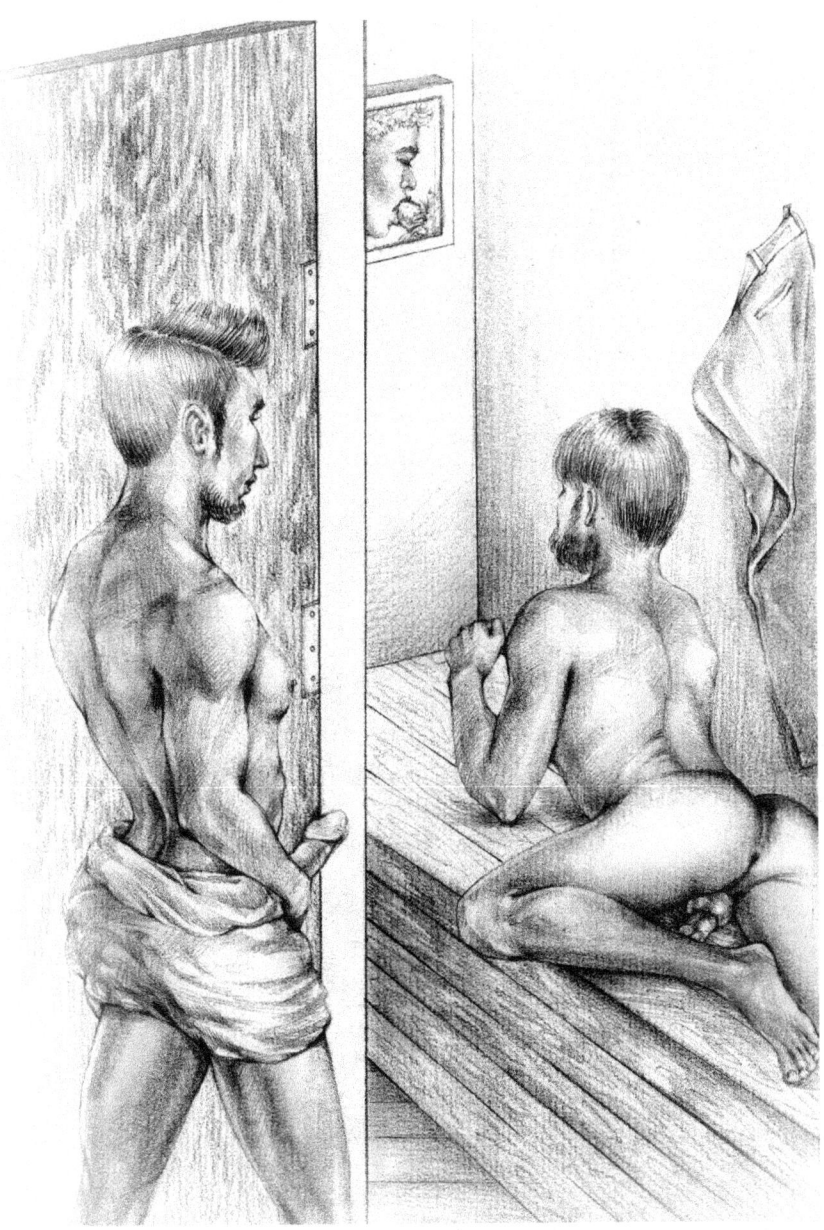

Years ago, before the practice of safe sex, I would go to a bath house in LA called the Corral Club. It was easy to find a willing partner for any form of sexual encounter you wanted in the two-story building, with rooms for any type of play. I had never seen a sling, and the staff had set one up in a large room. When I entered the room, there may have been ten to fifteen men watching a guy in the sling taking a huge cock with ease. The room was dark except for a spot light aimed at the sling to show off anyone using it.

I stood watching, and as my eyes quickly became adjusted to the dark, I realized there were men watching and others on their knees sucking those watching. Soon a mouth was latched on to me, and with the excitement I came quickly. Soon another unknown mouth was on me. After giving up my third load, I walked out of the room and explored the other areas. Fascinated with the activity in the sling room, I found my way back again. The same two guys were still going at it, but the bottom was now covered with cum from the men standing around, watching and jacking their loads onto him.

During the two hours, the same guy was in the sling, and as I kept going back to watch, I came seven times. Yes, I was maybe twenty-four at the time, and to cum three to four times in an hour without the help of pills was common. I will still jack some forty years later, remembering my first experience of watching guys in a sling.

On a recent mini-vacation, my partner and I decided to visit a bathhouse for a couple of nights of anonymous sex. The first night was a bit of a bust with limited guys in the room. A couple of nights later, we decided to try again—not a huge crowd but a bit more choice. We split up, and I went to one of the rooms showing porn. There was an older dude lying in the room, supposedly asleep and buck naked with his junk exposed. I watched the movies for a bit, occasionally reaching over and playing with his flaccid cock. Maybe he was really sleeping, but I think he was hoping to get fucked. I went over and began to lick his balls and cock, eventually getting his cock to stiffen.

My partner entered the room, and I motioned for him to join in. We both took turns blowing the dude, and then my partner, the top in our relationship, began to play with his ass. This eventually led to his fucking him. By this time, we were getting a bit of an audience who began blowing each other, and me as well. This went on for some time, and I eventually wandered off to find a hot cock to fuck my ass. Soon after, a very hot younger dude came over and asked if I would come to his room. Well, I'm a sixty-year-old man, and it's not often I get the opportunity to play around with a hot, smooth, younger man who was likely in his late twenties or early thirties. Of course, I followed him to his room.

Once there, he quickly grabbed me and started kissing me, all the while wanting me to pinch his nipples. He then asked if he could fuck me. Well, what's a guy to do! He had me in just about every position we could in the confines of the small room. All the while, all he asked in return was for me to constantly play hard with his nipples. He fucked me for what seemed like hours, like only someone of his youth and stamina could—all the while telling me he wanted to fuck me for days as he watched himself fucking me in the mirror. I was in heaven. Eventually, I started to feel somewhat guilty, thinking my partner would be wondering where I had disappeared for so long. We took a break, and he went looking for his buddy whom he had come with. Unfortunately, we never did get back together that night. My ass hasn't been fucked that long and hard for a long time. Definitely a night to remember.

I'm forty-nine and live in South Florida. I ventured out to a sex club in Ft. Lauderdale called Slammers 321. It usually has a range of men from late twenties to sixties. All shapes and sizes. The dress code ranges from fully clothed to a couple guys completely nude. The venue has glory holes, booths, slings, a completely dark room with fuck tables, and a large open room with a large, padded, circular, fuck ottoman where bottoms get on all fours to get bred by any and all takers.

As a bottom cock sucker, I choose to walk around in a jock, socks, and sneakers. My story begins when I was standing in a dark cubbyhole/booth with no door and with this hot guy grabbing his dick through his jeans right across from me. He came into my booth, pushed me to my knees, and put poppers to my nose for four long, strong hits—I loved it. He then told me to suck his dick, very quickly grabbed the back of my head, and made it go down my throat. He was a good seven inches, so it was manageable. He really started skull fucking me, and I was able to take his dick well. The poppers helped.

As he fucked my throat, he held me down with one hand on the top of my head and the other on the underside of my neck—to feel his dick inside me, I guess. He then flipped me around and started fucking my ass and pushing my face into the dick of a guy watching. So I sucked this guy while getting fucked. My stud flipped me again, made me sniff more poppers, and worked my throat. He made me gag and throw up slime THREE times. Flipped and fucked me two more times and finally came inside my ass. Then he walked away.

Hot as hell! I could have followed him home! I thought my throat would be sore the next day, but it was completely normal. I guess I'm getting better at deep-throating dick!

I found a bathhouse many years ago in Columbus, Ohio. My first experience ever at a place like this. Nervous as hell, I undressed, wrapped a towel around me, and began looking/cruising around. I found a row of glory holes, fuck stations, and the shower/steam sauna areas. Before long, I was at the glory holes traveling one to another. Some very good sucking going on. Then I noticed a crowd gathered around a fuck station. We stood around and watched and listened to a very loud bottom moaning and groaning while a huge dicked guy thrust in and out like I've never seen before. After they finished, the crowd dispersed, and I found myself fucking the guy all by myself.

Then I headed for the sauna. That's where the crowd had gone. I entered cautiously, a new experience again, and there were so many men in there it was almost elbow to elbow. Well, this cute, delicious, tiny Asian boy began sucking on me. We kissed, caressed, and fondled each other until I thought I was going to lose my mind. He goes back down on me. It cleared out somewhat so I could lie down, and for the first time ever I had someone deep-throat my seven inch, uncut cock. I let him continue that for several minutes until I told him I was cumming. I've never had anyone swallow before, and he doesn't move off my cock.

I explode in pure ecstasy. He doesn't release my cock but continues to roll my cock around in his mouth. He stayed on it for fifteen or so minutes. Finally, after recovery, he orally manipulates me into another erection. It took me longer to cum second time around but another explosion. Again he leaves my cock in his mouth for another fifteen minutes. This time he releases and lets me go. I hurriedly showered and fled away!

When I was in college, I lived on the Lower West Side of New York City in the Chelsea area. I was invited to a Christmas party which I went to and enjoyed myself, even though they were all straight friends. I

Bathhouse

took the subway home back into the city. Even though it was after midnight, I decided I was going to the baths. The Everard Baths was originally a Turkish bathhouse that opened in 1888 and eventually became a gay bathhouse. There were multiple floors, a swimming pool on the lower level, and a huge steam room. The main floor was lockers and the top two floors were the rooms and the orgy room. It was a fun place to visit, and I always found a way to release my energy. Plus, it was close to home. Tragically, the bath house had a bad fire in 1986 and closed forever.

It must have been a real busy night at the baths; when I got there the line to get in was out the door and down the stairs to the front entrance. I asked the guy in front of me what's the hold up and he said there were no rooms or lockers available. So we just had to wait till they opened up. It was a cold night, and we were all standing in the cold. The guy behind me and I started to chat. He was from New Jersey and missed his train home for the night, so he was going to kill two birds with one stone—a place to stay and a place to get laid—then go home in the morning. He was a nice looking gent as well. Mind you, I am a twenty-year-old and in college, and he was in his thirties, I found out later. It was getting really cold and my feet were frozen, so I suggested to my new friend that we go back to my place and he could stay the night. It's warm and clean, and I have the whole place to myself for the holidays. Without batting an eye he asked how far, I said five blocks cross town, he said let's get a cab and go.

We were so cold when we got to my place that I said let's take a warm shower. Well, we got undressed, and, boy, was I in for a surprise. He stood there, this very good-looking specimen, lovely hairy chest and a nice seven-plus inch cock with a wonderful hairy bush and a nice firm, hairy ass—all my favorite things. We got in the shower and started getting warm and then got hot. While still in the shower he got nice and hard. He started stroking his cock, got down on his knees, and started to suck my cock. I said we have time for that later, so let's get dried off and get in between the sheets.

We got into bed but the sheets were kicked to the edge. We started kissing and playing and exploring each other. I wanted his cock and butt so badly. It was like a dream come true—a hot man in my own bed—and we were really getting it on. This guy knew just how to get the balls rolling, his finger up my hole, his mouth on my cock, and my hands all over him. I was so horny I shot my load right into his mouth, and he swallowed every drop. Me being in my twenties, I got hard really fast again and went for his cock. This time, he shot his sweet load in my mouth and said, "Don't swallow yet, hold it," and then he started to suck face with me.

Bathhouse

That was one of the hottest face suckings I had ever had. He had me lie on my back and proceeded to give me the hottest blowjob I'd ever had, and never had again. He sucked my balls, got between my legs, and rimmed me. I had never been rimmed before; it was an amazing feeling. Then he started to suck me again. He sucked and sucked until I was about to cum, and the second load was hotter than the first. Wow!! I let out such a scream of passion that I'm not sure if I woke up the neighbors. With that, he came back to my mouth with my cum in it, and we sucked face again. Damn, he makes me horny. I was hard again. He said I wore him out and he needed some rest, but we could do this again in the morning. Yes, we did it in the morning, and again twice that next day. He stayed the weekend and finally said he had to get home to go to work. We exchanged numbers, and I went to visit him a few times when I was home on weekends. But the first time is always the hottest, exploring new hot men.

I went to the Continental Baths a few times and I remember the hot times I had there! It was on the Upper West Side and since I live close by I was like a kid in a candy store! I was there after Bette Midler, but I was there one night when they were filming the movie *Saturday Night at the Baths*. They let us in for free that night to have bodies present for the filming. I was not in the film because I was busy sucking cock! It had the largest orgy room ever, with wall-to-wall mattresses in one room. There were cat walks and rooms everywhere. It was delightful and great experience.

The other wonderful place was the Everard baths that was three floors of fun and also with a hot orgy room! I spent a lot of time there as well since I was in school a few blocks away! You could go there almost anytime of the day and have some fun. I was there the night before the big fire. All those guys on the street with their towels! Yikes! I felt sorry for them but glad I was not there! They fixed it up and reopened a few months later. Then they closed it down when they had the big AIDS epidemic and never reopened.

We have a FLEX bathhouse here, which as I understand is the best of the ones that are in the US. I have been there on two occasions; the first one was not impressive.

However, the second time was from about 9:00 pm until? I could have stayed until 5:00 am, but after a lot of hot play, I got my trigger off, so I left.

It was only $9 at that time. Monday is their half-off day, and there are tons of guys. There are so many they have to park in the road. It was nice that night as it was not packed and there was a mix of ages; consequently, age was not a factor and a good time was had by all. Loved the guy who wore thongs with his hole quite available and who hung around bending over so he could be fucked all night.

They have all sorts of neat things, but one has to search for them. The first time I was there I was not aware of that and just rented a cabana—will not do that again. So the second time I just rented a locker. Met this guy in the hot tub, was on his way from the mid-west to visit his lover in Albany, NY, and probably always made that stop on the way to and from. We got to making out and ended up in the steam room, the sauna, and the room with the sling. I had always wanted to be fucked in a sling—going there is like going into a dungeon. I got in the sling, and he fucked me royally. Other men around us were fucking each other too. There were two bunk beds in the room, so men were taking turns fucking on those. Later, I talked to a man who was in the sling and who had been bred three times with nice warm loads of cum dripping out of him. I licked every drop. Openness is the name of the game there.

It does have an official workout section, a porn theater, and a straight theater, but do not ask me where the straight one was. Mattresses all over the place for guys to fuck on. I fucked in the porn theater that one time, a man was in there and bent over and got the nicest fuck of his life. Age was not a factor—fucking, sucking, rimming, swallowing, breeding, and seeding were the norm for everyone. Plus, they do have some very upscale, hotel type rooms that can be rented for the night.

Dead night. Forty-four rooms, five cars in lot. Zero men in evidence. Made multiple rounds looking for action. Nothing. Where are the drivers of the five cars in the lot? Resigned, I returned to my room to watch porn, door half open. In about fifteen minutes, the door was swung wide open and a thirty-year-old, 6'4" trim, smooth, not defined or cut, sporting a towel barged in. His first words clipped: "I've never done this before, never seen another man's dick before. I drove from Youngstown—six hours away. Don't know what I want but had to come here." I doubted his story but only for an instant. He was wild-eyed, muscles tense, shaking, pits dripping nervous sweat.

Bathhouse

I offered a massage to start relaxing him and suggested he lie down. He sat instead and presented his back. I massaged his back and shoulders, tight as if rigor mortis had set in. Ditto glutes. I noticed he was jacking under his towel. He did not resist when I moved my hand under his towel, and soon I was able to suck him, but only briefly before he turned away. He stroked me briefly and continued to beat himself under the towel. I sucked him again but his towel remained tightly wrapped. "I'm going to cum," he said. "Give it to me," I replied. He did. I swallowed. And he was out, as abruptly as he came in, "I gotta get some air," his adieu. The entire encounter lasted little longer than it took the reader to get to this point. Satisfying? No. But I honor and respect the extreme risk he took on his own behalf, and hope this was the beginning of a journey toward a proud, gay sex-positive identity. Wish him well.

Back in 1969 I was just back from my six months in the Army Reserves in Fort Polk, Louisiana, where it was a hot summer. I had fooled around with a few anonymous cocks in college and knew I liked dick, although coming out was not for me. No girl friend at the time and getting off with a like-minded guy was so much easier, and cheaper. I had not finished college, so money was tight as my part-time job paid for no more than gas money. I read about the bathhouse in town in the SF gay newspaper. No internet back then and no Craigslist, but the gay paper did have personal ads to peruse. The bathhouse caught my eye.

One Friday night I decided take a drive to finally see it all for myself. It was a gigantic big step. I stopped at a local watering hole around the corner for some liquid courage to build up the nerve to venture in the front door. As I approached the bathhouse my knees were shaking and my stomach turning. Shit was I ever a nervous, straight, twenty-three-year-old white boy about to push his limits.

Once inside, I changed into a white towel and nothing else. The place was jumping, probably sixty young men of all types roaming the halls and cubbies. Three floors of delightful young bodies to explore and enjoy. I saw my first blowjob—other than my own—two guys in a corner going at it in full glory. Damn, was that a sight, couldn't take my eye off them. But after a bit, I proceeded to venture upstairs. I met another fair-haired guy in the hall, and we struck up a conversation. He said it was his first time there and he was apprehensive that he might run into someone he knew, as was I.

Bathhouse

Soon, the two of us found an empty cubby—no door, but dark. It was the first time I sucked and got sucked by a guy with whom I had actually had a brief chat. I actually knew his name! It was wonderful. No towels, no rushing, no time limit, no hiding, no concerns. A few cruisers stopped in the hall to watch us. Damn, did that turn me up to the next level. Back then, it was no kissing and no cum in the mouth. He felt the same. What little did we know about the joys of two mouths and tongues locked in wet, sloppy, French kisses with another man. Two fun boy ejaculations were left on the floor, and we parted ways hoping to see one another next time. This was before cell phones so it was difficult to connect.

I wandered up to the third floor, which had porn movies playing on a huge screen with pillows and mats everywhere on the floor. As I recall, the room was about 25 x 25 with a dozen guys sprawled around here and there, some kissing, hugging, stroking. I found a nice spot adjacent to two of them at the back wall and could hardly take my eyes off them to watch the porn as I stroked my fat cock with spit and more spit. Why bother, I had real live man porn not two feet away. Then it happened; they started to fuck. OMG, what a show! I was glued to the sex right in front of me, hypnotized by the movements and thrusts of two men having anal sex right before my eyes. Even though the room was very dark, the porn on the screen provided plenty of light for a fantastic view. I finished rather quickly, and then they finished. Before they got up to leave, they rolled over and both gave me a big smile which made me feel so warm and connected.

I went home and jacked off again and did so many more times in the weeks ahead with the image of two guys fucking right next to me. Absolute Bliss! Eventually married with three kids, I'm still firmly in the closet today and very thankful for the joys available on the internet, thanks to a porn buddy and Grindr.

BEACH, RESORT, PARK, and HOTEL

I'm not sure when I started thinking what it would feel like to have a man suck my cock, for me suck one, but I think it got a big push when I got my first computer and went online. Somehow I stumbled on

Beach, Resort, Park, and Hotel

some gay porn sites, and all I knew was that I got instantly hard. Several years later, I heard of a place south of town, just off the interstate, where a nude beach was located. It was in the middle of three ponds, and on summer weekends the place was packed with couples and singles lying around naked, catching some nice Midwest rays. Most of the people were spread out on the east and south sides. After visiting the first time, I found out that the west side was the gay side. The only access to the pond was from the west side so everyone driving by could see some of the west side action, though much of it was hidden by the dense underbrush that surrounded most of the pond.

My third visit was on a Sunday. I got there a little after 1:00 pm and, after finding an open spot, I parked my truck and proceeded to get set up on the sand. The hot sun beating down on my naked body sure felt good. Looking around, I could see one large group of people in a corner area. The rest of the sunbathers seemed to be couples, with a few singles like myself. After about an hour, it was time to hit the water to cool off a bit. I floated my little air mattress out about twenty yards and just let the wind drift me around. All the while, I kept watch on the people around the pond. I noticed that one lady and her husband left the one large group and started walking around the pond talking to the other people. Just my luck that I was out in the water because she was a very nice looking woman.

Returning to shore, I resumed my sunning and reading a book. As the afternoon went on, some people left and new ones arrived. By late afternoon, most of the people had headed home with just a few couples left. The sun wasn't far from disappearing under the horizon when the last two couples from the large group walked out about waist deep into the water. They stood there for a while, watching the sun, and then they headed back to shore. As their lower bodies came into view, I saw one of the men was half hard, most likely from his wife playing with him while they were watching the sun go down.

When they drove off, I was the only person left, or at least that's what I thought. From across the pond, I saw a lone man emerge from the underbrush and start walking along the south side towards me. I'm not sure what propelled me, but I got up from my chair and started walking towards him. We met along the south side, and after a little small talk he asked if I wanted to walk back to where he came from. I nodded my head, and we started walking back to the west side of the pond.

Not a word was exchanged as we walked side by side, but out of the corner of my eye I saw that he was stroking his half hard cock! That's all it took for mine to start growing. After a couple of minutes, we were at his spot. As we embraced, he started giving my nipples small kisses. My head was swimming. I'd never done anything like this before! Both of our hands slowly worked their way down the other person's body until we were fondling each other's hard cocks and balls. I had only felt my own hard cock before so this was a whole new experience. I liked the smooth feel of his mushroom head and the way his heavy balls rolled around in my hand. In my mind, this went on forever, but I'm sure it didn't last more than a few minutes. I had no idea of what to do next. Should I drop to my knees and take my first hard cock into my mouth or wait and see what happens? That thought no sooner was in my head when he slowly dropped to his knees in front of me. "My God," I thought to myself, "He really is going to suck my cock!" The only way I could describe the sensation of his taking my cock into his mouth was "hot velvet."

It took only a few seconds to realize this was the best blowjob I had ever had. His tongue and lips were the only things that touched my cock. I never felt his teeth at all. The feeling was truly heaven. My knees were about to start shaking; it felt so good. I put my hands on his head and felt the motion of his head moving back and forth. Looking down, I was mesmerized by the sight of my cock going in and out of his mouth. It was such an incredible sensation that I never wanted it to stop. All of a sudden, I could feel my balls start to tighten, and I knew I was about to cum. He must have felt my stirrings since he slowly let my hard cock drop from his mouth. He grasped my cock with his hand and slowly started stroking me. With his face just inches from my pulsing cock, I came harder than I can ever remember. My cum spewed all over the sand.

Truthfully, I didn't know what to do next, so I ran back to my side of the pond, got dressed, and headed back home. But the feelings I experienced that day stayed with me for quite a few years, until I satisfied my curiosity and finally sucked my first cock. But that's another story!

During the eighteen months I lived at the beach, I got a lot of cock. I met Ron, years before, right out of high school when I lived with my parents. He had just moved in with his aunt and uncle across the street. Tall guy about 6'5", blond hair, blue eyes, built like a brick house, and a beer or two short of a six pack, if you know what I mean. I didn't imagine sucking him at the time, since I wasn't that active then. Though I knew he

Beach, Resort, Park, and Hotel

was very popular with the ladies, always getting what he wanted for services given. His last two were with older ladies, free room and board for a free fuck. When I moved to the beach, he lived in the area with other surfers. Casual pad, lots of naked cocks around.

One night, I was kinda drunk, walked down to the beach bathrooms. Very active at the time, could always rely on getting a cock or a fuck when I went there. I cruised the stalls and found a nice cock to suck—looked like a drunk, straight guy needing to release a load. We went over to the urinals, and I took his hard cock in my mouth. I was sucking him when we heard someone approaching the door. We stood up and pretended to be pissing in the urinals. A guy walked in and went down to the stalls. My guy didn't seem to move, so I went back to work on the guy's cock. A few minutes passed, he arched his back, drove his cock in my mouth, and unloaded a big, creamy, warm load of cum in my mouth. The guy pulled up his pants and zipped up while I stayed on my knees, savoring the load I had just received. The guy tapped my shoulder, pointed in the direction of the stalls. I looked over. There in the corner was Ron!

The first guy left, and there was no denying what I was doing there. The bigger question was what was Ron doing there? What did he want? I walked over to him as he dropped his swim trunks. It was at this point I realized what all those ladies craved from Ron. He had the biggest cock I had ever seen. A cut cock, a good nine inches, semi-hard, with a beautiful pair of cum-filled, low hanging balls. I wondered why I had never attempted to suck him before. I got on my knees and took his cockhead in my mouth. As my lips got slick with my spit, I was able to take more and more of his humongous shaft. Soon, I was deep-throating his shaft, even though my eyes were watering heavily.

We took our shirts off, and he stepped out of his shorts. I grabbed his tight ass orbs, driving his cock into my mouth as far as I could handle it. I licked his balls, his curly pubes, his crotch, his shaft. He whispered in heavy breath that he was cumming. I braced for the coming flood of his white, warm, creamy nectar. He started to cum, he filled my mouth, I swallowed, filled again, I swallowed. He filled my mouth again. This time, his cum slipped out of the corners of my mouth. His cum ran down to my chest. I pulled away, and his last drops came to rest down my back.

He stopped, but was breathing hard. Ron reached under my arms and raised me to my feet. He asked me what I was doing there? I grabbed his cock; we smiled. He said he never knew. At the same time, we both remarked about

Beach, Resort, Park, and Hotel

all the time we had wasted when we could have been fucking! We laughed. After that night, Ron frequented my apartment many times; spent the night numerous times, with no one knowing what was really happening when I closed my bedroom door. I sucked him many times, and he fucked me with his monster cock. He sucked me a couple of times, but I was more interested in his cock! And I did suck and was fucked by two of the guys he lived with. Ron and I stayed friends for years, even though he moved from place to place.

I was about forty or so and staying at my favorite gay resort in Palm Springs about thirty years ago. I was average looking, by no means a glamour boy. There were any number of very young, good-looking, West Hollywood types there that were very much into themselves and paid no attention to anyone else.

So I was lying nude by the pool one morning when a very good-looking young guy came and sat down beside me. We started talking, and I found I had actually seen him on my flight to California. After a while, I told him I was very hot and was going to take a shower. My room was nearby. While in the shower I heard someone say, "Can I join you?" It was the pretty boy, and yes, he joined me, and we actually spent two nights together.

I was walking by the group of stuck-up queens one morning and one of them called me over to their group. I knew something was up, so I went over. One of the little assholes says to me, "We were wondering how someone like you could get the best looking guy at the hotel to spend so much time with you?" I looked back and said as nicely as possible, "Go fuck yourself," and walked off. The looks on their faces were priceless. Everyone needs a good day like that every once in a while.

Had to tell you about my group experience last night. A buddy invited me to join a monthly group of men that meet at a hotel once a month. I missed last month, but made a point to go last night. It goes from 6:00-9:00 pm or until the dicks go soft. We arrived at 6:10 pm. There were already five naked guys sucking and one getting fucked. Another one was blindfolded with his ass up on the bed. I got naked and went to town sucking a guy's dick. He was already busy sucking another one. More guys started knocking and were allowed in. Soon there were fourteen or fifteen naked, horny guys in the room, sucking and fucking, ranging in age from forty to seventy.

I soon found a guy lying on the bed, wanting to be sucked. Being the cock expert I am, I took his soft penis in my mouth and went to work with my oral skills. Well, I brought that limp dick to life, and he showed me that he's a grower. I sucked him for sometime, and then I got on top of him to ride his cock. First, I just rocked back and forth, then, I got up squatting over his cock and rode it with full trust. Soon the bed was squeaking like crazy, had him close a couple of times but couldn't get him to cum by riding him.

I found my big dicked massage therapist there. He had already fucked two guys and blew his load. I still sucked him, letting that big cock of his swell in my mouth—and what a mouthful. Wanted him to fuck me, but he said two loads and he was spent. The host of the group soon saw me taking a break and came over. I went to work on his cock, getting him hard again. The bed being full, he pulled out the desk chair, and I put my head in the seat while he fucked me crazy.

The evening ended with me sucking this other big-dicked dude with two guys working his nips, and my finger working its way to his hole. I soon found his prostate. I fingered him until my arm was sore. I suggested he lie on the bed and I'd get my Njoy and massage his prostate. Well, after five minutes of ravaging his prostate, he had a massive orgasm. There were four of the guys lapping it up and licking it off his nuts.

Soon we all went home.

I am ashamed to say that I was a child who grew up in a city that, until I was a senior in high school, did not have a single black person who lived in his city, so I never knew anything about them at all. My sexual experiences began at the early age of eleven and continued to grow and become a great deal more varied, some might even say kinky. Anyway, one day when I was sixteen, I skipped school and went to the beach early that morning. I went directly to the nude area and walked even further down and into the gay area. I found a very secluded area and laid my blanket down, set my little water cooler down, and stripped. My body was not so great and my hair was always kept long, but I knew I had a nice cock and was proud of it. It was seven inches cut and very thick when it stood straight up, and my balls were large and pendulous. I lay on my stomach with my ass ready to be taken by anyone who wanted it. My legs were spread just a little bit to show I was open for business. There was just enough hair on my ass to show that my balls would be nice and hairy and that when spread, my hole would be nice for eating.

It wasn't long before I had my first new friend. He was about forty-five and lay down beside me. He propped his head on his hand and started the small talk that always preceded the sex. He was dark and had black hair and a beard which I was a sucker for, blue eyes, and the hairiest chest I had ever seen. As I moved my hand closer to his cock, I felt what had to be a ten inch cock which was almost as big around as a beer can. I was going to enjoy this. He started to kiss me, and I kissed back. His tongue took me to places where I had only dreamed of.

As he laid me over and began to work on my nipples, I felt another mouth on mine. I opened my eyes and saw the most handsome black man I had ever seen in my life. The first man whispered, "It's alright baby, he is my lover, and we both want you. We are going to do things to you that you could never dream of. Let's get out of here, and let us show you the world." I couldn't get my clothes on fast enough. The black man drove with me—it was my time getting head in a car. He would look up every once in a while and tell me where to turn or something then go back to work on my cock, never letting me cum, only teasing me.

When we did get to their place, the black guy whose name was James told me to strip in the car, and I did. He followed me out of the car on my side and placed his hand on my ass. I felt his fingers as they probed my ass and I began to dance. His other hand began to stroke my nipples, and he nibbled my neck. I felt the eyes of some of the neighbors watching and didn't care at all. His lover, Robert, had stripped and stood at the front door, and we walked to him. As we got there, he placed my hand on his cock and asked me if I wanted it. I said, "Yes please." And he said I would get it and much more.

We went inside and directly to the bedroom. They put me in a sling. Robert slid underneath me, and I felt his huge cock at my hole. I had no idea what was going to happen and didn't care as long as I was fucked by him. He turned my head, began to kiss me, and fondled my cock and nipples. I began to feel James as he entered the picture and also fondled my nipples, then sucked them and then licked and ate my hole expertly. I was moaning and almost crying it felt so good. He stood up and began to suck my cock and kiss me. Then I felt Robert's cock begin to enter me. I had seen and known

Beach, Resort, Park, and Hotel

it was big but had never realized how big. "Relax, baby, it will be okay," he said. I relaxed and began to feel his twelve inch black cock enter me.

My first black cock ever at the age of sixteen, and I loved it and was hooked. I screamed for more and for him to fuck me deeper and harder. He asked me if I was wanting something special, and I yelled, "Yes, anything, just keep fucking me." Somehow, he picked me up without ever removing his cock from me, turned me over and laid me on top of Robert, who began to kiss me and whisper that this was going to be one of the most special days of my life. I loved the feel of his fur against me, and I whispered how good he felt against me. He said it was only the first of many, many times we would be doing this and that was a promise. With that, he began to slide his cock into me along side James's, and I began to moan with the most wonderful feeling of joy and extreme sexual completeness between the three of us. The feeling of two cocks inside of me was nothing I had ever felt before but was something I would feel a great many time since then, especially the feeling of black and white and black and black.

I recently visited Boston with my wife, daughter, and her family. On our arrival at the hotel, this very tall, good-looking man was walking out as we were walking in. It was lust at first sight for me. I thought to myself, store that image for jacking off to later.

The following day, we all took a break from sightseeing at an Au Bon Pain—best coffee and sandwiches on the planet miles away from the hotel—and soon after we sat down. The man whom I lusted sat at the table across from us, directly in front of me. We made eye-contact. He smiled, winked, and started reading a newspaper. How damn rude, how can I lust after someone hiding behind a paper? Until I looked down under the table and saw the biggest damn package I think I ever laid eyes on. I can't tell you how hard it was to keep up with the table conversation, feeling my third leg getting hard and trying to eat at the same time. But I think I pulled it off nicely. Needless to say, I now had even more jacking material. As we were getting ready to leave, I said, "See you back at the hotel!" And he replied with "You betcha!!" and another smile and wink!! As soon as we were outside, my wife whispered, "He seems friendly." If she only knew what was going through my mind.

The third day was dedicated to shopping and that they did. My son-in-law took their kids to the duck pond after the first store, and I was the designated backpacker. When it reached fifty pounds, I just couldn't carry any more, so I said I was going back to the hotel to unload, get something to eat and drink and that I'd come back and find them. I got to the hotel; the only thing on my mind was getting something to eat—until I laid eyes on Mr. Hottie. I nearly stopped in my tracks, as he was sitting in the lobby, in shorts and t-shirt. His legs were covered with dense, dark fur. My knees went limp. I headed for the coffee urn, dropped my backpack and proceeded to pour coffee, all the while watching him. What a sight. Just as I was popping the lid on the cup, he was right beside me.

I am 5'6"; this guy has to be 6'4", if not taller. My eyes were level with his tummy. Along with his hairy legs, he also had chest hair sprouting over his neckline, and the hair on his arms was as thick as the hair on his legs. He said, "This is the first time I've seen you alone." I told him that I left my family in the Backbay while I came back to the hotel to unload. He reached down and grabbed my backpack, saying, "Let me give you a hand with this. Holy shit this thing is heavy." We both laughed. I pleaded that he didn't need to and that he probably had other things to do, but he just said, "Lead the way."

We got to my room, and I really did think he would just hand me the sack and go away. Instead, he walked in and put the do-not-disturb sign on the outside of the door. I then asked how he could possibly know that I wanted him to fuck me like a bull. He said my eyes gave me away. So much for acting cool, eh?

As luck would have it, the maid had not gotten to our room yet, so I told him I needed a shower. With that, he whipped off his shirt and dropped his shorts. I couldn't believe the size of his balls, low-hangers, like two baseballs, with a slowly growing uncut penis. He then reached over and pulled off my shirt while I was trying to take off my pants. In the movies, this always looks so easy to do. For me, it wasn't anything graceful, let me tell ya. Probably because I still had my shoes on. After a bit of awkward hopping and sitting, I was finally naked. He pressed me close to his chest. My hands were all over him. We managed to work ourselves to the bathroom and got in the shower. I lathered him up with shampoo, and he used me like a sponge, rubbing my body all over his. We took turns finger-fucking each other, rinsing, sucking, soaping. I love to edge, and I guess he did too.

We finally got out of the shower, dried off, and proceeded to the bed. He lay down on top of me, and we just rubbed bodies together. It felt awesome. He worked his way down my body and gave me the most incredible blowjob I think I ever had. He swallowed every drop. I really did want him to fuck me, but since neither of us had rubbers I ended up just rubbing his cock up and down my pucker hole. Then I swallowed him whole. I love to deep-throat, and he had the perfect sized cock—his foreskin was just loose enough to have fun with. When he came, I thought the back of my throat was going to rupture. I never had anyone come so hard in my mouth before. The afterglow was long-lasting; I know I "tingled" for a long time. Then we headed back to the shower again, got dressed, and left.

What is really sad is I never got his phone number or email address. I guess he must have checked out the following day, because I never saw him again.

My years of going to adult bookstores, truck stops, and county parks in New England and Pennsylvania allowed me to see and do a lot of things. Most of the time, it was just vanilla, sucking cocks at the rest areas, roaming the trails of the county parks searching for cock. One of the times that I was in a county park, I came upon a group of guys deep into the woods and off the main trail. They were all naked and stood around one guy who was reclining on a flat rock waiting to be gang banged.

Most of the guys were in their late twenties or early thirties. The guy who was being gang banged was in his early twenties and had a rather large dick that some of the men were sucking while others were fucking him. I stripped and played with my seven-plus incher and ended up jacking off on his chest, as did a bunch of the men. Only a few fucked him while I was there. I did do some licking of cum off his chest, along with another guy. We then snowballed!

I talked to some of the guys, and they said that the fuckee came to the park often. I looked for him many times, but never saw him again. I learned that favorite spot with the flat rock was a famous part of the park, and I visited it frequently.

News from the trenches. Just back from a hotel sex party. Not a lot attending, but quality prime beef from those who showed up. There were six of us. Everyone kind of sampled what was available, but two of them paired up. That left four of us to figure out what to do. OMG, I love their imaginations. Picture this as it happened. No. 1: Thirty-year-old, nice build, nice cock, average sized. Not all that much into sucking but did love to be sucked. No. 2: Young bear, maybe fiftyish with nice equipment. He had seen me at earlier parties, topping an occasional bottom. He really wanted to be fucked but not in front of the others. Eventually, he let me have his load, massive. I love the feeling of a cock pulsating in my mouth as it unloads.

No. 3: Probably fiftyish also, shaved head, massive cock with a head hard to get in my mouth. He was versatile, really worked the thirty-year-old and me together, but he didn't want to cum yet. No. 4: Me, seventy-six with an eight inch hard-on, thanks to Viagra. No. 3 and No. 4 (me) soaked him with our cum after he had sucked us for about fifteen minutes. Fun to shoot together. After coming down from an ejaculation high, I asked him if he wanted me to take his load. No argument there. He also had A+ equipment and a head that filled my mouth. Again, I was reminded how great it is to feel a loaded cock discharge and fill my mouth. I've become such a cum whore I can't believe it. I'm pretty sure I'll be there again in ten days. Life is a ball, just suck on two of them.

Back in the day when I was living in Queens, NY, and had a car at my disposal, I would cruise this park a short ride from my home. It was called Forest Park. It was notorious for evening cruisers, especially during the warm summer months when all the trees were in full bloom and there were plenty of paths to take. Some were close to the parking lot and could be lighted by the street lights so you did not have to go in deep to get a quick blowjob or suck some dick. But this afternoon I was home during the week and decided to see what was going on. I put on a pair or elastic waist shorts, a t-shirt, and went commando. This would make for an easy escape, if needed.

When I got there, there were a few cars already parked and none were filled. Said to myself, gonna get some today for sure. I walked on the closest path to the lot and saw nothing interesting, so decided to really explore. I was walking down another path, and this guy circled around me, then walked past me and signaled me to follow him. So off I went to follow him. We kept walking and walking, and then he went off the path and a bit deeper into the wooded area. Finally, he walked around these thick hanging vines and I followed. When I got behind the vines, I noticed that you can't be seen from the path and that it was very secluded. Also, by the time I was face-to-face with this guy, he had his pants open and down and with his shirt open.

Beach, Resort, Park, and Hotel

First words out of his mouth were, "Join me and get comfortable, nobody can see us and if they do they only want to join in." We locked lips and kissed and touched each other all over. I was loving this hot, cute, hairy body, and he was sucking on my nips. I had a raging hard-on. I said slow down or I am gong to cum. He smiled and said bring it on, so he began to suck my cock, and for sure, in the middle of Mother Nature, I blew a load right down his throat.

He stood up and said, "Got any more of that." I said, "Give me a moment." We kept kissing. I wanted to suck him off, but he said, "Wait, I don't want to cum until you shoot another load for me." When I was young, I could shoot three loads in an evening and still be hard. But now I am in my sixties and am only good for one hot load a night. So this fine, hot guy started to suck my cock some more and kept sucking while playing with my balls. Finally, after a few minutes, I said here I cum, and he swallowed my second load. As he was sucking and I was cumming, he gobbled up the goop. After he drained me, I took his cock in my mouth and was ready to swallow his load. But he said don't swallow, let's share it. And that's what we did, kissing so hard our tongues were in knots.

We put our clothes back on and walked out to the cars. We exchanged numbers, and we feasted on each other a couple more times. It was just as hot or even hotter when we don't have to worry about being caught.

Back a number of years ago I was on vacation at an all-inclusive resort on one of the Caribbean islands. The resort was family oriented so there were some kids around and many families enjoying the sand beach. I was on a lounge chair by the pool where it seemed fewer families hung out. Lying on the lounge chair, I could see the people by the pool and also the people that came up to the poolside bar for their drinks instead of waiting for the waiters. There was one couple that my eyes often wandered back to. There was a young man about fortyish and what appeared to be his twentyish son. Both were in nice shape, and they both wore the same type of swim suits, pouch type brief suits, and both filled out the pouch very well. The father had a heavy load, but the son had an even more impressive pouch stretching set of male equipment, almost like it was stuffed to the breaking point. And both had no problem strutting about with their half-covered asses and full pouches. But the boy was far more impressive.

Beach, Resort, Park, and Hotel

Some time passed and I moved into more shade. The warmth felt so good I think I fell asleep for a while. When I awoke, the pool was nearly empty, and the bar boy was there in his white shorts and colorful shirt offering me a new drink. I was covered by a towel and seemed closer to the bar than I remembered. And there by the bar on a stool and with his half clad ass was the boy wonder with his ass crack showing as prominently as his packed pouch, having a drink and talking to the bar man. I ordered my drink from the bar boy waiter and lay back to enjoy the view, nice ass. The boy turned and noticed I was awake and told me he hoped I did not mind that he had covered me with the towel. I was sound asleep in the sun, and he thought I looked like I had had enough sun. I couldn't help but stare at his crotch and wonder how he kept that suit from exploding open as it was packed and stretched out the way it was. I think he noticed my staring and shifted so that I got a better view. And he cupped his package and adjusted it a bit and made it look even more impressive. Then he got up and left. I seemed almost ready to explode under the towel into my swim suit and didn't know how I was going to get to my room with me so hard. I felt like a teenage boy with his perpetual erection.

I finally got up and headed for my room and was glad it was a poolside room on the ground floor. Once I got in the room I grabbed my package and was enjoying the feel when there was a knock on the door. When I opened the door, the young man I had met at the pool was standing there. He came into my room, closed the door, and said that he noticed how much I had admired his package. He wondered if I wanted a closer look as he put his thumbs inside and began to strip that tightly stretched swim suit off, letting it drop to the floor. His balls were like a bull's balls, large and plump, and his cock was magnificent, big and full, standing straight up against his belly. I got instantly harder than I already was and just stared unable to think of anything to say. The lad then headed for the bed with me in tow and told me to get on my back, put my head on the pillow. He was going to fuck me. I obeyed. He took some lotion I had on the night stand and lubed his cock; then he lubed my ass. When I was fully covered with lube, he got on the bed, pushed my legs up toward my chest, aimed and pushed his way into my love chute, my ass. I was either too tight or he was larger than I thought because the stretch of my ass gave me such pain I called out, and he just smiled. He pumped away nice and slow, going deep into me with his long, thick wanger. And I both writhed in pain and really loved the invasion. When he was done, he headed to the showers, put on his swim suit, and left.

The next day when I went back to my room, the kid was there at the door. We entered my room, and he again dropped his suit at the door. He pushed my face down on the bed and rammed his huge cock into my ass without a word being said. The next day was a repeat of day one. The next day, he showed up early in the morning and then later that afternoon, each time specifically for a fuck and a shower. And each time my ass got more and more sore. When he plowed into me, I hurt more and more but wanted him more and more and couldn't stop the cycle. I wanted him filling me up with his cum.

After about two weeks, he stopped coming by, and I found out he and his dad had left to go home. I was sore for about a week after but remember his loving even now. He was raw and wild and uninhibited. He was brief, and he stretched my ass beyond what anyone had before. He forced his way into my body and my memory, and I wish even today he would do it again.

Rehoboth Beach, Delaware, attracted gay beachgoers from Philadelphia, PA, and Washington, D.C. metro areas. It was a small town with one gay bar/restaurant and one gay nightclub.

It was the late 1980s, and I had bought a small beach house in Rehoboth Beach. I rented it out by the week for most of the summer, mostly to LGBTs and organizations, and then for a few weekends at other times of the year. On one of the summer weekends, my doctor partner and I decided to go to the beach and stay at a gay guest house, so I could check out how my house was doing. After a great relaxing day on the beach, checking out the gay wildlife in swimsuits, and enjoying the water, it was time to head home. It was late Sunday afternoon, and we had checked out of the gay guest house earlier, but we came back to the guest house to take a shower before our drive back to the northern Virginia suburbs of Washington, D.C. To our pleasant surprise, the guest house's outdoor "very gay" shower was floor to walls to ceiling mirrors. How erotic!

First, it was nice to see our bodies in the mirrors. Then, it felt just great to get the sand and sea salt off our bodies before we began the two-plus hour drive back home. Somehow, after the fun cleaning, we were touching each other, and then stimulating each other. We had a great craving to have sex in the shower. It became a MUST DO! With more touching and stimulating and with more water running, we both lost our self-control. We were insatiable and sex happy. I sucked, kissed, licked, and grabbed all parts of my partner's great body, while he was turning me on more and more when he did the same to me. The mirrors, the water, the soap/lubricant, the relaxed time of the day, and our relaxed bodies, all turned into this constantly growing great sexcapade. I rubbed, and sucked, and fucked him. He rubbed, and sucked, and fucked me. In reality, who was doing what and when was impossible to remember.

It was an explosion of desire and sexual energy. We were insatiable. We both went wild. We came. What more could we do? We went on and on until we were finally more than satisfied. We were also more than happy and grateful that this surprise in our sex life had moved us up to a new level. A forever, happy, memorable part of that relationship.

Well, here we are in 2017. I will be turning sixty-three this year. I finally remembered something that happened around 1989. Moved from Michigan to California in 1985, to Laguna Beach. In some polite discussions at the Little Shrimp, I found out about places where men and boys could go to enjoy the beach, sans clothing—really? Oh fuck, I am in, tell me more. Well, I learned that if you have a car, there are a couple of places to check out. First, is way to the south, near Del Mar, north of San Diego, Black's Beach. The drawback is the cliff you have to descend to reach the miles of naked men.

There is also a closer beach. I like closer, so where is it, I asked. Seems it's south of San Clemente, very near the nuclear reactor, and at the northern border of Camp Pendleton, Marine base. I was told where to park and how to find the gay area. Seems there is a fence, an old, almost non-existent fence at the far south end of the state park. Since nude people were not allowed in the state park area of the beach, I was told to just walk around the end of what was left of the fence, go about a quarter mile to the south, and I would find the gay men's area, passing the naked families on the way.

Sure enough, when I arrived, I was like a kid in a candy store. Young, old, middle aged, fat, slim, buff—oh shit, all these swinging cocks, paradise! Off came the speedo, down went the towel. Let the drool begin. Well these guys were VERY friendly, and I was new meat. I was warned that upon occasion, rarely, but it was possible, that the Marines would come and kick people off the beach. It was, after all, a federal Marine base. Even back then there were lots of lawsuits about the beach being public everywhere, so not to worry too much about it. The worst that would happen is being asked to leave. Then the fellows on the beach were telling me about the areas to go to have a good time. After all, the park rangers could not do any thing if you were naked on federal land, but if they caught you fucking, you would be arrested. So the canyons that were wide on the beach would lead back inland and narrow the further back you went. So, that's where I went. I was back there having about four hours of great fun and so many new friends.

I was making my way back out to the beach when all of a sudden I heard helicopters and shouting and saw about fifty or sixty uniformed men repelling off the 100 foot canyon walls with rifles on their backs. So, as a naked queer just moving to CA from MI with a new job, I ran toward the beach, got to my towel and cooler and started to make my way back to the fence line. Ordered at gun point to halt, damn right I did! Scared shitless, dropped the towel and cooler, did have my suit back on by then—that was a sight all unto itself, me trying to run and put on my speedo.

So it turns out that back then you have two choices. This is way before Homeland Security. You can be arrested for trespassing on federal land, or they will give you a $50 ticket, which you have to pay in person, in cash, at the federal court house in San Diego. So, then came the questioning. I had no identification; it was locked in the trunk of the car. I was warned that if I lied they would find out. Mom taught me well not to lie, EVER. So I took the ticket, had to be paid within thirty days. I went back there many times, and this never happened again.

I did learn a valuable lesson from all this. Pay attention to your surroundings, listen over the waves, and if you hear anything weird, move out now! I did go to Black's Beach many times, too, because I just love to be naked with shiny men who want my cock. Not so anymore, unfortunately. I will always remember those hot Marines. I never did hold against them what happened. They were following orders. I did have many opportunities after that to offer them my body for pleasure, the 4th street baths in San Diego was their playground too! Hubba hubba. On a later trip, I met some film legends, Jim, Rod, and Tim, and enjoyed watching their films even more after some of the fun we had there. And after I moved to West Hollywood, they were always at the parties.

I have always enjoyed nude beaches, especially if there was a gay section where you could head off into semi-secluded areas for play. It was Labor Day weekend of either 1991 or 1992. I had hoped to be at Black's Beach near San Diego, but I was going to have to settle for Oval Beach on the Michigan side of Lake Michigan. I had been there before, so I

Beach, Resort, Park, and Hotel

had a room in a local motel nearby. As I remember, you park your car at the public beach, then pay a fee to cross over to a privately owned area in the Sand Dunes where women had their area, and men had their places to wander or lay out nude. It was fairly common to see pairs or groups of men engaged in sexual activity. After all these years, I do not remember anyone's real names, but this is the afternoon as I remember it.

I had recently climaxed with someone else and was just walking around the dunes when I saw this tall, dark, hairy, Italian-looking guy with one of the longest dicks I had ever seen. He was definitely over a foot long, soft, and of reasonable girth. He was rubbing the massive soft dick but was showing no interest in anyone as he walked past me. My mouth fell open in awe as "Long Dong" passed me by. I was in my early forties, 144 pounds, 5'8" with a respectable seven-plus inch, uncut dick of my own. As he passed, I saw another man also with his mouth open and staring. "Bob" and I started talking and found we had similar tastes and thoughts. He was definitely the businessman type, maybe a lawyer or banker or an executive type, perhaps early fifties, 6' tall and also decently endowed. It soon became clear we were both tops, but we enjoyed each other's company and started walking around, evaluating the available meat and asses.

There were men and boys of all types hanging around that day. Long Dong would pass by showing no emotion or friendliness to anyone. Bob and I were both outgoing, so we would get group conversations going for periods of time. Sometime into the afternoon we met Cliff. He was about 5'10", dark haired, a small business owner himself, and was wearing as much leather as he could and still be comfortable. It turned out that Cliff was versatile but loved to bottom. He finally said he would love to have either Bob or me top him, or we could take turns. We decided to take him up on his offer.

Instead of finding a secluded spot, we spread our towels out on a sand dune where we were in view of many. Bob and I put on condoms and started taking turns pleasuring ourselves in Cliff's gorgeous ass. None of us were in any hurry. I do remember that Cliff was getting too hot in his leather so that all slowly came off. He lay there naked but happy being filled with dick. Within a few minutes, several more of the nicer looking men whom we had talked with earlier came along and also put on condoms. We all were enjoying watching each other as someone was always fucking Cliff's ass. A couple was actually ready to leave for the day when, as they were walking to the outer sand dunes to return to the public area, they saw the action on our dune, came back, and joined in. Most of us had already climaxed earlier in the day with someone or some other group, so we were not in any hurry. We all were enjoying being a part of this live porn action.

It was now early evening with the sun getting low on the horizon. All of a sudden Long Dong stepped up to the group and started to play with himself in earnest. As that monster got bigger, he started groaning. Everyone watching pulled off their condoms, and all of us were jacking off. Nearly all together, we shot our loads over Cliff's naked body lying before us like an altar. WOW, what a climax that was. Cliff was drenched in cum. He had a broad smile coated with cum!!

By now it was starting to get dark, so we hurriedly had to find our way out. Bob and I were carrying Cliff's leather since he still had cum running off him. All the others headed to their own vehicles. Bob had planned to drive back to Chicago that evening, and Cliff was staying in a house with a bunch of friends. Instead, they came back to my motel room. The three of us showered, picked up food and liquor, came back to the room, and played most of the night. Bob did drive back to Chicago in the morning. Cliff and I went back to the dunes area at Oval Beach the next day. It had been too dark to clean up the area. I found eight condoms in the sand. Long Dong and Cliff never had one on. That makes ten guys that shot on Cliff that late afternoon. No wonder I can still remember that afternoon and evening with pleasure.

Well it was a nice summer day in the Silicon Valley. I was coming from work one afternoon, and I was driving west on the 101 FWY going up to Santa Clara, CA where I live. I was driving my little Black Mata, and I noticed this hot guy in a car that was on my right side in traffic and realized he was looking at me. He was so hot and had a nice beard. I kept looking at him and smiling at him, and then I made a gesture by putting my hand by my mouth, like putting his cock in my mouth, and he laughed. We proceeded to smile, and I wanted him bad. He pointed to follow him, and we got off the FWY. He led me to a park. He was tall and hot.

He went to the bathroom area, and I followed him. He pulled his thick big cock out, I went down on my knees, and started to suck on this hot man that I just met on the FWY. He was so hot looking and had a nice thick cock, so I sucked on it for a while. Then he turned me around and put his hot, thick cock in my ass and started to pump my ass good. It hurt for a little, and then he started to pump it hard in me while other men were outside cutting the grass. He pumped his hot load in my hot ass, and then he said thanks. He said he just moved in the area and was living with his girlfriend. He said my BJ was so good and my ass felt so hot, and he loved it. Then he left the bathroom. My ass was so full of the hot load he just pumped in me. I wiped his load off, and then left as well. I'll never forget this hot time on the 101 San Jose FWY. Welcome to San Jose, CA!!

I live about an hour drive from a very delightful gay campground in Florida. It is busy all winter months with a deluge of northern snowbirds and vacationers. During the summer, it is busy on weekends as the place has several bars. Much of the daytime activity takes place at the salt water pool where nudity is the accepted and often preferred dress. The pool is also a good place to meet other men. It is not uncommon for men to reach out and start checking each other's equipment under the water. For some, it is like shaking hands. Those handshakes can lead to a lot more. Because food is served in the nearby bar, the rule is that any full sexual activity needs to be done in other spaces. Some men attempt to deflate before exiting the water. Occasionally, someone walks out of the pool with a raging hard-on. I think, "Good for him!"

Near the pool there is a bathroom complex. One door from the pool says MEN with toilets, urinals, an open shower area with four shower heads and two sinks. On my first trip ever to the pool, I went to use the urinal. Shortly, I was visited by a nice-looking guy from the pool, who leaned over and laid a deep kiss on me while I was still pissing. I immediately started getting hard. After my stream stopped, I turned to face him. He immediately was down feasting on my engorged penis. Since it was my first time there, I asked, "Can we be doing this here?" I assume he thought I was shy. He stood up, waved his arm, and I followed him to the other side of the building where a handicapped bathroom has an entrance. We went in, he locked the door, and he returned to his knees, feasting on my cock. Of course, I offered him my first climax at this facility. That handicapped bathroom proved convenient several times more. I have fucked several guys in that room. One slower summer day at the pool, I saw a guy who kept changing swim wear. Each different thong focused attention on his great endowments. I, of course, was in the pool with nothing more on than a cock ring. He finally took off his swim thong, came into the pool, and started playing with my cock. He said, "I think you are the only person here today that can compare to me in size. Let's both get hard and then measure." We fondled each other to full erections. Then we both walked out of the water proudly and fully aroused, proceeded to the handicapped bathroom, where he took photos of our equipment, side by side. We decided we were close to the same size. I am uncut, he was not, but otherwise I might be a little longer, while he had an area in the middle that was slightly thicker than me. Later that day, we completed a thorough examination down on the trails.

More recently, three of us started getting very familiar with each other in the pool. Needing a place to continue our play, I said, "Slowly follow me. Try not to be too obvious." I went in the men's side and back to the handicapped door only to find it locked. The other door from that side leads into another area where many overnight tenters and cabin guests clean up. We may have thought we were not being obvious as we three moved into the shower area. So much for not being obvious. We were quickly followed by four other men who apparently had been watching us from their chaise lounge chairs. One did not step into the shower area to join us, but six of us were soon having a nice orgy. A guy giving a good blowjob got my load as another guy watching jacked off, shooting onto the head of the one giving me the blowjob. I realized later that the partner of the one giving the great blowjob had just walked back to their cabin. Mr. Blowjob followed us, got his afternoon snack, and then returned to his chaise lounge before his partner returned. I wonder if he ever confessed his indiscretion.

The most notorious place for sexual activity is the "Trails" on the wooded area of the property. It is several blocks from the pool but offers spaces, some hidden behind fences, some in plain sight, for full sexual activities. In the open area towards the back there is what appears to be a wooden foot bridge. It would be fine for crossing a stream, but it sits in a place without a stream. If you want to receive a blowjob, you stand on the bridge. If you want to do the blowing, then stay on the sand below the bridge. During the day, most persons use the private areas for sexual cruising, but at night, especially if persons have had a few drinks, the bridge can get very busy. One late evening, I was giving a blowjob when I decided it was time for me to receive my blowjob. I got up on the bridge standing next to the guy I had been blowing. My mouth on his dick had been replaced immediately by another man's. I started deep kissing the guy getting blown as he fondled me. I felt him climax while my tongue was sucking his tongue. I was very aroused. The man who had just swallowed his load then started giving me a great blowjob. It was totally dark. The man sucking me did not remove his mouth but momentarily stopped sucking. I quickly realized that he had just readjusted as someone had entered his ass. Once the guy fucking got his rhythm going, I followed suit. As the man blowing me received what felt like a deep thrust from behind, I fucked into his mouth simultaneously. You could tell we were all grooving together. I can be very loud, screaming out in pleasure when I have a wild climax. It was totally dark, so I could not see anything. But from what I felt and heard, the person in the middle was filled with cum from each end, as both of us were very vocal as we climaxed together.

I like to visit the campground on Mondays, since most of the weekend visitors have headed home. I enjoy swimming the short laps when I do not have to keep a watchful eye for persons in my swim path. I also enjoy meeting and talking with both old and new friends. One Monday morning I was introduced to a new person. He was fair complexioned and wearing a hat and swim trunks. A couple of hours later, I was again trying to swim when a guy in a different hat said something to me. I stopped, said hello, realized it was the man introduced to me in the morning, and then quickly followed with a nice caress to his genitals. He responded accordingly. It was a different hat, but he was extremely nice looking and possibly could be the age of my son. We were getting very familiar when another guy came and joined us. It turns out this man had blown this great looking guy when he had visited for his first time a few weeks earlier. The man who joined us was one of those guys who could go under water and give a short blowjob before returning above water for air. This scene was a big turn on. It was a hot, muggy, summer Monday afternoon. I mentioned the air-conditioned, handicapped bathroom and all agreed to try it there. It was locked again! Maybe management had decided to keep it for use only by those handicapped persons who needed it or maybe to keep us horny men out, or maybe it was just occupied for pleasure purposes.

I suggested we could head to the trails. We three walked the several blocks to the trails feeling each other as we went. Then we walked all the way back to the bridge. The younger man had not been back there. In the pool, I had realized that he enjoyed my merely finger-fucking him. It was also obvious that he was very innocent and very tight. He was wearing the big hat because he was a very true blue-eyed blond, and could easily sun burn. I explained what the bridge was for and invited him to join me on the bridge. I had brought my poppers and offered them if he liked. The other guy was now giving the newbie a great blowjob. He asked if we would not cum in his mouth but instead shoot all over his hairy chest, which he loved. As the younger guy was getting blown, I was behind him, nibbling on his neck. I was also rubbing my decent-sized dick in his crack, teasing his ass hole. Stupid me, I had not grabbed lube. Anyway, the younger guy inhaled the poppers, climaxed without warning, and the other guy was 'forced' to swallow the whole load.

Now it was my turn. Again the guy giving the blowjob asked if I would blow my load on his hairy chest. That is a real turn on for me. The hairy guy was giving a great blowjob. Only one other guy was back on the trails. He stopped and was watching our action while he jacked off, which was another turn on. Then the younger man started deep kissing me as he caressed my nipples. Another real turn on. I was getting close, so I took a big hit on the poppers, pulled out my dick, and started jacking myself. My guttural scream came from deep inside me. Then I saturated the guy's hairy chest with a super-size load of cum. In that heat, I was nearly wiped out from that climax. Definitely a Monday afternoon to remember.

I've had the absolute pleasure to attend numerous hotel room sex parties in the SF Bay Area over the years. I used to help organize them with two buds. We would start at 4:00 pm and finish by 6:00 so everyone could get home to 'Mama' on time. My task was to reply to the Craigslist men who asked to attend. We always required face and body pics of the invitees so that our married regulars, including me, would not run into a colleague or neighbor. We would meet during a fifteen minute window at a cafe around the corner to verify the new people actually looked like their photo and at that time give them the name of the hotel and the room number. Yeah, I know, Homeland Security paranoia. I'm a photo nut so I was the official cameraman at the parties. "No Faces" was the absolute rule and anyone could review and delete their pics in the camera before they left. Condoms were a strict requirement for the bottoms—bottoms kept their socks on for easy identification. It worked like a charm for a decade.

A couple of years ago, I was invited to a small afternoon, downtown hotel sex party by a married friend, Bill, whom I had played with about a dozen times prior—lots of oral, kissing, rimming, sucking, and safe fucking with a couple of threeways thrown in. We are both married to women with children and firmly in the big old closet. He was thirty-two and I am now sixty-six. This party was hosted by an older visitor whom Bill had played with on other trips. The room was actually a suite in one of the top hotels in SF. I was excited to attend and found a stiff dick in my underwear a couple of times that morning in anticipation of the 4:00 pm soiree. Bill opened the door and introduced me to the four men in the suite, poured me a drink, and we sat down for a chat until the others arrived. About five minutes later, a knock on the door. When Bill opened the door, I recognized one of my real estate business clients, another married guy with kids—also in the closet. OH SHIT! I freaked, buried my head in my knees, and covered up, hoping he had not seen me. First thing he asks Bill, "Where is the bathroom." With that, he walks in and walks right by all of us on the couch, my head down and covered, and goes into the bathroom.

I grabbed my coat and bolted for the door, telling Bill, "We'll talk, got to go." I stopped at the lobby bar for a stiff drink and was soon on my way back to the office. For those of you who are out and proud, this probably is not much of a story, but for those of us who are still in the closet it was a frightening experience. From then on, I insisted that I see face photos of all attendees prior to my showing up. And as you can guess, I've not attended many hotel sex parties since then. I find it better to invite some of the regulars I know and ask them not to bring any new people, just us fuckers.

I'm not the most wanted guy for not being young and not being in great shape, so I put ads in Craigslist, describing myself close enough so guys don't get surprised when we connect. I'm Latino, hairy, chubby, fifties, bottom, and a great cocksucker. I say in the ad that I am hosting at my place in Southern California. I include a cartoon of a chub man sucking a guy, and I embed my cell phone number in disguise in the picture. So, this guy texted me and asked to get together. He was staying at a hotel in my city since he was working in town and asked me to go there because he is not familiar with the city. I could not go that day because I had an interview and assessment test that day.

We could not meet at night because a co-worker is staying in his room. So, we set it up to meet the next day. He is less than three miles away, so I agree to go there. I had asked him for his age to make sure he is at least eighteen; he said he was thirty-five. I was not familiar with the hotel. When I got to the entrance, I found a guard, so I parked on the street and texted him to find out how to get in. He said to let them know that I was there to see a construction company and gave me the name of the company and a room number. I gave the information to the guard and was able to drive in.

Soon, I see a lot of remodeling going on—roads and landscape—and the road splits. I turned left and parked at the first parking area. Since my car was the only car parked there, I was not sure if it was the right place. I got out and could not see any room numbers. All I saw was a pool, the office,

Beach, Resort, Park, and Hotel

and some cabanas by the pool. I texted the guy again. He asked me where I was and said he would come to meet me. I see a construction guy heading my direction—brown work boots, tool belt, khakis, white, dirty t-shirt, and in great shape. Part of me was wishing this was the guy I was supposed to meet, but I thought that would be too good to be true. The other part of me thought that he was coming to ask me to move the car because of the construction.

He greeted me and told me to drive to the other side of the property where the rooms were. He gave me the key to his room and told me to follow the road to his room, go inside, and wait for him there. He said he would follow me there. I was nervous, kinda scared, excited, and wondering what I was getting myself into. I found the room, went inside, and saw the two undone beds, clothes lying around, and a case of beer with half empty bottles in it.

About five minutes later, he comes to the room. I hand him his room key, he grabs my hand, and pulls me toward him. I started touching his firm pecs, and he started taking off my polo shirt. I moved to his khaki pants and started undoing the belt. He pulled off his pants and pushed my head towards his semi-hard, uncut cock. I usually like to get the balls in my mouth first, but his balls were so big that I could barely cover them with my hand. I proceeded to suck that great cock which kept getting bigger, and he kept moving my head up and down his thick shaft.

After a few minutes, he said, "I want to fuck you, but don't have any condoms." I said, "Don't worry, I have condoms and lube." While he was putting on the condom, I lubed my ass, and before I could think, he turned me around, threw my face on the bed with my feet on the ground and my ass up in the air while he forced his cock into my asshole. It hurt for a few seconds, but I could not make any noise since the cleaning crew was cleaning the room next to his. I could hear ladies talking in Spanish while I was feeling the big cock moving in and out of my ass.

I thought I was going to moan some, but my face was pushed against the mattress. After a good fuck, he pulled my head by my ponytail and turned me around while he took off the condom. He pushed my head to his hard cock to suck it some more and forced my head against his crotch while he shot his big load. I had to swallow three times to get it all down. Then, he picked up the condom, lube, wrapper, and tissue, giving it to me so his roommate wouldn't see it.

Beach, Resort, Park, and Hotel

Years ago I went to an all male party hosted by a friend at a local motel. I was having a great time with the thirty or so men that were there, but I noticed this one man that was obviously there for the first time. He still had all of his clothes on and remained near the food, just watching and not seeming to be having any "fun." The host was naked and standing near him, but he did not make a move. Just standing, talking and watching. Since I knew the host quite well, I walked over to chat with him. While I was there, he introduced me to the man who was quite handsome but very nervous. I started talking with him and then just unzipped his pants and went down on him. I swallowed his load when I finished him off and he quickly exited the party. A few days later, he contacted the host via email and asked if the host had a way to contact me. The host gave him my e-mail and we have been "friends" since then. That was about ten years ago. I love making friends like that!

In my late thirties, while still closeted, I began exploring my attraction to men. I am an avid naturalist, and one day while hiking in a local park I noticed a naked guy about sixty from the trail who was standing with his back toward me and leaning against a tree. Naturally, I was very excited and quietly snuck up on him to get a closer look at his naked torso, hoping to see his cock and balls.

At that time in my life I was still very naïve, and the male sexual freedom movement was just getting started, so I was quite shocked to discover that there were actually two good-looking, naked, hung guys, mutually blowing and jerking off each other, in the open public place. Although I never got the courage to get very close at that time, I watched from a distance as the guy leaning against the tree began to moan loudly and started pumping his hips into the other guys face while he shot his hot load into his partner's mouth and down the other guy's throat.

By now, my cock was raging hard, and I gripped it beneath my jeans with a clenched hand as I watched my first live male orgasm. The guy giving the blowjob stood up smiling and positioned himself next to the guy who just shot. Fortunately, I could still see both their cocks as I watched from the side. It was now the other guy's turn to get off. I watched as the first guy spit on his hand for lube and began rapidly pumping up and down the shaft and head of the other guy's uncut cock. By now, my uncut cock had leaked copious amounts of precum into my foreskin and underwear which made it easy for me to pump my cock in and out of the fist I had clenched around it.

Beach, Resort, Park, and Hotel

That first-time scene was so fucking hot for me, that I shot one of the hottest loads of my life into my pants, even before the other guy came all over the hairy chest and forearm of the guy pumping his cock.

As far as I know, neither guy saw me watching them that day. At least they didn't let on that they did, so I felt my attraction to men was still somewhat safe.

Seeing those guys get off gave birth to a voyeur fetish that I enjoy to this day. Traveling as a salesman, I would seek out remote wooded areas near densely populated cities with the hope that I would see more man-to-man action as hot as my first encounter. And see them I did, and as time went on, a whole lot more too.

One of my memorable events was when I was visiting Vancouver, Canada, a number of years ago. I was chatting with a number of guys in a chat room, trying to get someone to meet up in my hotel room. Finally connected with this one guy who came over. Being a little shy and fairly new at meeting up with guys, which I had discussed during our chat, he came in and took control. We did some kissing, he slowly undressed me and laid me down face down on the bed. He proceeded to get undressed, sat on my legs, and started massaging my back and butt. He worked me over and rimmed me deep with his tongue, moved on deep with his finger, and then slowly he went deep inside me. He felt wonderful as we moved into many different positions. He was very experienced and showed me a really good time.

After I exploded with him jerking my cock and his cock hard in my ass, he pulled out. He still hadn't cum and he started to clean me up. I asked him if he was going to cum and he said no, it was all about me and he wanted to make sure I enjoyed it. He started to get dressed, and I put on my robe. After he was dressed, he stood there looking at me and finally said something about getting paid! I asked him what he was talking about, and he said that he only came over as he was expecting I was prepared to pay for his services. YIKES, I had hired a male prostitute. I was really embarrassed and didn't have much cash on me. I gave him a few bucks, apologized, and he left. Never made that mistake again!

Beach, Resort, Park, and Hotel

Back at the beginning of summer I met up with a BateWorld (BW) guy for a hotel bate. He left the room door ajar and said to let myself in when I got there, since he would be naked and bating on the balcony. I walked in, stripped off all of my clothes, and joined him. I was hard before I got to the balcony. There is something very primal that comes from meeting another man for the first time when you are both naked. I really enjoy that a lot.

He is a very hairy bear. He asked me if I would like to try on one his rubber ball stretchers. I had never worn one and was eager to try it on. I loved it as soon as he put it on me. He also introduced me to Albolene for the first time. He worked over my slicked up cock and balls for quite a while out there on the balcony. He wouldn't let me play with his dick, but I kept myself busy playing with the long fur all over his chest and back. He was so hairy; I was in heaven. Finally, he had me lie down on the bed, and he stroked me until I came. The attention he paid to my balls restrained in the stretcher was intense, and I wanted some more of that. Definitely an excellent experience for my first BW hook up.

I was in Vegas for a few days and had a few hours free before dinner meetings so I started surfing Craigslist. I looked at this one ad, "Want to give a guy a BJ while he's smoking a cigar."

So I replied. We did the usual exchange of stats and pics; he liked mine and I liked his. He was around forty, 5'8", 165 pounds, six inch cock, in Vegas with his partner. He said his partner who was gambling downstairs was cool with this. He only wanted to give me a BJ while I smoked the cigar and blew smoke in his face while he jacked his own cock. We set the time for an hour later. He was staying at the Flamingo Hotel right next to me. I cleaned up, slipped my big thick metal cock ring on, and headed down to my casino floor to find a lady walking around selling cigarettes and cigars. Bought my big ass cigar and headed next door to the Flamingo. I was fifteen minutes early, so stopped by the bar to have a couple whiskeys to settle the nerves.

Finished these and headed up to his room. He was on the thirty-third floor. Knocked on the door. He was even better looking in person than his pics. His room overlooked the strip, right across from Caesar's, with full length windows from ceiling to floor. He knelt in front of the window and wanted to give me the BJ there. I lit up the cigar, stripped down, and he started to suck my uncut cock hard. Standing there in front of that window, smoking a cigar, getting a buzz off it as I was puffing on it pretty hard to blow smoke down at him. He was a great cock sucker, could take all of my cock down without gagging. I was nervous at first, thinking his partner could come up anytime if he was done gambling, even though the guy said he wouldn't come up. I think I lasted fifteen to twenty minutes before he sucked my load out and drained my nuts! I wish I would have taken my camera along! Zipped up and went to my hotel to get ready for dinner with a smile on my face all night.

I had some lovely fun in the park the other evening after my run. I was cooling down, walking around—OK, cruising, too—when I encountered two cute Thai boys in their twenties, one about to raw fuck the other. So I indicated I wanted to join in. I sat down and watched for a few minutes. The top pulled out to let me have a go; I slipped in very nicely, fucked him for a few minutes, then pulled out for the other top (I know how to share). The other top did the same, and we took turns for a bit, then the bottom started to make it clear he wanted our cum. The top let me go first, and I shot a lovely load in his lovely ass. After I shot, I pulled out and watched the other top do the same until he came too. Then I pulled up my shorts and walked away as if nothing had happened. That was really hot, and I loved it. I thought afterward I really should have eaten that cum cocktail out of the bottom's ass; it's one of my favorite activities. Next time.

Back in the day when I first started playing around with other guys, the only site I knew about was gay.com. I had been talking to this older guy from a nearby town and he mentioned a park outside of town where people go to have sex. He wanted to meet at a bar, have a drink, and see where things went. So we did that. We decided to take a drive out to this park. He had an SUV, so we parked, and he laid down the back seat. We started making out, and he wanted to ride my cock. I lay on my back, and he crawled on top of me and slid up and down my rock hard cock. We fucked for quite some time, and I shot my load. Afterwards, he kept riding me when all of a sudden I saw headlights coming down the driveway of this park. I yelled, "Someone's coming, get off, get off!" He was still loving the feeling of my cock apparently because he didn't understand what I was saying and asked, "What?" I said, "Get off me, someone is coming!" Just then a spotlight shined in the windows. It was a cop! He comes up to the door and opens it.

The only thing I could do, since there was no time to get dressed, was to hide under some blankets and hope he didn't notice me—I was young and just wishful thinking! He asked what was going on, and my new friend just said, "Having some fun is all." He shined the flashlight at me and told him, "Tell her to get dressed." The cop thought it was a woman hiding under the blanket. He told him it was another guy. I took the blanket off and got dressed, but another cop showed up. My worst fear was coming true. I wasn't out, and now I was probably going to jail for having sex in public with another man!

The cops separated us and asked me if I was there on my own will or was I forced. Then they asked how we met. I told them the truth and apparently so did the other guy. They finally brought us together, and told us they didn't care what we did in the privacy of our own homes, but to leave it out of the parks. Then they told us to get out of there and that they didn't want to see us back there again! I couldn't believe we were getting out with just a warning, but who was I to question it?

I chatted with that guy again after that, but we never met up again. As scary as it was to get caught, I still love the feeling of having sex outdoors. I did return to that park a few times after, but with smart phones and hookup apps, the parks aren't cruised as much anymore. It didn't stop me from checking out a few other parks and trails I found on Squirt.

I like older men and really do enjoy group sex with older men. Many years ago, I went to an unofficial gay nude beach on one of the Keys before you get to Key West—likely, it's been destroyed by Hurricane Irma. It's difficult to get to, so it's mostly locals in the know who go there. As I was exploring deeper along the shore and into the mangroves, I came upon a burly, masculine, hairy man in his mid-late sixties lying out on the sand on his towel and stroking his rather large cock, maybe about nine inches and very thick. I really do like a mature, hairy daddy with a thick dick. He said, "Hello, son, would you like to join me?" I agreed, and he stood up as we began to explore each other's body. He had a very hairy ass crack, something I like. I rubbed my spit-covered finger all around his pucker, and began to jack off his fat daddy cock. He was moaning and telling me, "You're going to make daddy cum, son, do you want me to shoot my sperm for you?" to which I replied, "YES SIR!!"

Beach, Resort, Park, and Hotel

I began to massage his prostate and tighten my grip as I stroked his growing dick. Soon, he mumbled, "I'm cumming, boy, here it comes!" and shot out about six or seven thick, white ropes of daddy-cum that squirted up into the air and landed on my hairy legs. He thanked me and said, "Now, it's time for daddy to make his boy feel good!" He began to rub his hands all over my hairy chest, in between my thighs, down my back and ALL AROUND my furry butt and ass-pucker. He gently nibbled and teased my nips, which is one of my favorite things, while slowly but FIRMLY masturbating my hard shaft and making my long-hanging balls smack up against his fist. He meant business as he jacked and asked, "Are you gonna cum for daddy, son? You got a big load for him?" He moved his other hand to my sweaty, sticky, musky asshole and pushed a finger deep inside until he hit my cum-nut and began to rub it back and forth, making it get bigger as it filled. I could feel my hot cum bubbling up my cockshaft and some precum was already leaking out of the head.

Suddenly, his voice deepened and got louder as he said, "Gimme that milk, boy, make your daddy proud of you!" He pushed his body against mine, and I couldn't take it anymore. I shot about 8-9 huge volleys of white cum shots as he aimed the squirts at our hairy stomachs and chests, until my dick was just dribbling the last drops of my cum. He then grabbed the back of my neck and pulled me in for a hot, slobbery kiss. I loved the feeling of his mustache and grey/white beard rubbing against my face. We kissed for a while. I told him I needed to go to the bathroom and he responded, "Let me help you with that, boy." And that's a whole other story. Turns out this daddy was VERY piggy and raunchy too. I always remember this as the best day at the beach ever!

Years ago I lived near a large city park where cruising was a regular thing. On this particular day, I made eye contact with a hot, straight-looking cowboy type guy, and soon we were going at it. We traded BJs but since both of us had to leave, we made plans for later that evening. At the scheduled time, Mark came by to pick me up, saying we were going to his place. To my surprise (and slight discomfort!) we drove miles out into the country. We came to a locked gate; he got out and opened it, then drove even further into the dark. I felt maybe I had made a mistake, maybe he was one of those straight guys who went nuts after they had gay sex, but at that point I had no choice but to go through with it. I had a wild side but was not super experienced and was usually more cautious about going off with strangers.

Beach, Resort, Park, and Hotel

We parked by a horse barn where he opened the tailgate and forced me onto my back, pulled down my shorts, and proceeded to fuck me good with just spit for lube. His uncut eight incher was stretching me and making me feel good as I started to really relax and get into it. That's when he really got aggressive, pinned my hands over my head, slapped me in the face, and spit on me. I was just as turned-on as I was scared! He took his time, told me to take it, chewed on my hard nipples, and blew a big load which made me cum as well, both of us crying out at the same time. He pulled out, then reached over to a cooler in the back and grabbed us a beer. I tried to stay calm as we talked and drank. He saddled up a horse, telling me he wanted us to go for a ride. My fear came back as I thought, "This is where I get killed, and he buries my body out here in the woods."

He climbed up, pulled me up, and off we went further down the road, my ass still wet and tingling from the fuck. Naked, we rode for a while and the sensation of my hard dick rubbing against his ass and my arms around his hairy chest was awesome. After we came back to the barn and put up the horse, we drank quite a bit more beer. Soon I got on my knees and sucked on his hard cock and long foreskin, but suddenly he grabbed me up, spun me around, and shoved his cock up my ass as we both stood by the truck. He was hammering me good, and I was definitely enjoying it when he suddenly stopped and said firmly, "Be still!" He pulled hard-on my nipples, chewed on my ear, and I could feel his cock throbbing and pulsing. I asked if he was cumming, but he said, "Shut up!" and slapped me hard several times. We stood together as he held me tightly for what seemed like forever, then suddenly I felt it. What I expected to be a big cum load was a torrent of piss gushing down my legs and flooding my shoes. He was using all that beer to flush out my guts!!

As the piss and earlier cum load flowed out of me, he shoved me back onto the tailgate and sucked on my ass, slurping up the rest of the sloppy juices. I thought I had gone to heaven as he took my cock in his mouth, and I blew my load, shaking and trembling like nothing I had ever experienced before. Later, we talked, laughed, drank more beer, and took our time fucking each other on the bed of the truck and in the barn until sun up. With my inhibitions practically gone and a new found appreciation for piss in my ass, we made our way back to my place and spent the rest of the day together. Over the next year or so, I learned a lot from Mark, both giving and receiving!

Beach, Resort, Park, and Hotel

I lived in Utica, NY, when I was younger, and all the gay men knew that Proctor Park was a cruising area. So one Saturday afternoon, I drove to the park to see who was out. If was a nice summer day about 75 degrees, and a cool breeze was blowing. I drove around and ended up parking near the trees to watch and see who was around. Within five to fifteen minutes, this adorable guy came riding through on a ten-speed bike, short brown hair with the most adorable smile and a swimmer's body, dressed in shorts and a t-shirt. He cruised by me about three times before he stopped to chat.

Well, the next thing I knew he was following me to my apartment. I was in my early thirties, and he was in his late twenties. Once inside my apartment, we sat and chatted for a while, listening to some music and having a beer. We started kissing on the couch and things got hot. I led him down to my bedroom, and we continued to make out and got undressed. This guy's body was rock hard, nice tight ass, and the legs were perfect from riding his bike. Once we were totally naked, we got on the bed, and I got my first full look at his beautiful, seven inch cock and balls. His cock stood straight up, pointing to his chest, and it was pink and perfect. His eyes were deep blue, and he wore a choker around his neck with a medallion on it which he said was a Polish symbol. We continued kissing and grinding our bodies together, and I slid down and began sucking on his beautiful cock.

OMG I was in heaven. The smell and taste was out of this world. I lay between his legs, sucking his cock and balls, listening to his breathing becoming heavy. He pulled me up to him and kissed me like there was no tomorrow. He rolled me over onto my back and kissed me some more, then went down to suck my cock, which is about six inches. We ended up in a 69 position with him lying on top of me and my arms wrapped around his body while I continued to suck his cock. Next thing I knew, he was sliding down to rim my hole, which felt incredible. We continued like this for about twenty minutes, and he finally asked if he could fuck me. I was more than happy to say yes. I went to the nightstand, got a rubber and some lube as he lay on his back with the most beautiful smile on his face and his eyes just glistening in the light from outside. I put some ky on his cock, put the rubber on, and then proceeded to mount his rock hard, perfect pink cock.

Once I got him inside me, my head started spinning with so much pleasure. It was totally incredible. We fucked for what seemed an hour, me on top, riding his cock and kissing his soft pink lips. He finally said to me that he was ready to cum, so I told him to go ahead. He grabbed my cock and started stroking me so that we could come together. It was amazing!! We shot our loads at the same time, and I fell on top of him, completely satisfied. We both took a moment to catch our breath with his cock still inside me and still rock hard. We began kissing and hugging each other until his cock finally came out of my hole. We lay side by side in total silence, until he noticed it was 6:00 pm, and he needed to get up to shower, and go home.

That was just one of many perfect Saturday afternoons I spent with my hot friend from the park.

A friend and I went to Yellowstone on vacation. We stayed at the historic Old Faithful Inn and took day-trip drives to various areas of the park during that week. However, I loved to walk and hike for exercise, which he didn't enjoy at all. So occasionally, off I'd go. I got to see a lot of the less-traveled areas of the park, so that was terrific. However, one afternoon turned out to be very special. I have to first admit to being abnormally shy and self-conscious. I guess that was the direct result of growing up being the chubby kid on the block. Even though I've fought to keep my weight under control and was often told I was good-looking, I still would shy away from social gatherings. I never cruised the local parks and wouldn't think of going to one of the gay watering holes alone. Even though I'm now a senior citizen, I still am as shy as ever, perhaps even more so now because of the gay focus on youth and beauty. My social life is near zero. Be that as it may, I reflect on this special event of nearly forty years ago.

Flowing directly north of the Old Faithful Geyser is the Fire Hole River. North of that are some remote hillside areas with narrow pathways leading to seldom visited geysers and pools. I decided to head that direction to hike up the mountainside and investigate. Ironically, the first geyser I came across was called Bear Cub. Even though I was a few years past the "cub" stage, I was certainly a bear. I waited there for a while, hoping for an eruption (of the geyser). Didn't happen. So I journeyed on. Further up the pine-covered mountain's winding path I eventually happened onto another geyser with another ironic name—Solitary Geyser.

Since I hadn't had good luck finding a permanent life-partner at that time, I considered my situation as solitary too. My personal "geyser" went off often, but alone 99% of the time. Again, I waited for this Yellowstone version to erupt. The area around this geyser seemed more scarred and damaged, so I figured when and if this one went off, it must be pretty spectacular. While I waited, I enjoyed the sights, sounds, and smells of the pine forest, deep blue skies, and mountain air. What I didn't expect were any other humans to be up on that side of the mountain. But as I stood there looking at the still dormant geyser cone, a very attractive fellow bear emerged from the trail on the other side of the forest opening. Like me, he was wearing cut-off Levi shorts and a tank top.

I couldn't help but notice his huge, muscular and hairy arms, and the thick muscles of his hairy thighs and calves. His legs were like tree trunks. He obviously either spent a lot of time at the gym or else he had a very physically taxing job. He looked at the sputtering geyser, then over at me. We nodded, but didn't speak. There soon became an uncomfortable, yet exciting, atmosphere as we both stood there on opposite sides of the seemingly dormant geyser. Neither of us walked away.

To my surprise, he reached down and rubbed his hand across the front of his body. By now, he was staring at me rather than at the scenery. I couldn't believe this handsome bull would be interested in me. I was in good shape since I did marathon walking for exercise. But totally lacking in self-confidence, I didn't think my body anywhere near compared to his.

However, our subtle signals continued for a few minutes. Then we both started to walk around the geyser toward each other. When we finally got close, we simultaneously reached out and gripped the back of each other's neck. Instantly, we were in a passionate kiss. Even though the area was quite remote, we worked our way through the underbrush to a very secluded spot where we could continue to kiss and hug without fear of interruptions. Soon our clothes were on the ground serving as a makeshift blanket for us to lie on. Lots of body exploring followed. I'd never had someone lick every square inch of me like this stud did. Soon I was returning the favor and loving it. Two bears rubbing and licking each other. I was in heaven.

The smell of pine trees and sulfur geysers just added to the special scene. Eventually, we locked together in a 69 suck. Legs wrapped around each other's head as we hugged the other guy's furry butt. Hair-covered chests and bellies rubbed. The mixing fur crackled as we ground our bodies against each other. It was like we became one ball of hairy bear flesh. Feeling his body rubbing on mine, along with his determination to drain my hard cock made me want to do the same for him. It didn't take long before we were both feeling the throbbing dick in our mouths pump cum down our throats. We filled each other with seed at exactly the same instant. There were many long minutes of sexual afterglow that followed. Neither of us wanted that special moment to end. But it eventually did. We dressed and shared yet another passionate kiss before he turned and slowly walked away.

During the rest of my week-long vacation in Yellowstone, I kept looking for my heart-throb bear at every tourist stop, store, and restaurant. I hadn't told my friend about my experience. However, he'd noticed that I seemed distracted and didn't have my usual focus at the wonderful natural phenomenon we were witnessing at the park. To my surprise, I did see that special bear again. It was at another of the geysers that required a short public hike to get to the view area. However, to my disappointment, he was with someone, just as I was. But I got the feeling his relationship with that fellow wasn't a platonic friendship like I had with my buddy. Almost on cue, the four of us walked back to our two respective cars. My dream bear flashed me a loving look as he got into his car, and they drove away in their white Ford Taurus with Wyoming plates. If nothing else, I was given closure to one of the most magnificent events of my life.

I have a story of discovery. The summer that I was fifteen, I worked at a beach club on the Jersey Shore. I was locker boy. We were supposed to open the beach lockers for customers that came in to change clothes and store their clothes for the day while they used and played on the beach. My coworkers from the years before had drilled small holes in the back of some of the lockers, so that they could peek at the female customers changing. Well, I found out about the holes and would peek at any of the hot looking men that would come in to the beach club.

One weekend when I was on duty, I had a really hot guy and a few of his friends come to use the lockers, which were actually little, private, walk-in closets. I was busy most of the day since it was the weekend and a great day for the beach. I was admiring the hot guys all day since they were right below us on the beach, and we were on the boardwalk. I heard one of them say he was going for a walk and decided to change back into his street clothes. When he called for me, I followed him to his the locker. Getting very close to him and looking up at him and his hot, hairy chest, I could just imagine what was in his swim trunks. I also noticed that this was one of the peephole lockers. I quickly went around to the other locker and looked through the hole. Boy, was I surprised to see one of the nicest cocks I could remember ever seeing. It was not huge but a nice seven inches with a great dark bush as well. I was thinking, "Damn, I want to put that cock in my mouth and suck on it for hours."

Next thing I noticed was an eyeball looking back at me through the little peephole. He said, "If you want to see more come on back over." So I immediately told my coworkers that I was taking a short break and ran back to the hot man at his locker. He was waiting for me for sure and quickly opened the door and let me in. There he was standing in front of me, completely naked and hard. He said, "If you want it, take it," and that is exactly what I did. I started sucking on this delicious cock that tasted like salt water from the ocean but still felt great in my mouth. He kept sliding it in and out, and all I could think of was that delicious cock in my mouth.

Before he was ready to cum, he knelt down in front of me and took my fifteen-year-old cock in his mouth and gave me a very hot blowjob as well. I was so anxious that I shot very quickly, and he just gobbled it all up with out missing a beat. Then I finished him off. It was the first time I had swallowed a complete load rather than just a drop or two. I took all of his man cum and swallowed it all. When I said that I had to return to work, he said, "Well, let's do this again later. I know my friends would enjoy meeting you too." I never did get to meet his friends there at work, but I did bump into them on the boardwalk and was introduced to them as the little cocksucker. That is exactly what we did, back in their hotel room that night. It was my first of many orgies I would experience in my life, with four guys in their early twenties and me a fifteen-year-old chicken.

ADULT BOOKSTORE

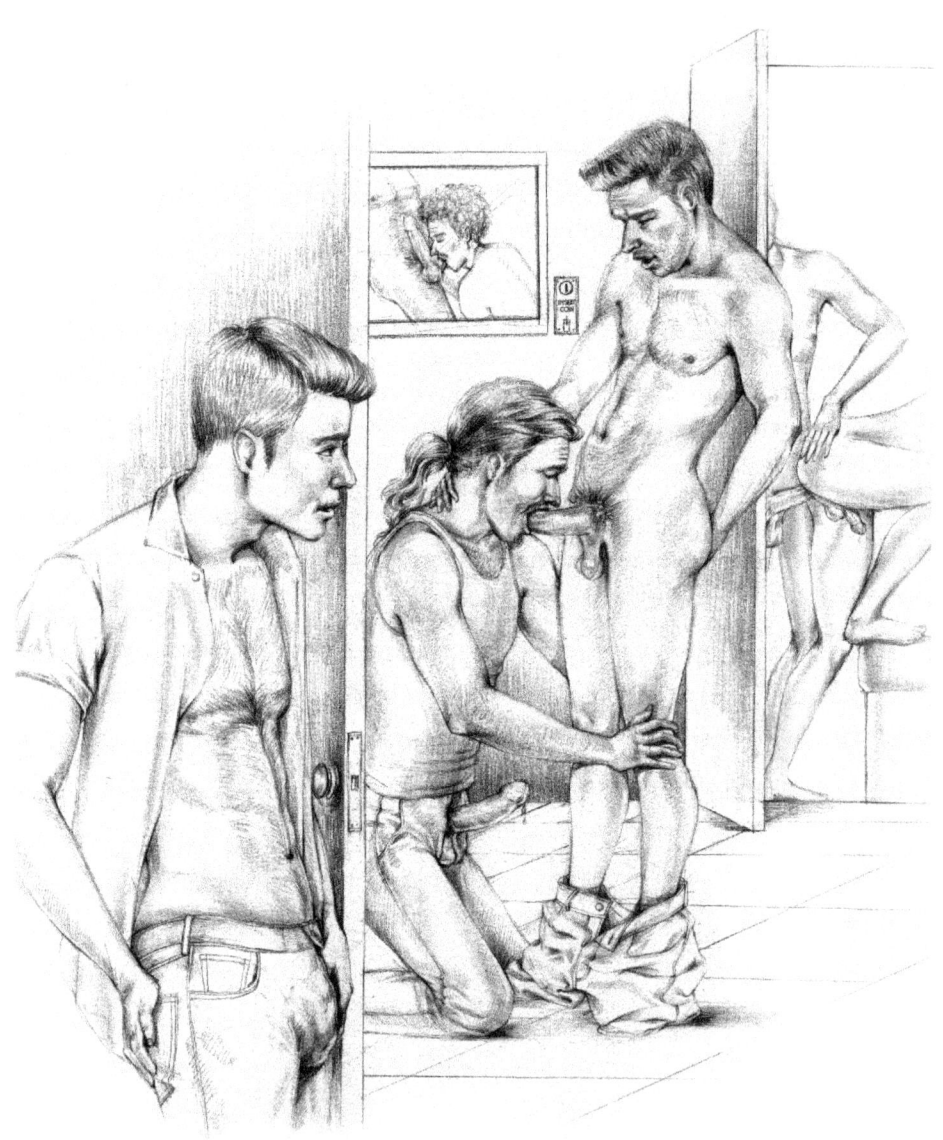

It was a hot September night, and I was in the mood for some fun. Did not want to do the bar scene so I went to Adult World, an adult bookstore with video booths in the back and guys cruising each other for a pick up. I just pulled into the parking lot around 9:00 pm and sat in my car to see who was going in and coming out. Within five minutes, a good-looking guy walked out, dressed in jeans and a white polo, wearing a ball cap. So I followed him to where he was parked and pulled my car in front of his, along side of the building. Shut my car off, and within a minute he was at my driver's side door, asking me if I was a cop. I said no and asked him the same question.

Well, to skip ahead, he got into my car, and we exchanged names. He asked what I was up to. Told him I was horny and looking for some fun. He then put his hand on my thigh and started rubbing it, getting closer to my package, so I returned the favor. He unzipped his pants and lowered them so I could get a look at his cock, which was semi-hard and about seven inches, with a nice little bush of hair and shaved balls. We started kissing. I was stroking his cock and said to him, "Why don't we go to my place where there is more room to play."

He was about 6' tall, slender body, and had a bald head and mustache. Beautiful six pack, and did I mention a nice cock? We drove to my apartment and went to my bedroom where we started kissing and undressing each other. As we were standing face-to-face, rubbing each other's body and undressing each other, he bent down to remove my jeans and slowly started sucking my cock. Wow, could this guy give head. I returned the favor and licked and sucked his cock. He pulled me up, kissed me, and guided me to the bed to lie on my back. Got between my legs and continued to suck my dick and caress my balls. He then proceeded to finger my hot hole, getting it loose and moist. Then he brought himself up to my face so I could suck on his cock and play with his asshole. This went on for a while, and we ended up in a 69 position so we could suck cock and finger each other's hole. I was on the bottom, and I moved my self up enough to rim his hot, tight, pink hole. I was loving every moment of it, having a hot guy suck my cock while I was rimming his hole. I was in heaven.

He moved himself down on me so he could return the favor of rimming me. Oh, my God, the feeling was amazing. He then rolled off me and got on top, taking a condom from my night stand, opening it with his teeth, and slowing putting it on his rock hard cock. Once on, he spread my legs apart, then bent over to kiss me as he slowly put his cock into my ass. I was in so much pleasure with his seven inches entering me that I could hardly contain my self and blew my load. He slowly began fucking my ass and kissing me, and the tempo increased as he pumped his hot, hard cock into my ass. My legs wrapped around his waist, his cock deep inside me, pumping at a nice rhythm. This went on for over a half hour. I was in heaven. This guy really knew how to fuck.

Did I mention that he had a rock hard body with a six pack that you could use as a wash board. Strong masculine arms and a nice golden tan. We continued to fuck until he was ready to explode, pulling his cock out and removing the rubber to let his cum fly across my chest—only to grab onto my cock and stroke it until I came. He lay on top of me, covered in our cum, kissing me and holding me tight. We finally got off the bed and went into the shower together to clean each other off.

The other day, I went to my favorite bookstore. Hadn't been there in a couple of weeks—I was busy, then out of town. Anyway, I was surprised that the guys had told a cute hottie with a BEAUTIFUL BIG COCK that if anyone could take his swollen dick, it was ME. I was touched and suddenly VERY horny. I was introduced to Trevor, and we quickly got started. He pulled down his pants to show me a semi-hard, uncut cock, nice round balls, with furry pubes on top.

I took his monster in my mouth, where it quickly grew to the RAGING point. I sucked on his balls, licked his shaft, played with his foreskin, did my tongue action for him, and he moaned with delight. I stood up, lubed his massive tool with some lube—I carry some because you never know when a monster cock comes your way. I lubed my hole, his cockhead, and then we gently pushed. I felt his cockhead enter, then we paused. I took some more of his cock, and then paused. Within minutes, I had his WHOLE shaft in my tight hole. He started to stroke, then more, faster, and pretty soon we were enjoying his entire shaft, doing full strokes in my hole.

I could feel his cock in my hole, stiffening, getting ready to explode! He grabbed my nipples and licked my neck as I grabbed his ass cheeks and pulled his balls so he would enter me deeper. He gave out a native moan. As he EXPLODED in my tight hole, I could feel his creamy cum gushing out. As he came and came, my hole filled up. Creamy cum started to drip down my legs. He held me close as he unloaded. I felt him grow soft and he pulled out. He took a deep breath, and said his girlfriend NEVER gave him a fuck like that. I felt proud. I'm going to see him again; we exchanged numbers, and perhaps I can lure him away from the girlfriend.

Adult Bookstore

I would LOVE to be one of those bottoms that gets fucked, time and time again. I just love having a raw cock in my ass, plowing to release its creamy cum. My usual hung, married stud's wife is pulling the strings, more or less. I think she has gotten wind that he is getting sucked and fucked elsewhere, since she won't give it to him. Anyway, the guys at my local bookstore have taken his "leave of absence" as a time when they can now get into my tight ass. I have the reputation of being a really tight, good piece of ass that loves to get fucked.

Last week, I had this Cholo that had been eyeing me last couple of times. I have had his thick, uncut chorizo in my ass before, so having him fuck me again was my pleasure. But now, since I am under no pressure to have him wait in line, Ramon is usually the first. I suck his awesome cock, playing with his foreskin, nipping it, putting my tongue between his skin and his shaft. I get him really hard and spit-lubed. Then I stand up, turn around and have him ease his thick cock in my tight hole. It takes a few minutes, but soon I have his shaft all the way, pubes to my ass cheeks. Then he slowly starts to stroke his shaft in and out of me. He plays with my nips because that is what really turns me on.

He picks up the pace as he strokes harder and faster. I reach back and grab his ass cheeks to drive his shaft as far into me as he can. I feel his pubes and balls slap my ass cheeks with every stroke. As he starts panting, he nibbles my ear and neck. Soon he explodes with such force that his creamy cum sometimes spills out and down my legs. I brace myself against the wall, with his cock still inside me as we catch our breath. He gets soft, and then he pulls out. Mmmmmm. Until the next week. He knows that even when John does come back, it will be a toss-up if John or Ramon fucks me first.

On the average, you would be surprised how far $20.00 can get you. Last year $60.00 got me all night of sucking and being fucked by two hunky, hot, go-go boys. There are some precautions you should take—don't get too drunk, know your surroundings, NEVER go into a seedy area, and during the night case out the "boys" you want to take back to your hotel room. Don't be reckless.

When I was in my thirties and forties, I used to drive over to Coralville to a bookstore called Just Different. Mostly it was a backroom with an adult book and novelty store out front. For $5 you could buy a day pass to the backroom where there were four rows of painted plywood

Adult Bookstore

cubicles with individual TVs playing porn in each. There were large rectangular holes cut between for glory holes, and there were even built-in benches and handy shelves with tissue for mopping up. I used to go about once a week. Some days the traffic was sparse, but there were times when it was crawling with men.

Once in a while, you'd see somebody you'd recognize, but mostly it was traffic from I-80—and lots of truckers. It was very easy to find a hot man who was willing to suck cock and to find a nice cock for sucking. There was often an old woman working there, or maybe just one other clerk. No matter who it was, they knew very well what went on in back and never bothered anybody. You were free to do whatever you wanted.

One of my favorite memories is of a hunky trucker with a thick, black beard. He had his face in the glory hole sucking on my cock like there was no tomorrow. Fantastic talent! At one point, I pulled out of his hot mouth to keep from cumming too soon, and he said, "Man, I'll take everything you've got." So, I gave it to him.

Another time, I remember driving over and seeing a guy in a car behind me. I could tell he was cute and hot, and when he took the same exit off the I-80, I wondered if he was heading where I was. As luck would have it, he was! He must have just come from work, because he was in a white shirt, neck tie, and dress pants. He was handsome and fit too, and he was soon on his knees in a booth next to mine asking to suck my cock. After sucking for a while, he said he wanted to eat my ass out—always a fave of mine! His being dressed nicely was a huge turn-on. So I told him to join me in my booth. Instead of locking the door, we left it ajar. I had taken off my pants and had one of my legs up on the bench so he could really have easy access to my hairy asshole. His tongue got way up inside, and he was able to get his lips around my anus and suck while he fucked me deep with his tongue. I began to see stars!

Pretty soon, a younger guy in a white t-shirt popped his head in and needed just a nod from me to get down and start sucking on my cock while the other guy sucked out my asshole. I was moaning pretty loudly, because it felt incredible. The kid sucking my cock was also squeezing my nipples under my shirt, and the guy eating my ass was gently squeezing my balls. Talk about heaven! Pretty soon this farm dude in tight jeans, a plaid shirt and cowboy hat and boots pokes his head into the booth. He got up on the bench, and I undid the big buckle on his belt. I peeled his jeans down over his bubble butt and hard thighs as far as I could. He had the biggest black bush

Adult Bookstore

that I'd ever seen, with a treasure trail up his flat stomach to his navel. His cock curved up like a satyr's and had a huge mushroom head. His balls were perfect—like big eggs hanging up tight to his crotch, ready to burst. I sucked that big head for all I was worth, working the shaft with my right hand, fingering those big balls with my left while getting my ass eaten like it'd never been eaten before or since, and having my cock sucked. I don't remember who came first, but we all came fairly close together. The guys sucking my cock and eating my ass had been pounding their cocks with their fists. We all just kind of collapsed on the bench together. My knees felt like rubber. We had a very hot group kiss, complete with cummy tongues. It was the hottest thing I've ever done. The stuff wet dreams are made of!!

The only regret I have is not getting names. It would have been great to get together again in a big bed. Oh, well, can't be too greedy!

Unfortunately, that place was torn down several years ago and the whole area has been developed into a boring common-place kind of area that you see in every burb. Last time I drove by, the Perkins restaurant was still there. It was always nice to fuck and suck at Just Different, then go and eat some pancakes with the taste of cum still on your tongue!

When I was about twenty years old, I heard of cock rings but never had any experience with them. Finally, after a few days, got up the nerve to go to an adult video store to purchase one. I was completely nervous, heart racing, a little sweaty, as I'd never been to a video store before. I was so excited when I entered the store, I popped a bone looking at all the leather wear, dildos, movie covers, etc. I was the only one in the store with exception of the clerk. Decent looking guy but didn't pay too much attention since I was trying to hide my boner. I went over to the cock ring section and, with a lump in my throat, started to look at the packages. There were so many. How was I to choose?

Then I heard his voice, "Can I help you find something, buddy?" I turned around, and the clerk was watching me from the register. I told him I never had a cock ring and really wanted one, so he offered to help me—even so far as allowing me to take them into the dressing room to figure out size. I took a few styles into the dressing room and really started to stress out—how do I get these damn things over my hard-on?

Adult Bookstore

Then a knock at the door. He asked if I was ok, I must have been in there a while. I said yes but was having trouble figuring out size, etc. He asked to see, so I opened the door with my pants at my ankles, hard-on straight to the ceiling and stretching the cock ring in my hand. He started to put the ring on me, as he was kneeling. Then he started to gently caress my cock and said, "See how good it feels with a ring? This one is perfect for you." I said I agreed and told him I would take the package and he replied, "Not so quick, young man." As soon as his sentence was over, he deep-throated my cock, burying his nose into my twenty-year-old pubes. He held his head in there until my eyes started to water and he heard me moan. He then gently and lovingly made love to my cock with his mouth, up and down and very wet from slobber.

He stopped, only to tell me to warn him when I was getting close, because he didn't want me to cum in his mouth. He then kept sucking my seven inch, thick, cut cock until my eyes started to roll. I told him I was getting closer to cumming, and he pulled his pants down, bent over the open dressing room door, and shoved his pre-lubed ass around my cock. Three thrusts later he was being filled with my cum. It was amazing! When done, he said I could come back any time, and he let me keep the cock rings. I still wear them, thinking about that time with him every time I breed a smooth ass like his.

Just a little story that happened to me about a week ago. There is a bookstore that I go to from time to time. I meet a guy there, white guy, only about 5'9", a little bit of fur but not much, just enough to cover his chest. BTW, he's married. Anyway, he has one of biggest, thickest cocks I have seen in a long while. His monster has got to be about ten inches and four to five inches around. Really defined cockhead and round, tasty balls. LOVES to get sucked AND to fuck, but most guys are scared of his girth. He loves to fuck and to fuck without cumming, because he knows what a gift he has between his legs. One day I was sucking him and he kept on lubing my hole with his spit. I told him if we did, it would have to be slow and easy. He agreed. I took his cockhead in my hole. We must have worked his cock to stretch my hole for about twenty minutes.

But the best part was when I had the entire cock in my hole. I worked him in and out, in and out, to help me take his girth. Soon, I was driving his cock in my hole. It seemed with each stroke, he was getting harder and harder. I was snorting poppers all the time because I needed that cock and it felt so damn good. He was pulling my tits and licking my neck as we built up our feverish pitch. I grabbed my cock, as it was apparent we were both close to cumming. I shot my creamy load high in the air as his cock twitched in my ass, unloading his sticky, creamy load. A little bit dripped down my leg as he gently pulled out of my well-fucked hole. We talked for a bit; he told me was so glad I agreed to let him fuck me. He was getting tired of blowjobs because guys were afraid to let him fuck them. I told him my hole is always open to his massive cock—I LOVE to feel a big cock in my ass. We agreed to meet again this week and weeks to follow.

I was in the closet, married, and still am. At the time in my early twenties, I was working at night, so after work I was able to stop off at the bookstores for some quickie sex, j/o, glory hole sucking and cum before going home. One of the bookstores was quite busy at night. This was in the days before the AIDS scare when the bookstores in my area all closed their cruising and video booths. I got to know this one guy. We met every Friday evening about 11:30 and would play in the booth until we sucked each other off.

One night, he said he wanted to suck my toes. This probably doesn't sound like anything special or new to many of the guys reading this but for me at the time it was something very special and new that I had not experienced before. Wow, it was really erotic, got me so hot I was ready to shoot my load as soon as he put my cock in his mouth. This is a short story, but it was a long relationship. We enjoyed playing with each other for a couple of years before the bookstore closed their booths. Wish there were still bookstores around so those of us who are still in the closet would have a place to meet other guys for some fun times.

Way back in Lansing, Michigan, the main street to the state capitol building was Michigan Avenue. There was one block that had three bookstores and two gay bars. Well, I still thought I was a straight man, married with two daughters. Here it was, thanksgiving weekend, I had Friday off, but had to work Saturday, so I left the family in northern Michigan with Mom and Dad, to go back on Saturday afternoon and pick them up to return to Lansing. Got back Friday about 3:00 pm. With frigid wife, I thought I would go to one of the bookstores to watch a movie and beat off. A reminder, in the mid-80s there was no internet and the 8mm movies were $50.00, and where do you hide that? I didn't have 50 bucks to my name since my wife controlled all the money, so I figured I could at

Adult Bookstore

least spend $5 bucks on the 25 cent movies. So about 4:00 pm, I got in my '73 Buick Le Sabre and went downtown—nervous as hell that someone would see me in that area. Stupid me, if they saw me, what were they doing there? Now I am sixty-four and don't give a rat's ass who sees me where.

So I gathered up my courage and made the trek, parked in a back lot and made my way into the store. The first thing that hit me was the smell. Got a hell of a hard-on. There was a clerk on a raised platform behind a counter, big fat guy in a wife beater. Gave him my $5 bucks and got a hand full of quarters. Turned around to see the black hallway with very dim lighting and a couple of not so attractive guys milling around. The movies were in plastic boxes on each door of the cubicle, each cubicle had two movies. Toward the rear of the hall, one of the movies was gay and one straight. Being curious about the other type of movie (gay) I found an empty booth, closed the door, and slid the bolt to lock the door. There were two coin boxes, A being for straight, and B for gay. They were 8mm, no sound movies so someone on the outside would not know which you chose. So I started with the straight movie. Put a couple of quarters in and it started—awful, jumpy, out of focus. Four minutes later the movie stopped and the dim light came back on in the booth. I heard someone enter the booth next to this one, lock the door, and drop money.

I put more money in; this time I tried the gay movie. Next thing I hear is a "psst." There's a hole in the wall between the booths and there's a finger wagging in the hole, and he says, "Put your dick through the hole, and I'll suck it." Well, I freaked the fuck out and started shaking, thinking how nice that would feel, but yet he might bite my dick off. I was so afraid and so hard; I was dripping precum like crazy. Well, the dick won the battle. I shoved it through the hole and oh my god, heaven on earth. I just could not stop shaking. I was so very nervous and worried what might happen. The guy actually stopped and whispered thru the hole, "Man, are you gonna make it or are you gonna pass out?" I told him, "I am just very nervous," and put it back thru the hole. When he asked me the question, it calmed me down somewhat and about a minute later was spurting down his throat. Zipped up and hustled out of there back to the car and spent a good ten minutes trying to calm the fuck down. I just kept saying to myself, "Wow that felt SO good." So, as I'm sure you have already guessed, that was the first time, but sure as hell not the last time.

I was married for ten years, had two girls, probably fucked her eight times in that ten years. Grew up knowing I was different but not knowing why. When I saw that first gay movie, I knew right away why I felt different all that time. Crazy thing was that she fell in love with my best friend, who was in a heavy metal band with me. Divorced me to shack up with him. A year later, I moved to California to be who I knew I should be. Met a guy after being there for a month, moved in, then spent the next thirty-three years together. Got married back when it became legal in Washington state. Then we found out he had syphilis for the last forty years. We were both tops, so I never got it from him. The VA treated him for it, and that was four years ago. Now he is suffering the effect of the disease—lesions on the brain—and he has gone into stage three dementia. Says he's gonna divorce me, and I'm all for it. What a waste. I take a couple of days off and go into Portland to have fun and relax. Now living in a very rural area, but thank goodness for the internet and a buddy who sends me porn movies and stories to keep me sane.

Part of my graduate program was to intern for a university in the Midwest. I arrived late August to "Smalltown, Middle Country" and soon realized that my up-till-now active sex life was probably going to nosedive until I left in December. Everything man-to-man (if there was anything man-to-man) was undoubtedly underground. I looked hard (yes, I searched everywhere, and yes, I was sometimes hard while I looked.) Nothing. No bars, no darkrooms, no T-rooms, no gym or locker room action. Nothing.

Well, maybe something. I was assigned to work in Rick's office. Rick was single and early thirties. Tall, lanky with slim hips. Blond with sun streaks and deep tan marked him as more of a surfer—but two thousand miles from a coast. I loved how his sinewy tan arms showed off an expensive watch nestled in his blond hair. Beautiful blond, hairy arms. What else was hairy and blond? As the only two younger (I was only twenty) single guys in the office we became friendly. He told me about another town about thirty-five miles away. He laughed that there wasn't much to do in our little college burg so he enjoyed the time away visiting.

I liked Rick, and I liked to watch him move. His movements were graceful in a way; his long body seemed to glide. When he leaned back in his desk chair with his hands behind his head, he was so slim, flat with the only bumps being his well-formed nipples showing through his dress shirts and the fabulous bulge, big but not tight. In my fantasies, he was definitely a boxer's man. I jerked off thinking about him, wondering what else lay beneath his office clothes. But he was my boss, off limits in my mind, and I

Adult Bookstore

was resigned to just wondering. Not acting. I didn't even really imagine he enjoyed men; his girlfriend was pretty hot.

A quiet Saturday (Hell, there was nothing but quiet weekends.) I decided to check out the other town. A thirty-five mile drive might cool my jets. Driving into town, I saw what appeared to be Mecca to my man-deprived self—"The Rodeo Video Store"—I knew it had to be an adult bookstore. I pulled in to check it out, at least I could get some new porn. Hopefully more. Yes, video booths!

It wasn't really that crowded. The movies warmed me up, and I had my shirt off, pinching my nipples while I stroked myself. I enjoyed a few men through the elongated hole in the plywood wall. First a guy in a uniform of some sort, nice thick five inches, shaved so deep-throating him was awesome, no gagging. He shot a big, creamy load pretty fast and scurried off satisfied.

Next, a nervous married guy (I could see his ring) that shot in probably less than a minute. The place was deserted for a while, so I watched some more movies. Naked now, why not be comfortable! I was edging myself so as to enjoy my new gay wonderland for as long as possible. I heard the door in the next booth, and in an instant a new dick pushed up to the hole. Long, probably seven limp, not very thick, like tall, lanky guys have. Gorgeous blond thatch. Uncut, not the pruney kind that makes it look shriveled up, but the hooded type that gives a hint as to how much it's going to grow and maybe give a little musky smell that is distinctly masculine.

I was on my knees fast. I took the covered head into the front of my mouth and began to roll my tongue round and round and felt him relax and lean in, excited for what he knew would be an amazing blowjob. Slowly, I took him deeper, still rolling my tongue around his cock as it stiffened more and more. It was rock hard as it pushed against the back of my throat, and I began to bounce my head up and down, and my mystery man began to moan quietly. He tried to pull back, and I never slowed down with the grip I had on his long, hard dick. He did pull away and whispered he didn't want to shoot yet. As he pulled back I saw his arms—shit. And I saw his watch and those beautiful blond, hairy arms. Shit, not really knowing what to do and for the moment not wanting him to know his intern had just deep-throated him, I stuck my hard dick through the hole. Immediately, I felt the warm, wet, welcoming mouth of a man, a feeling that I hadn't felt in over a month. I felt like I would collapse as his lips and tongue made love to my erect penis and my loose hanging balls. I was a little afraid I would cum too soon but he was expert, speeding up and slowing down, teasing me from the head of my dick to the base of my balls between my legs.

I heard him say, "Turn." I did, and his tongue slid into my ass. So sensitive to me, the tongue, the lips, even the teeth all around. My pink hole relaxed its tightness, and I was ready for what I had missed so terribly, a man sliding deep into me and loving me, and banging me senseless. I ached to feel the head of the hard cock that was aching for fucking a tight warm hole. I heard him whisper, "Open your door." If I did, he'd know that I knew his secret. If I didn't, I'd potentially miss out on a solid man fucking me. I wanted and needed a man so fucking bad. He could essentially flunk me, or we could have the rest of the semester sweaty and testosterone-driven.

I went with my testosterone. I unlocked my door, and he slid inside. In the dim flickering light of the video, his eyes raised up and recognition hit him. He paused, briefly considering the same things that I had. Looking confused, then concerned, his eyes narrowed and his mouth moved to a crooked grin. He put his beautiful arm around my neck and pulled with enough force to shift my whole naked body next to him. His tongue that had just been in my ass slipped into my mouth. I melted under the powerful kiss and the force. He pulled me next to him. His hands lowered to each cheek of my bare ass.

I looked down and saw those huge nipples hard with excitement through Rick's tight t-shirt. My hands, then my fingers went to manipulate them, and I noticed his hard dick pressing through his shorts against my naked crotch. I quickly pulled off his top and dropped it on my pile of clothes. My tongue began to manipulate the nips I had fantasies about. He moaned quietly, and I was reminded why he had asked me to open my door and why he had come hard and solid into my booth. I unbuttoned his shorts, and they fell to his ankles. He kicked them to the pile of clothes, and I turned and leaned over the bench—my ass forced high in the air, my pink, wrinkled hole quivering with anticipation. Still drippy wet from his spit, he slid in easily. He was so long he went deep right away, and I cringed a little bit. He leaned in and whispered in my ear, "Too much?" "Hell no, I've been wanting this day forever. Fuck me!"

Sometimes we crave something and when we get it, it doesn't measure up to our expectations. Rick's fucking me exceeded my masturbation-filled expectations. Even for a quickie in a video booth, he knew how to provide slow long-way-in-almost-all-the-way-out satisfaction, teasing my prostate with the rough banging hard up against my prostate. Honestly, it didn't take long with that stimulation for me to shoot a generous load across the black vinyl of the bench. When Rick saw my cum, he took one more thrust, shuddered, and shot his load deep in me, coating my prostate with his creamy juice.

Reality hit me fast. I had just been fucked like a cum slut by my boss/mentor. Now what? We both stood up, and with the sweet crooked smile he told me, "Get dressed, let's go, let me buy you a beer." That beer was the gateway to a semester long affair that literally gave me goose bumps every time we were together. Sometimes a weekend away, sometimes a blowjob under the desk. We were inseparable till I had to leave. Internship grades are funny. Who fails an internship, right? Well, I got an A+.

I decided to go to a local adult bookstore the other day, watch some porn and see what else might be going on. The place was packed. I walked into a big booth, and in one minute another guy joined me, good-looking, nice body, looked like a nice bulge in his shorts. He pulled my shorts down and started jacking on my uncut cock, sliding my foreskin up and down over my now swelling cockhead. I reached over and pulled his shorts down, nice cut cock, hanging balls. He got on his knees and started sucking my cock.

As he was sucking me, another guy walked in. I had seen him in this place before, and I knew that he loved rimming my hairy ass. He got behind me and spread my ass cheeks and started eating, licking on my ass, and tongue fucking my hole. Fuck, it felt great getting sucked and rimmed at the same time! The guy who is rimming me reaches over and starts jacking on the other guy's cock. Before long, he moves and starts sucking his cock. He stood up and asked him to fuck him. The guy smiled and said ok. He put some lube on his cock, turned around, and slid his cock and balls deep into his ass. They started fucking, moaning and moaning. You could hear his balls slapping against his ass with every thrust! Damn hot scene.

Then a young black guy walks in and seeing the action, takes out his cock. Nice cut cock. Jacking on his cock, the guy that is getting fucked starts sucking on his cock, then shifts back and forth between my cock and his cock. Damn nice.

In another minute, another guy walks in, also black. He takes out his cock. I started jacking on his cock, and then I bent down and started sucking on it. It was a total orgy! So fucking hot, all five enjoying some hot man-play. Then, another guy walks in. The two are still fucking, and he says he is close to cumming. He tells him to shoot, and he does. The whole place had to hear him moaning when he shot his cum load up this guy's ass. The other guy that had walked in dropped his shorts and asked the black guy to fuck him, so he spits on his dick, rams it in his ass, and fucks him like crazy. Again, we could hear his balls slapping against his ass. At that point, the guy that had already been fucked leaned over and started sucking on my cock again. I told him I was close to cumming, and he told me to shoot my load down his throat. I started blasting my cum load. He swallowed every fucking drop of my manjuice, licked every drop off of my cock, and slid my foreskin up and down a few times to get every last drop—mmmmm, damn nice afternoon!

I visit my local adult bookstore from time to time and generally nothing or not much happens. Several months ago, I visited and walked around the booths looking at guys. I figured this was another nothing day. I didn't notice a young (twentyish) blond guy come in. As I walked around like the other guys, I saw the kid in a booth with his shorts and underwear down. Boy, did he have a beautiful ass. He was facing the monitor screen and sniffing what I figured were poppers.

I finally got the nerve to join him and asked if he minded my being there. He sort of quietly grunted something—he just wasn't talking. I touched his ass since it was there looking for attention. He made a pleasing sound, so I continued touching his ass. I reached around to touch his nice cock which was up against the wall. I think he moved somehow, indicating that he did want his cock touched. I kissed his ass and then put a finger up it. He really groaned and wiggled. Well, that was all I needed. I pushed three fingers in his ass. I noticed that he was pre-lubed with the slippery, stringy stuff, don't know what it is called. I had never fisted a man before and this cutie was giving signals that he wanted more. I was amazed how easily I got my hand up his tiny ass. This was one of the hottest things I had ever done and with a drop-dead handsome guy.

After my hand was in, I decided to touch his beautiful cock again. He didn't seem to mind, and his cock got hard. He was tight up against the monitor so there was no way I could suck him. I tried two hands, but since this was my first experience I was hurting him some. He was so cute, and I didn't want to hurt him. I asked him if I could see him again, and I didn't really get an answer. By the way, he was very clean. My hand had nothing but goo on it.

I love to gently bite a guy's ass. I gave him a couple of bites. Man, was I flowing with precum. I put my hand in and out several times. I didn't know how far I could safely put it in, so I was cautious. He just purred with my hand up his ass. He was thin, slender, and good enough to eat and kiss all over. I finally had to leave, so I said goodbye, but hardly got a response from him. Talk about hitting the jackpot. I left with my cock wet and my underwear all wet. I got my $10 worth of that cute guy.

I went to my local adult bookstore yesterday. It was sort of quiet. You never know if there will be no one there or fifteen guys all looking to suck on some cock or get sucked or fuck or get fucked. I had on my cock ring, so my cock and balls were pretty pronounced in my gym shorts. I am sixty, look younger, clean-shaven face, average build and looks. As I walked around checking the booths, a guy came in, around forty I would guess, shiny wedding ring on that left ring finger. He clearly was looking at my crotch bulge and when he looked up I smiled at him. He nodded at me and walked into a big booth, turning around to see if I was following him.

I put several tokens in the machine and the porn started. This guy was clearly hungry. He was on his knees in no time, yanking down my gym shorts. He smiled and said this is what he was looking for and started stroking on my uncut cock. He told me he loved uncut cock. I said great, go ahead and enjoy, and he did. He started by licking on my cockhead, sliding my foreskin up and down as he did so, fondled my hanging balls and then deep-throated my cock! Damn, it felt great. When does a blowjob not feel great?

As he was sucking on me, another guy walks into the booth, young guy as well, in his thirties I would guess. He watched for a while as this guy is sucking on my cock. He then started rubbing on my nipples, then lifts my t-shirt, and puts his mouth on my nipples, sucking, licking, and kissing. Then he leaned up and started kissing me deep and hard. The entire time the guy on his knees is sucking me, he reaches up to this other guy's jeans, takes out his rock hard manhood, and starts sucking on him. He continues to kiss me, and then says he wants to suck on me as well. I smiled and said go ahead, so he kneels down and starts sucking and pumping on my dick. Two hot guys all working on me. Damn, it was nice. Soon I tell the guys I am going to cum. Both of them are there on their knees with their mouths open. I pump on my cock and blast a long stream of my cum load into both of their mouths. They take turns licking and sucking my cock and taking every drop of my cum. Damn, it was nice day!

DUET

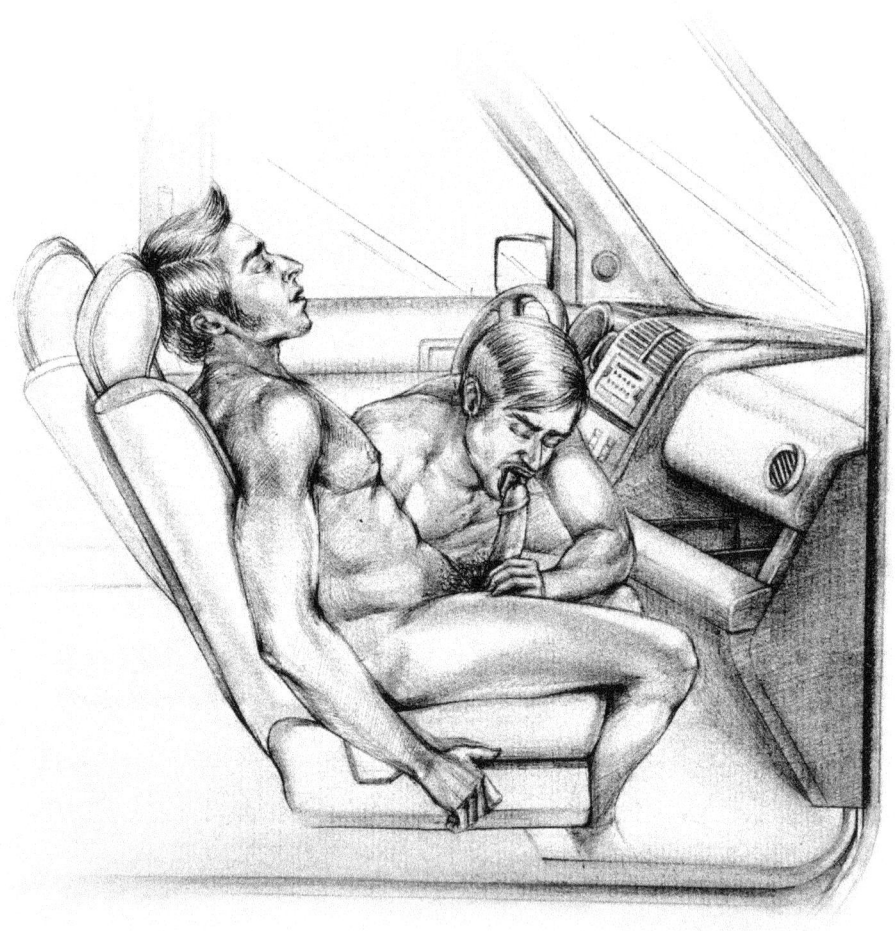

I got an early education in the world of sex. I had an older cousin that taught me how much fun it could be to suck and get sucked and how fun it could be to get fucked. At that time he was fifteen; I was eight, but this isn't about that time. Let's fast forward a few years. By this time, the word had gotten around to some of the more, let's say, receptive guys in the neighborhood. I was a popular alternative to the frigid cock tease girls in the neighborhood who loved to tease, but never put out. Jesse was only a couple of years older than me, and we had started to hang out, playing video games, riding bikes, going fishing, and then it turned to what I was always good at; we started to fool around a bit. I started to blow him at various times when we would find reasons to disappear for long times.

One day, Jesse calls and tells me to hurry up and come to his house. I didn't hesitate and rushed over. He explained his mom and stepdad were both at work and wouldn't be home anytime soon. We had the house to ourselves! We spent little time getting undressed so we could play leisurely and not worry about somebody coming around and finding us. I got down between Jesse's legs and teased his cock, which was pretty big for a guy his age at the time. I had learned the lessons of how to deep-throat, and man did I put it to use! I sucked and teased and fucked my own throat with his cock. We had never yet gotten to the point of his fucking me; we were too scared of getting caught. This time was different! Things progressed, and for the first time, Jesse had started to fuck me silly, the all too quick rabbit fucks of youth. Since we were alone in the house, we didn't pay much attention to making noise. I had just been pulled up to a doggy position, and Jesse slammed his dick in, so naturally I ended up squealing about the rude entry.

"Holy shit what was that?" I said. "I don't know. What was what? I didn't hear anything! Let me back in, this is feeling so good!" We carried on and finished our session. We had a few more times when we could play again and not worry about getting caught the rest of that summer. At the end of the summer, Jesse tells me the bad news I figured was coming. His mom's ex, his real dad, wanted him to move in with him and go to school in the next state. I was crushed. There went my buddy, just like that. Two weeks after Jesse had left, I was riding my bike around and Jesse's stepdad, Johnny, comes to the fence, "Hey there bud, where have you been? I haven't seen you around for a while." "Um, not much reason to come around if Jesse isn't here, is there?" "Well, you know, he did leave his game system here. Wanna come in and play a few games?" he asked.

Well now, I could ride a bike outside in the heat, or I could be inside a nice air-conditioned house playing video games. I chose the video games over the bike ride. "Just put your bike in the garage and shut the door so no one will take your new bike," I was told. Being the good kid, I did what I was told. I shut the garage door behind me and went into the kitchen. "You don't mind my coming by and just playing video games?" "No, bud, in fact I'm glad to have the noise. The house is entirely too quiet now that Jesse is at his dad's." "Yeah, I wish he was back, I miss him," I easily admitted. "Well come on over any time you want to play a game or just hang out." I played the games for a while, and Johnny asked if I wanted a Coke or something to drink. "Sure that sounds great."

He opens the cabinet for a glass, and a magazine falls out onto the counter. Johnny walks over to the fridge and pours me a Coke. I move closer to where the magazine fell out, and I see a dirty magazine. Johnny notices me looking at the porno magazine, "Better watch yourself there, better not let your mom and dad know you saw that! But if you wanna look at it, go ahead. A young man needs to get his education sometime, ha ha." I pick up the mag and leaf through it. There are all the images of naked women. UGH! I leaf quickly through the pages until I come to a screeching halt. There is a layout of a naked man and a woman! Woo hoo! I took my time looking closely at those pages, at the good-looking guy with some porno bimbo. I was practically drooling.

"Like that, huh?" Johnny asked. "Kinda noticed how you went pretty fast through the naked women and came to a dead stop with the naked guy. Do you like naked guys?" My mouth went dry, and the color drained from my face. Holy shit, here I was getting busted! Man, oh man, was I going to be in trouble! I could just picture what punishments I was going to get from my parents when Johnny tells them how their teenage son was getting hard looking at naked guys. Panic starts to set in. "Whoa, little buddy! What's wrong?" he says. I start to stammer and babble incoherently. "Hey, listen to me. It's okay, it's all okay," he assures me. I'm not going to tell anyone, not one soul!" I am freaking out a little less now.

"You wanna know a secret about me—to make us even? I like looking at the guys too! As a matter of fact look here," he points down to his crotch and there is the biggest hard dick I have ever seen! BOING! My dick gets stiff immediately! "Looks like you like those pictures too. Look at yours!" he says. I couldn't deny it; I was hard as a rock. Johnny walks over to me and just grabs me up in a hard kiss, my mouth and tongue tasting the Canadian Mist on his tongue. His hand runs down my stomach down to my hard dick. He rubs ever so gently, but insistently. "Wow, yours is so huge! You got a big one too, for a guy your age!" Now the smart ass in me starts to come out, and I ask him, "How many guys my age have you seen naked, Johnny?" "You're a little smart ass aren't you? Come on let's go back to the couch."

Duet

We sit together as we leaf through the magazine, and Johnny takes his time rubbing my crotch. I finally get so heated I beg to take my pants off. "Now listen," he insists. "This is important! This is something that if we start this, we can never tell another soul, understand? Your parents would have me shot. You wouldn't want that to happen now would you?" I promised to never tell a soul. I take my own cock out, and Johnny leans over and sucks me down all the way to the sparse hair. I see his dick throbbing in time with his heartbeat. I instinctively lean over and take his big dick as far in my mouth as I can take him. "Damn boy, I just KNEW I had to have you after I caught you two that time, but I could never do this if Jesse were here, he confessed. "That's why I suggested his dad take him for a while." I guess when you're a horny teen you're not too smart.

"I caught you two sucking and fucking. You and Jesse were going at it, I had come home early, and you two were making so much noise you didn't hear me come in. I would have loved to jump in and join you two, but how could I do anything with Jesse? First time I pissed him off he would go run to his mother and tell." "I miss Jesse, but I like this too!" I admitted. "I know I could never tell, but maybe if he ever comes back to visit, you could help us out by giving us some time together?" Johnny suggested that maybe he could take Jesse's mom out somewhere "to give you two little horn dogs some time to get off! Now get over here and let me and you get off together." We go back to the 69 session and take each other to blasting off. Youth never lasts long. His tongue was working wonders on my cock, and I shot into his mouth as he drank it down like a man dying of starvation.

He doesn't last long after that and croaks out, "Watch it, here comes mine, boy, take that daddy cum!" He blasts off, load after load, filling my mouth almost to overflowing. "Don't waste a drop, swallow that down like I did yours." I dutifully swallow his creamy load and realize that there was a difference between Jesse's and Johnny's taste. Our secret meetings go on for the next four years. I would go off for a bike ride, check to see if Johnny's wife was home. If she was gone, I would park my bike in the garage, shut it up, and go inside to Johnny and play around. He kept his word, and when Jesse did visit, he engineered time for us to be alone. Those times grew all too infrequent.

Then the dreaded day came when we were alone. Before I got between Jesse's legs to settle in for a nice long blowjob, he stopped me, "Hey man, I just wanna let you know that I can't do this anymore. I met a girl back at my dad's. We are dating, and I can't do this anymore, sorry." "Oh. Okay," I said. "I'm sorry I bothered you then. I'd better go. I hope you have a nice life with your girlfriend. I really have to leave now."

I left his house with tears starting to burn down my cheeks. I rode my bike and thought to myself, "Great, you just lost your best buddy and now what is going to happen?" Luckily, Johnny was there to make it all better. We continued to fuck around until I left for college.

In August 1984, I ended a four-year relationship with a man I respected and liked but came to realize I did not love. The past year had been quite frustrating since he did not understand nor agree with the breakup. So frustrating, in fact, that I decided that I never again would repeat the words "I love you" to another man. I was going to be free of such entanglements. You see, I had been married to a lovely and generous woman. Even though it was a good relationship, and she accepted that I was gay and needed sex with men, we had decided that after several years of dealing with this complicated marriage, we needed to divorce.

In October, a few months after the breakup with my gay friend and knowing I would soon be free of my marriage, I attended a conference in Chicago, planning all along to have some wild nights on the town, some hot adventures. It was an unusually warm Halloween, in the mid 70s. It must have been about 11:00 pm or so when I entered Manhandler, known as the best gay cruise bar in town. As one reviewer remarked, "If you can't get it here, you're a DICK." Upon entering, I noticed really hot gay porn playing constantly on the TV monitor. In a dark corner towards the back, a few guys were kissing and doing a bit of groping and fondling. When I noticed a couple of hot men going out a back door, I naturally had to follow. The inside bar had been noisy from the sucking and fucking activity on the TV. But once I went outside I saw a fireplace and several chairs and benches where guys were relaxing with their beers and with their new conquests for the night.

Since I was still looking for my conquest, I proceeded beyond the wooden stockade fencing at the back of the patio. It was dark, no lighting except for nearby streetlights. Several large, wooden tables in the center. Men were leaning against the fence, some lying on the tables, some sitting on benches. Wanting to fit in with the western theme of the crowd, I came wearing tight jeans, and an unbuttoned denim shirt. Holding my can of beer, I walked over to the fence and began to pose. Obviously, I hoped a hot man would approach and would not know I was married.

Half way thru my beer, I walked around the gravel playground and saw some great sucking, fucking, rimming. Two men had actually stripped naked. As I returned to leaning at the fence, this handsome guy approached me. "It's OK, I'm married too," he said. Truth be told, it was a real turn-off. I certainly did not want anyone to know I was married. He reached down for my cock and started to massage it. He then reached inside my shirt and began to work my nips. Little did he know at the time that if someone gets to my tits, my hot button, they're home free. I liked what he was doing, so I let him continue. The more he worked, the more I liked it. And I began to reciprocate. In the end, we both shot our loads.

He asked if I wanted to go back to the patio and join him with a glass of white wine. Happily, I agreed. I learned that he was a successful Realtor in the Western suburbs, was also married and planning a divorce and had recently broken up with his boy friend. As we sat and chatted, he remarked, "You know, it's too bad you meet someone you like at a place like this and you wind up never seeing him again." After a short pause, I answered, "So, what are you doing tomorrow night?" I couldn't believe I said it! I am shy and seldom connect at gay bars. Luckily, he was free the next night and invited me to visit him at his townhouse.

I remember that first night so clearly. We were all tangled up with legs and arms around each other, sleeping on a pull-out sofa bed as best we could. At one point the telephone rang, and when he stood across the room talking to a client, I realized, oh my God, I am falling in love. He was handsome, so loving, so beautiful. I drove home the next day. We talked on the phone almost daily, wrote notes and cards, and saw each other almost every weekend, even though we were 300 miles apart. We kept saying, "Now we've got to take this slowly, since we're both on the rebound." Too late to slow down now, since it was love at first sight, just like in a movie. By Christmas, just two months after we met, we committed to being together forever. That was thirty-five years ago, and our love is just beginning.

I chatted online for a bit with this guy who came by one evening. We were sitting on the sofa chatting, which led to kissing. We took our clothes off and were making out. He was going down on me, and I was enjoying it very much—got me hot and hard in a short time. I went into the bedroom and grabbed some lube. Got my dick all lubed, went back into the front room and had him lean over the back of the sofa and spread his ass checks. I took my dick and rammed it in his hole without hesitation in one quick thrust. He gasped as my dick hit its mark! He later stated that he felt like a torpedo was inside him, trying to open his ass up.

We fucked for a bit more before going to the bedroom. With me lying on my back, he slowly sat on my hard dick, and I raised my hips to meet him. We went at this for an unknown time, with us kissing, me playing with his nipples and jerking on his dick. We both got off. We lay on the bed for sometime and eventually started over again for a second encounter. He stated it was very enjoyable, and he left only to return a couple weeks later for repeat sessions. This went on for a couple months until I moved out of town. We kept in touch and even arranged to get together when I could come to town. We would rent a room at a local hotel for our sessions. I think of him now and then; too bad we lost contact after a couple months of moving out of town. He eventually went back with his old lover, and I was left to find others to find for enjoyment!

It was a boring December Sunday afternoon. I logged on to Adam4Adam and saw pictures of this hairy bear. He's a bit older than me but very attractive. We chat, and he asks if I want to come over. I drive to his house, and he answers the door in his robe. He invites me up to his bedroom. He takes off the robe, and he has all this beautiful fur covering his body. My seven-incher jumped to attention. He lies on the bed, exposing a gorgeous eight-incher with nice balls, also furry. We kissed, rubbed, sucked, and then he started fingering my ass. I was in heaven and he was nice and hard. I sucked him a bit more to get him nice and hard. He said he wanted to fuck me. I told him I had never taken a dick that big before, but I was going to try. He lubed me up with his cock. I lay on my back and raised my legs. I felt him push, gently opening me up. I moaned so loudly while he continued to slide in. He moaned, too, and kissed me deep. I pinched his tits, and we both went wild. I felt my cock harden, and he jacked me. His cock inside and hand on my cock sent me over. I shot a huge load all over my chest up to my chin. He moaned and shot his load deep inside me. Haven't been back yet but hope to—soon!

I was going to meet a guy for a hook up. When I got in my car it wouldn't start. So I contacted the guy and told him what was going on since

Duet

we were going to meet somewhere. He was in his truck and asked where I was. I usually don't give out my address, but this guy sounded interesting at 6'6" tall, muscular, and wanting to bottom. He wanted to have some fun with me, a 5'8" big ole bear, so I had to see. Well, he pulled up in his big ass truck with a super cab and out stepped this monster of a man. He was a walking wet dream, tall, fit, and bearded. We talked a little while and got to know each other. It was getting late and it was dark, so I suggested we have a little fun in his truck. I have never seen someone jump at a suggestion as he did. So we got into the back of his cab where he proceeded to strip and revealed a nice, thick, muscled body that was smooth, along with a crotch that was shaved, which only made his thick, long cock look huge. It was at least 9" and as thick as my bear cub wrist.

Needless to say, it did not take me two seconds to start sucking on his cock. He was hard, and I had fun trying to take it all the way down my throat. He was enjoying the attention and pulled his legs up to show me his hot ass. I can't resist a nice ass, so I started eating away while jacking his cock. He starts moaning, moving his ass up and down trying to get my tongue further up his ass. I was in heaven. This hot, tall, metal worker was enjoying everything I was doing to him. He said he wanted to get fucked so badly, but being in his big ass truck, his size and mine, it was kind of hard to do. I would have had to fold him in half because of how tall he was and that wasn't going to happen. So I got one of my fingers wet and slowly pushed it into his tight hole, and while doing that I went back to his cock. I got up to my first knuckle, and he let out a low moan. His cock let out a nice spurt of tasty cum. Next, he pushed his ass down all the way to the base of my finger.

So I started to finger fuck him, and he was getting into it. So I pulled the one finger out and replaced it with two. This got him breathing harder, and his cock got thicker, if that was even possible. So I worked them in and out while sucking his cock, which was leaking some sweet ass nectar. He lifted his ass some more which allowed me to get three of my fingers in him. He rode my fingers like a pro all the while I was sucking his cock like a pro. I got off his cock and started licking his bull balls, and they started tightening up. I worked down, licked his taint while slobbering some spit on my hand to lube up my fingers better. I worked them in and out of his hole and licked my way back up to his cock.

I knew it wouldn't be long as his balls were tight around the base of his cock. I worked his cock as far down my throat as I could and went to town fucking my fingers in and out of his ass. He was groaning loudly now. I looked up and saw his head was thrown back and he was panting with his mouth wide open. I could feel his ass tightening up around my hand, so I knew I would be rewarded with his special cream soon. As soon as I thought that, his asshole spasmed around my hand; his cock got bigger and shot a huge shot of cum down my throat. He pushed his ass down all the way to my palm and shot the rest of his hot load, which was a volley of about ten shots into my mouth. Very hot!! Once he was done shooting, his body went limp with my hand up his ass and his cock in my mouth.

I left everything where it was, sucking on his cock and just letting my fingers rest in his ass. He caught his breath when I let his monster cock slip out of my mouth. I pulled my fingers out of his ass and watched his asshole slowly close up, so I took one last lick to taste that hot ass. It took about five minutes for him to gather his senses. We then planned to get together again so I could really get a piece of his ass. We got out of the truck, and all I could think was that I hoped my neighbors didn't hear him or see anything.

I was working at a summer job and the urge to mess around with a guy had been growing for a while. Every night I'd wank off to gay porn, which increased my desire to feel another man's cock. I signed up to a gay hookup website and posted a nice nude body pic. I got to chatting to an older gent, who, despite being nearly fifty, was in pretty good shape.

After a few days of messaging, we agreed to a time and a place to meet. As I traveled to meet him, I was so nervous but super excited at the same time. I can still remember the feeling of my stomach doing somersaults as I got the bus to his place.

He met me at a shop beneath his apartment block. He was a good-looking, older guy in the flesh. He could tell that I was nervous, so he did his best to put me at ease. After entering his apartment, I went straight for the bed. I sat on the edge, he stood in front of me, and we both stripped off our clothes. Without saying a word, he immediately took my semi-hard cock and eagerly wrapped his lips around the head. I'll never forget how it felt. He used his tongue to massage the bottom of my shaft and head. I loved it.

He lay me down and started going to work on my cock. After a few minutes of that pure bliss, he asked me to get on all fours so he could rim me. Having never been rimmed before, I found the feeling was amazing. He eagerly licked and kissed my virgin ass. He'd lick the back of my ball-sack, smoothly continue to my asshole, and generously give it a lot of attention with his soft tongue. Oh the memories!

When I was twenty-five years old and yahoo chat rooms were big, I remember chatting with a guy from the next town over. He sent me his picture, and I was instantly hooked! We chatted online for quite a while, but could never make a meeting work out. Then, all of a sudden, he vanished from the internet. I recognized him as a local funeral director, but luckily I didn't have to use his business services. Years went by and there were always rumors about his liking guys. None of the people I heard it from, however, had ever been with him—just had heard stories and wanted to be with him.

One night, I was sitting at my computer and had logged in to Adult Friend Finder when someone started chatting with me. He turned his cam on, and I about lost it—here was my long lost crush from about seven years before. We started chatting, and then he invited me over. Wow, was this really happening? I was finally going to meet this hot guy that I had been hoping to meet for so long.

I drove to his house where he met me at the door. As soon as I walked in, he grabbed me and started kissing me, our hands all over each other. He took me up to his bedroom where we lay and just kissed each other for what seemed to be hours, rubbing our cocks together and occasionally breaking the kissing long enough to lick and suck each other's cocks. I pushed his legs against his chest and buried my face in his ass. Every part of his body tasted so good. We got each other off that night while we lay there and kissed. A few weeks later, we did it again. That night, after we were done, we just lay there and talked for a long time. I just wanted to get to know this guy as much as I possibly could. He admitted to me that I had been the only guy he'd been with for years.

We have continued to see each other when time permits and have become pretty good friends as well. The last time we were together we were lying next to each other kissing, and he somehow got hold of my tongue and sucked it into his mouth so hard that the other thing I could feel is the roof of his mouth on my tongue! It turned me on so much that I got harder than I had ever gotten. He must have noticed because he straddled my cock and started riding it so hard, all the while kissing me, holding my hands, and sucking my tongue into his mouth. I couldn't hold back any longer and shot my cum inside him! He then shot his juice all over my stomach and chest. Afterwards, we again lay next to each other, falling asleep in each other's arms. It was one of the most perfect nights I've had!

Winter is usually mild where I live, but a few years ago, a rare snowstorm was predicted to hit my city overnight. I had gone out to stock up on some supplies beforehand since even a couple of inches of snow paralyzes the town for a day or two. On the way home, I stopped at a local diner for a quick bite. Once seated, I noticed a somewhat familiar figure sitting across from me in a nearby booth. I strained my brain trying to place him, and then it came to me—he was someone I had gone to high school with almost twenty-five years earlier, someone whom I had barely known, but who had been a popular and well-known figure, enough for me to remember him.

I decided to say hello, even though I knew he wouldn't know me from Adam. And I was right. He had been in high school with me and he had no idea who I was. But we made some connections, made some small talk, and I joined him at his table. He was in town to get his deceased parents' home, which had been vacant for a couple of years, ready to be put on the market. He was headed to a motel because the central heating unit in the home was on the blink and he'd be without heat for a few days if he stayed there. Not a good prospect with temperatures in low 30s. He knew no one to ask for a place to crash, as he hadn't lived in the area since he had left for college and had no family here.

I offered to let him stay with me in my three bedroom home, which I occupied by myself after my divorce a year earlier. He was reluctant, saying that he didn't want to impose on me. I told him that it wasn't an imposition and he agreed, but said that he needed to tell me something and that I could rescind the invitation if I were uncomfortable.

He told me that he was gay and didn't want me to feel awkward about his staying with me. I told him right away that I wasn't uncomfortable at all and that I had been having sex with men since my marriage ended. He was curious about that, saying that he had never slept with a woman and had been sleeping with guys since college. I replied that I had buried my gay urges deeply enough to get married and have children, but that now I was liberated and could acknowledge my desires. I told him not to worry though, as I knew that I wasn't his type and that he would be safe. He laughed and said that he didn't necessarily want to be safe. Our eyes met for a moment and there were definitely leers shared between us.

We arrived at my place, and I quickly showed him the guest room where he would be sleeping. There was another moment between us as he grinned at me and said, "Yeah, right!" We came to the master bedroom, and it was basically all over. He grabbed me, and I grabbed him, and we started tearing off our clothes. We laughed as we each fumbled getting our shoes off and then our pants and shirts, leaving our briefs on. We hurried into a kiss and touched each other in all the right places. We fell onto the bed and stroked and kissed all over. Soon the briefs were flung away and he dived low, pulling on my dick and squeezing my ass. He explored me and felt me with his hands. Soon his mouth had taken me in and he was sucking my dick with abandon, while probing my hole with his fingers. I was ecstatic to say the least—I hadn't expected this at all. I felt my cum rushing to explode and I fought the urge to erupt, but I lost that fight and came in hot spurts in his mouth, which he swallowed with gusto. He pulled himself up to my level, and sank into the bed, and we hugged and kissed.

A few minutes later, I said that it was my turn to savor him. I crawled down and lifted his legs to get a great view of the Holy Three—dick, balls, and asshole. It was an awesome sight, and I maneuvered myself to kiss his hole. He moaned slightly, and I knew he wanted more, so I started rimming with my tongue. I was in heaven and he was too, apparently, as he was quivering with pleasure. I tongue-fucked his hole for several minutes, while pulling his dick and balls. Finishing with his ass, I went for his dick, licked his shaft up and down, and then took all of him into my mouth, sucking him fast. He fucked my mouth furiously and soon came in a torrent of gooey, delicious ooze.

We fell asleep, both exhausted by our sexual releases and didn't even notice that snow had begun to fall. We awoke in the middle of night, both of us a little unsure of what had happened. We remembered quickly, and then started our sexual exploits with each other again.

Thank you, Mother Nature, for providing a memorable couple of days. We were housebound for about thirty-six hours due to the snow, and we enjoyed each other many times during that period. Afterwards, we stayed in touch for a while, but never saw each other again.

Duet

I had a good time last Friday. It was just a regular session with a regular fuck buddy, but it had been a while, so it was good. Pretty much a lot of mutual suck action, but some hard core face-fucking and head over the bed action. He also has this great, meaty ass, and he's a regular horny-ass bottom when the time comes. I really opened up his hole with my fingers and spit. I'm always surprised at how receptive he is, how he just opens up, and that my whole hand pretty much goes right up, right away! He seems so polite and innocent, but you wouldn't know it the way he squirms and pushes back onto my fist. I was rock hard and ready to go, but it had been a while for him, so I wasn't really planning to fuck him. I just teased him a bit with my fat dick head, slipping it into his open hole and swiveling my hips a bit.

Well, he took the hint and pushed that fat juicy ass right back unto my thick cock. It slid right in, up to my balls, and he was riding back on my dick like I was paying him—he was so horned up! I started thrusting back and rode him like that, hard and pounding for about a good ten minutes, speeding up and slowing down, staying in there while he clenched onto my dick with his ass, rocking back and forth when he wanted more. We had to stop after a while though. It had been so long since he had been fucked that he was starting to feel it, and, besides, it had been sometime since I had fucked a hot ass and unloaded. I would've shot my load right up his ass sooner than later! So after some more hard kissing, rubbing and sucking, I couldn't take any more and had to blow. I straddled his face and fucked his mouth while he beat off. Just before I was about to cum, I pulled my huge, bloated cock out of his mouth, stood up on the bed, and sprayed my load all over his chest and face. I don't remember how long it had been since I had cum last, but it had been a while, and I had been edging all week for this day. I shot so much, spraying all over him, jet after jet of thick, ropey cum. The orgasm was so intense I almost fell off the bed. I was cumming for quite a while. Still with so much cum, I knelt down and put my still shooting dick in his mouth and had him finish me off while he himself shot a pretty decent load. Pretty hot afternoon, good time.

After teaching my classes one day, I stopped by a local hamburger place to get a bite to eat. I liked this particular restaurant because the manager had become a friend of mine after meeting him online. We both were in search of the same thing, M2M sex. He was a hot, young, black man, I, an older white guy whose interest lay with young men decades younger than me. Shortly after I finished my burger and fries, my friend asked me if I wanted to ride with him to the bank. I agreed, so we both got in his truck for the trip. The first thing I noticed was that he had had his windows tinted so dark they were probably illegal. We drove through the drive-through at the bank for him to make the restaurant's deposit, and we returned to the restaurant. He pulled into a parking place near the building. We stayed in the truck to talk.

It was only minutes before our conversation turned to sex, and even a shorter time before he unzipped his fly and pulled out his 9" boner, turgid and swollen with a drop of precum ready to drip from its slit. I bent over, took his manhood into my mouth, and began to suck him off. His cock was so thick I could hardly get my mouth around its flared head, but I did the best I could and continued to pleasure him, relishing the taste of his precum.

Suddenly, it dawned on me that maybe people going in and out of the restaurant could see our naughty tryst in his pickup truck, but he assured me that the windows were too dark. He chuckled and said this was the very reason he had them tinted so dark. I bent to continue sucking him off, but he stopped me, saying he wanted some of my cock. I unzipped, pulled out my smaller cock, and he took my entire cock into his mouth. I was enjoying his oral skills when I looked out the window and observed the assistant manager, a female, heading straight for our mobile sex mobile.

"Uh, Ron (not his real name), one of your employees is headed this way!" I said with urgency in my tone. I didn't want for him to stop, but it appeared we were about to get caught in the act in only seconds. "What?" Ron responded as he suddenly sat up. "Damn! That's my assistant coming to ask me a question or something." We both frantically pulled up our pants and tried to look normal when, instead, we looked like the cat that swallowed the canary, I'm sure. He rolled down his window, and the two of them chatted for a little while.

She turned to return to work, and Ron pushed the button making the window roll back up. "Well, that was close!" Ron exclaimed. "Indeed it was," I retorted, my heart still pounding from the experience. Neither one of us had reached climax, which was disappointing. At least we didn't get caught. Or did we? I've always wondered if she really knew what we had been doing in a truck cab in the parking lot of a well-known burger joint.

Many years ago in the late 1960s, when I was turning thirtyish, I had a best buddy with whom I hung around a lot. He was in his early twenties. We were almost inseparable. We met every night after classes and work and maybe played ball or watched a game or hung around a bar where guys like us would be. There was no personal contact; it was just spending time together.

Max one day decided he wanted to take a road trip and visit his brother and sister-in-law out in California. This was a time before the interstate system was complete, so most of the trip would be on regular highways and side roads and would take about three to four days there and three to four days back, plus the time he would spend there. It was therefore going to be a two-week trip, all told. He asked me if I wanted to go and share the driving. It took only one second for me to say yes, and I told my boss at work. Being it was the slow season anyway, I got the time off. We packed and were on the road in less than two days, a full tank of gas, money in our pockets, and using his car.

We drove along what was once the infamous Route 66, driving through Illinois and then Missouri, and spending the night in a small, roadside motel. I remember the place was painted pink with blue trim and awnings, and the room was nothing except a bed and a small dresser with the TV on top of it. The toilet was the bare essentials with a bath tub/shower, a toilet, and a smallish sink. No countertop.

Max grabbed a towel from the rack and went into the shower, leaving the bathroom door open so the steam would heat the cool room. When he was done, I went in to shower and shave. Coming out of the shower, I saw that Max was already in bed. I put on a pair of short pants pajamas and joined him. I was about 6' tall, but Max towered over me with his 6'8" height. I was about 165 pounds, and he was a massive full-back size of about 250. And everything else was proportionate, large hands, large feet, large male member. It was all there. I got into bed, and almost immediately Max rolled on top of me, saying he had always wanted to fuck me, and today he was going to shove his cock up my ass and I would like it so much I would beg for more. He pulled my pajamas down, lifted my legs, put them over his shoulders, and then moved up until I felt the head of his cock on my asshole. He reached over and took some lube out of a can on the bed stand, rubbed some all over his cock, on my asshole, and then slowly moved forward and into me as I shriveled up in pain.

I had not had a cock in my ass and his seemed massive. I thought he was going to rip me apart when he pushed his hard male appendage into me. He just kept going, and I felt like I had to shit and my ass felt so full and bloated. Despite the lube, it felt like he was ripping me open. When I felt his balls hit my ass, I knew he was in all the way. He stopped and let me calm down. He leaned forward and lay on top of me and kissed me when I was gasping for air. I found myself kissing him back. And then he started to slowly piston in and out of my ass. It hurt more, but the pain seemed to be almost enjoyably better. I grabbed his arms and held onto them with all my strength. And he worked my ass raw.

When he shot, he bellowed like a bull moose (yes, I have heard a bull moose bellow), as he collapsed on me and then rolled to the side. My ass hurt really bad. I was out of breath; his weight was crushing me, and my mind was swirling. I felt no joy or sadness. I just was. I lay there like a smudge of something that had been stepped on. My face was wet from tears. My ass felt like someone had scrapped it with a wire brush, and I could not move because Max was still on me, catching his second wind.

I said second wind because as soon as Max had rested a bit he got up on me again and rammed his newly erect cock into me a second time. The pain of the first time was still there, but this time, although the pain was new and raw, I felt differently about it. I wanted it, more of it, and did not want it to end. It took Max a lot longer to cum, but he bellowed again, and then slid off me, leaving me feeling like I wanted him to stay.

Max and I had sex several times that day. My ass was so raw it was almost impossible for me to shit without wincing. But I wanted Max so much that even as we drove, I kept my hand on his leg—no fooling around just being close in case he needed to have more sex. My thirties were really good years with Max.

I am reminded of an incident that happened years ago. I had played around in college and in the Navy, sucked a lot, and been fucked numerous times. At the time, I was living at the beach with friends, still kinda in the closet. My roommate and a couple of others knew, but I lived the lie, even with an ex- girlfriend. Our group consisted of my roommate, my ex-girlfriend, and her ex-boyfriends. She loved sex.

Anyway, one of my ex-girlfriend's exes, Craig, was a 6'1", dark stud with a thick, uncut cock. I think he had Italian in him. One summer, he went to the Bahamas and brought back some different rums. He invited me to dinner at his house, for food and of course for rums. I was a bit surprised when I got there that we were totally alone. We had dinner and then proceeded to sample the rums. Soon we were drunk and giggling. It was hot, so we took off our shirts and shoes. Somehow we got on the subject of fucking our ex, how many times we had fucked her, the different positions, odd places. We then got on the subject of our dick sizes.

Were we thick, thin, uncut, cut, big balls, whatever? He proceeded to show me that he was hung. Dropped his pants, showing a tasty, thick cock, uncut, round full balls topped with a curly mass of dark pubes. With those jewels fucking me, I would have never broken up with him. He asked me if I had ever tasted a cock. He probably knew the answer and I said, "Hell, Yes!" I bent down and started sucking him, and he became very hard in my mouth. During the course of our session, he never sucked me or did I fuck him, but he fondled my cock and balls.

I sucked him, he moaned and shuttered, stiffened, but didn't cum. He asked if he could fuck me. I said, "Oh Please!" I lay on my back, as he pushed his mushroom cockhead into my tight pink hole. I reminded him that this wasn't a pussy but a man's tight ass, so start slowly. He pushed, entered my hole, stopped as I adjusted to his girth, and then continued to insert his entire shaft. We didn't measure, I didn't ask but I'm guessing about eight inches. Soon, his entire shaft was pumping my tight hole—in, out, faster and faster.

Craig licked and sucked my neck, licking my ears, neck and lips. Then, as he exploded his creamy, warm cum in my tight, cock hungry ass, he kissed me! Locked his lips on mine and drove his tongue in my mouth. We kissed passionately. I held his head to drive my tongue deeper and to accept his tongue in my mouth. He finished cumming, stayed on top of me as he caught his breath.

He whispered to me that that was the best fuck he had ever had. I had to agree. We promised to never tell a soul and never tell our ex-girlfriend. We fucked from time to time after that, but he eventually married. Nice girl, he invited me to his wedding. I had to smile because I knew exactly what she was getting, every inch!

I met him by answering an ad on Craigslist. We talked for a while via email and while I had some limited experience with men, what was about to happen was beyond my wildest dreams. He told me that he enjoyed tying men down and then teasing them until they came. That sounded like fun, so we set up a time to meet. I arrived at his house, and he greeted me with a hug and a kiss on the cheek. We talked for a bit, and then he led me into his bedroom. He told me to disrobe. I did, and then I lay down on his bed. He tied me down spread eagle and my cock was already rising in anticipation. He then slid a blindfold on me.

He left the room for a few minutes and then returned. I felt him rubbing something on my armpits and then my groin area. It took me a few moments to realize it was shaving cream. In very short order, my armpits and groin area were completely smooth. I hadn't expected this, and the first thought I had was how am I going to explain this new look to my wife. As I was mulling it over, I felt him lower his face to mine, and he kissed me. A long, slow, deep, wet kiss. I had never kissed a man before, but it was amazing. Now I was as hard as a rock. He kissed and licked my armpits and then began working on my nipples. When he started on my nipples, I just melted. One of my many weak spots. You play with my nipples and I'm yours. As he did that, he began to ever so lightly caress my cock and balls. It was amazing. My body was squirming and my cock jumping. He kissed his way down and was soon kissing my balls, licking, and sucking my cock. I began to move near orgasm when he quit. He came back up, and we kissed some more. A very nice long, make-out session. He got up and I waited. Soon he was between my legs, sucking on my cock. It felt wonderful. Then his hand moved between my legs, and I felt his lubed finger enter my ass. He moved it in gently. I protested at first, but as he began to move it in and out it began to feel good. Then I felt a bit more pain, and he told me to relax, that he now had two fingers in me. He then kissed the tip of my cock and began to fuck me with both fingers.

Soon it felt good again. He was sucking and fucking, and as I neared cumming he got up. Damn. I felt him moving my foot and raising it up. Suddenly my right foot was up in the air and spread wide. When I felt him begin on my left foot, I began to panic. I was afraid of what might be coming. When I asked him to stop, he told me to relax while he tied off my left foot up in the air. I must have looked like a piece of meat hanging in the meat locker. He bent down and kissed my cock once again, and as he did he lubed up my ass hole. I begged him not to, but he ignored me. There was a pause, and then I felt him moving between my legs. I felt the head of his cock at my asshole. He then said there are two ways to do this. One is for him to simply force it in, or the other is for me to relax and just enjoy. I opted for the second choice. He talked gently to me as he pushed his cock in. It hurt for a bit, but once he was all the way in, he stopped. He leaned down and kissed me.

Our lips parted and our tongues danced in each other's mouth. Soon the pain was replaced by discomfort, but soon the discomfort was gone. He moved his hips slowly, and I sighed as he slid back in. It began to feel very nice. "Feel good?" he asked. I moaned yes in response. He moved gently in and out, in and out. It was simply wonderful. Then he began to move faster. It felt better than I had imagined. He began to pant and then moaned, "I'm cumming." His pace quickened, and after a few more thrusts he slowed down. I felt him lower himself on me, and we kissed—long, slow, and wet. I was amazed at how good it felt. Slowly, he disengaged and then moved down my body. He began to suck on me, his head bobbing up and down. It felt simply wonderful. I felt my orgasm begin, and I said, "I'm going to cum." He increased the speed, and soon I felt myself cumming in his warm sucking mouth. The feeling was amazing. I had cum many times before with women by hand, orally, with intercourse, and with a couple of men by hand, but this was the most intense orgasm I had ever experienced in my life. I felt that I was being totally drained.

Soon, I was done. He moved back up, and we kissed. I felt my cum draining out of his mouth into mine. We kissed passionately and long. It was the most amazing kiss I had ever experienced. He untied me and lay down next to me. We wrapped up in each other's arms, caressing, kissing, and enjoying each other's company. We would doze off and then reawaken to kiss and caress. Finally, I got dressed. He walked me to the door, we kissed, and then I left. I couldn't wait to get back to see him, hopefully in the near future. Hope you all enjoy my story. Have a great day.

I have never had a "rent boy," though I did know a guy that was a model, stripper, and escort. He made pretty good money doing that, plus he had a built body, gorgeous face and HUGE cock! First met him at a bathhouse on his day off, go figure. Anyway, I got to know him pretty well and ended up doing some business work for him when his manager and he had a falling out. One of the perks he gave me for my work was a personal, naked, lap dance! I'm a total bottom, which was his preference. I'd suck him, then he'd fuck me until my tight hole was stretched out and cum-filled. He sure knew how to fuck. If it wasn't free, it would have been worth the $200 per hour!

I was working in New York City in a retail store during the holidays. It was my late night and the store was open for the last minute shoppers. When I left the store around 11:00 that night, it was snowing. I had to walk three blocks to get my train home. On the way to the train, I was approached by a young man asking if I was looking for company. I kind of smirked, "You're barking up the wrong tree with me. I just got off work and am really tired." I could see he was shivering. He was not really dressed for the cold weather, and I could see he had a great body. It was the holidays. I felt bad for him. Then I said to him, "Look, it's slow out, it's snowing really heavy, and you're not going to score tonight, so why not just come home with me. You can have a hot shower, and I will make something for you to eat. Stay the night and I am not asking for anything in return." He thought about it for a few seconds and finally agreed. So we took the subway home to my place.

When we got into my apartment, he stripped right in front of me and asked for the shower. This guy had a body you'd die for—smooth, light fur, six pack abs, a chest with light blond fur on it, and nipples you could have a meal on. Don't start me on his cock; it was slightly erect with dark blond pubic hair and the cock was a nice 8" cut. It was just dangling there. Oh, how I wanted it, but held back, just looking and admiring. I gave him a towel and showed him the way. That ass as he got into the shower was just delicious to look at, nice and firm, also with light blond fur on it as well. I made him a sandwich and some soup and he kept saying how grateful he was. I asked him when the last time was that he had eaten. He responded yesterday. He used up all his money to go to the baths to get warm and sleep, but his time was up so he had to leave. I offered him the couch or my bed. He took to my bed! We watched a little TV, and finally I said I had to go to sleep. It was almost 2:00 am, and I had to work late again the next day.

It must have been about 5:00 am when I woke up to a hand on my chest. He was looking down at me with those big brown eyes and said, "I really want to thank you—no one ever did this for me before, even in NYC or at home." He told me he got kicked out of the house because he could not get along with his stepfather, and also because he was gay. He was from Indiana, twenty-one, and no place to go. He hitched to NYC and started to hustle. He had been doing it for three years, since he was nineteen. Living on the streets he said is not pretty. He started rubbing my chest and sucking on my nipples, and I got hard right away. He knew what to do and did it well. He started nibbling on my belly and finally pulled my shorts off and sucked my cock, playing with my balls and fingering my hole. He gave me a rimming the likes of which I've never had before or ever again; I learned a few new techniques as well. All I wanted was to suck his cock and he said, "No, this is all about you. You didn't approach me and you kept your promise, so this is a gift to you from me."

He covered every spot of my body from top to bottom, front to back. I kept looking at that erect, hard cock of his, holding it in my hand, jacking it, and fondling it for what seemed like hours. I have been laid before and had some great times, but I was never serviced like that before and never was again, except by him. We shot our loads in each other's mouth at the same time and then kissed, sharing in the wettest and sloppiest kiss ever. We took a shower and went back to bed for a while. I finally had to get up to go to work. On the way to work, I said he was welcome to come home with me after work if he wanted. I went into the store with the biggest smile, wondering all day if he was going to meet me. Well, I got off work again at 11:00 pm and started walking. There at the corner was my new friend. I was so glad I did not have work the next day, because we were up playing all over again! That was the last time I ever saw him and do not know what ever happened to him. All I have is the memories of my being a decent person helping out a hot-looking hustler who became my friend.

Some men I will never forget because of unbelievable talents they have attained during sex. Several years ago, I met a man at an area gay establishment. It was a slow day and near closing time, so we were able to talk. We found out we had some common interests, and he gave me his number before I left. I am a top and oral. He turned out to be an unbelievable bottom.

He had lived in California for many years but had recently returned to his native Florida to help watch out for his mother after his father died. He lived in one of his parent's rental properties that needed work. He also supported his pot habit by working three days a week in the gay entertainment environment where we met.

By the third date, he had learned I also enjoy a buzz while having sex. This day at his place we got a good buzz, and then we both did poppers. When I entered his glorious anal area, all of a sudden I found his most sensitive spot. This man had taught himself to climax without cumming. I enjoy being in another ass as they climax since I love the milking my cock gets. Once I hit the right spot, his climax just went on and on and on. I am able to go for a long time without climaxing myself, so we were enjoying that feeling of climax for what seemed like forever.

From that point on, a usual love making day would start with a buzz, then a good fuck until he reached that dry climax, sending us both into unbelievable pleasure without cumming. Then we would rest a little before a repeat performance. One day when he did not have to work, we had five hours of repeats. Once I had hit his trigger, he would start near convulsions the second I reentered him. In five hours, he had reached very extended climaxes seven times. I feared my dick would be worn out soon when he said, "I need to cum."

This time he asked me to lie on my back. He climbed aboard, riding me as he faced me. His main negative was that he had one of the littlest dick's I had ever enjoyed. No wonder he was such a well-trained bottom. He masturbated as he road up and down on me. Then he reached his cum climax. The cum shot out of that tiny dick with such force! The first two bursts splattered the wall behind the bed. It was only the third volley that hit my face and hair, the remaining bursts on my chest. Of course, all the action triggered my climax, which was also very memorable.

We had several more very similar sessions. Unfortunately, when we were out with some gay friends, I teasingly alluded to his tiny dick. Our mutual friends had never seen him with his pants down and laughed at my joke. He was so offended, he has refused to talk to me since.

It would be hard to forget those great sessions. I wish I had known how hurt he could be over my mention of his tiny dick. I never intended to hurt him, but I certainly remember his talents.

I recall a twentyish-year-old who had been sleeping (well, not sleeping really) at the baths a few times a week and was horny as a loon. There were a few adult bookstores back then and, yup, I was there quite a bit. One of the guys was a young, hot Gumba. We both had eyed each other but never had a moment. Then there was a night. I'd been out, bars had just closed, I was walking around waiting for the urge to check into the CBC (bath house) when up drove a car. Who should it be but the hot freaking Italian looking for me. We were both heated up and were trying to make it work in the car. It wasn't happening, so he drove down some back streets, and we arrived behind a factory with a loading dock. Suffice to say I was pummeled sweetly and loaded. My back was all torn up from being fucked on the concrete, but I couldn't feel the pain. The Fucking Pleasure was too great.

"Bang me HARD. I need it." Was the headline of his profile on the cruising app. I had checked in early afternoon at my hotel, and the app also indicated this guy was only 1400 feet away. Global positioning has some limits, but I know that's pretty damn close. I messaged him and asked if "now" worked. Right away, he responded. He wanted confirmation that I was a solid top and hoped I had stamina for a long and hard fuck. I confirmed both were true. He worked across the street at the hospital and was knocking softly on my door within fifteen minutes.

Dressed in scrubs, he explained he was a resident at the hospital. He had no time for relationships, but he had a definite need for hard, sweaty sex— that's why he only met through the apps and had hard, brief, safe, hopefully passionate sex. He kicked off his running shoes as he took off his jacket, then his loose scrubs hit the floor. I could see that he was fit and toned, but the long hours with little rest and irregular eating had taken a little bit of a toll on what probably had been a very "gym body" in his undergraduate years. Just a little belly and a little muffin top over just a jock strap.

He got on his knees and mouthed my hardening cock through my jeans. He unzipped me, and with my not wearing briefs he pulled my semi-erect cock out. It was at full eight inches of attention and covered with his spit and precum within just a few minutes. He was deliberate in his technique but also insistent. Seeing his passion for cock, I grabbed the back of his head and bounced up and deep down his throat as he gagged and teared up. Seizing the opportunity when I broke stride to let him breathe a second, he pleaded for me to fuck him now. Hard.

I'm aching to bang. I slide on a condom and slide into his already lubed hole (I love when a bottom has prepared well for me). I slide in, in one deep motion, and he groaned. He muttered through clenched teeth, "Make it happen, daddy, fuck me like you mean it." I banged him like a crazy man. He could take it, and with every gasp and little cry he made me plow harder. Every minute or so we would adjust to get a different angle, or a deeper thrust. We went for close to twenty-five minutes and were both dripping with sweat when my orgasm spasms shook both of us. One last deep thrust, and I stayed in him while I held him, and we let our heart beats drop.

As I slowly pulled out and showed him the amount of cum captured in the condom, he smiled and said this was exactly what he needed and wanted. He could go to his long work shift satisfied and relaxed. He glanced at his watch, "Shit, I gotta go. I'm going to be late." Threw his clothes on and headed out the door.

After a couple of late afternoon sales calls and late dinner, I slid naked into bed thinking about my cute young doctor, looking at his profile pic on the app. I started to work my hard nipples, caress my smooth, low hanging balls, and the tender spot between my legs. A message popped up on the app, "Are you still awake? Do you want some company?" Oh hell yes I wanted him back with me for round two. I messaged back, "The door is unlocked. Join me." A few minutes later, the light from the hallway flashed for a second; I heard those scrubs drop to the floor, and I felt my good doctor slide in bed with me, naked.

This round we had more time to explore each other, kissing and sucking. He was a very attentive lover, sensing when I enjoyed a particular touch and working hard to please me. I wanted to do the same. I knew what pleased him. When it was time, I mounted him and banged him HARD. I flipped him so I could see his face while I fucked him over and over, until I knew he would cum with me if I pressed behind his balls on his prostate. We both exploded. I with my multiple spasms, and him with kind of a high pitched scream. We melted into each other's arms and slept together, our bodies cuddled and cradled together the whole night.

Back before HIV and cell phones, if you got a busy signal on your land line you could hear people talking between the beeps, looking to hook up. Some people called them "Teen Lines" but I always called them "Beep Lines." You would have to practice to get used to passing your messages between the beeps (what's – beep – your name? or what's – beep – your number?). I got a guy's number who did not live too far from me and who wanted to hook up. I called him, and after some conversation, he invited me over. It was night time and he instructed me to take off my shirt as I approached his front door, and he turned off the porch light.

He opened the door and greeted me in the nude. I unbuttoned my shorts, and they dropped to the floor—I was wearing no underwear. His hands were immediately on my junk and mine on his. He had a beautiful solid eight inch dick and a pair of hangers. He pressed down on my shoulders, and I slid down onto my knees. I greedily sucked his cock and fondled and sucked his balls. He had me stand up, and then he led me to a staircase where he lay back on the stairs and raised his legs, inviting me to eat his ass, which I willingly obliged. I licked his hot hole while I jacked his cock. He then led me downstairs to a bedroom and we 69'd for a time. He then mentioned that I told him on the phone that I wanted to get fucked and asked me if I still wanted to. Hell yes! I ran back up the stairs and retrieved a bottle of good poppers from my shorts and went back downstairs. I lay on my back with my knees drawn up and him kneeling and facing me. I took several hits of the poppers then said, "Okay."

He impaled me in one thrust. I yelled, "Whoa," and put my hands on his chest and stomach. He remained fully inserted inside me while I adjusted to his cock. After a minute or two, I gave him the go ahead and he started fucking me, gently at first. He quickly picked up that I was digging his fucking me, and he dialed up the pace. I felt his hangers banging on my ass and felt his big dick filling my hole. He was thrusting all the way in and most of the way out—I call that long-dicking, which I love. He was hitting all the right spots, and I was moaning. He pulled out, and I asked why he stopped. He said that he thought that I was cumming and wanted to cum with me. I said I was not cumming but that I was close. He rammed his cock back into me, and I did not touch myself because I was so close. After about ten to fifteen pumps, I announced that I was cumming without touching myself—the only time that has ever happened to me. He pulled out and came on my balls while I was shooting untouched. My new buddy was about twenty-five years my senior, and he got me off better than most of my contemporaries. A treasured memory!

John has been my daddy for the past twelve years. I see him on about a weekly basis. This was my last visit. I got to his house after dinner. After a few minutes of visiting, he said, "Why don't you go downstairs and get yourself ready." I went down to the playroom in the basement and stripped to just socks. I put on a black jock with an aluminum cup with a hole for my cock to stick through. Into my urethra went a cock screw. I inserted a metal, bi-polar, butt plug in my ass. The cock and cup were wired to be attached to an Erostek power device as was the butt plug. My nips were in suction cups to make them larger, so daddy could torment them. I took the cups off and wiped my nips off. I put a pair of cuffs on my wrists and another pair on my ankles. I was ready for daddy to come down.

When daddy joined me, he locked the cuffs. He put ear plugs in my ears and a gas mask on my head with the lenses covered so I could not see and my hearing was restricted, which concentrates my senses on what he is doing.

Duet

He put a collar on my neck. I backed up to a sling frame and my wrists and ankles were attached to it so that I am spread in an X and am open to his administrations. The wires from my cock and ass were attached to the Erostek and it was powered up. It was turned on a setting to where it was on the edge between pleasurable and somewhat painful. He hit the ramp button where it dropped to a lower level and occasionally bumped up to a higher lever. There was a bit of a jolt each time the level increased. A cotton ball with some poppers was put in the canister of the mask. A few deep breaths took me to my 'special place.'

Then the real play began. Daddy loves nipple play and, over the years, I've been using suction cups to enlarge my nips so that he can work them over better. I can definitely see the difference when I wear my cycling gear. He started pulling and twisting my nips. He then put a clamp on each nip, sending initial shocks through me but settled down a bit. The clamps are connected with a chain so that he can hang weights from the chain or use it to pull on my nips. After pulling on the chain for a while and hanging weights from the chain, daddy then took two battery-powered, vibrating tooth brushes and started using them on the tips of my exposed nips and tightened the clamps.

The feelings can be painful, but they can also be fantastic. I'd say they are the same level as an orgasm, although I've never actually cum doing all of this. I think that's part psychological since I become hypersensitive when I cum and am really afraid that combining that with the electro may be too much. He sometimes puts the toothbrushes through the rings connected to the clamps, freeing his hands to play with my cock and/or spank my ass. After several minutes of this treatment, I'm both ready for him to stop, but wanting more. Eventually, he decided I'd have enough of that and removed the tooth brushes and took off the clamps. There was a huge surge of pain when he took off the clamps, added to when he started massaging and pulling on my nips. Again, I both wanted him to stop, but also wanted more. He quit that, but then chewed on my nips with his teeth. He finally decided I'd had enough and released my arms and legs from the sling frame.

We moved over to the couch where we engaged in some deep kissing and rubbing of each other's cock and balls. I got on my knees and dug his cock out of his pants. I sucked on his hardening cock until he dumped a big load down my throat. I'm not allowed to cum, but I was stimulated so much earlier, that's not a problem for me.

After a cool down period, he took off the cuffs and allowed me to remove the electro gear and get cleaned up. He headed back upstairs and, after getting cleaned up and putting everything away, I joined him upstairs for a snack before I headed home. I'm looking forward to my next visit. We're going shopping, and I will be wired up under my clothes and experience the electro while in public. Wondering what other shoppers would think if they knew what adds to the scene.

You never know when you'll find a playmate, be it a one time stand or a longer relationship. I was in a small UMC church in Alexandria, VA, during my time there. I joined the small choir and we made good music. There was a guy in it that I took to bed, but it took some convincing. He'd lost his wife who ran off with a younger guy, and he was suffering. He was a normal guy.

He responded to my suggestions about getting relief by getting a good blowjob from a good person, and I was such a person. One day we'd had a run on one of the trails around my building and had come back to my apartment. I gave him some fizzy water to drink and said now might be a good time to provide the fellatio he needed. He said, "OK," so I proceeded to open his running shorts to reveal a very nice, cut six inch cock. I had him sit in an easy chair while I knelt in front of him to begin worshipping his cock with my mouth. He moaned the whole time, and I suspect had never had a good blowjob before. I sensed he might cum soon, so I worked to let it play out much more slowly for him. He was a great guy, and since I wanted to play with him again, I wanted to make sure he left hungry for more.

Finally, he began to convulse, and he squeezed my head so hard I thought I might not survive. He let loose with a forceful spray of cum in at least ten bursts of ejaculation to the back of my mouth. He stayed hard for a long time, and I kept my mouth on him until he finally slipped out. "Man, you have great tasting semen. I would love more when you want to do this again."

He was taking a while to calm down and finally said, "Holy shit, that was great. Never had one like that before, and never from a man. Again? We can do it again?" I told him, "Yes, and there is much more pleasure where that came from." We showered together, and I got him to let me kiss him and put my tongue down his throat. To my surprise, he kissed me back and became quite intimate there in the shower water.

At that same church, the pastor had also recently lost his wife. She divorced him for some reason, and he'd become quite sad. This pastor came on to me asking, "What am I to do without her in my bed?" Well, I suggested an alternative way to orgasm and release, and he was rather immediately interested. Long story short here, I sucked his cock in the church basement. He had a pencil dick that was easy to suck, about seven inches in length. His semen was watery but good tasting, and he came pretty quickly. He seemed relieved.

So our potential partners are everywhere. Just divining which ones they are is the tricky part.

Here is the story of an event that happened to me over ten years ago. It really did change my life. My name is Mike and I'm fifty years old, six foot tall and about 195 pounds with dark hair and dark eyes. My wife decided I needed a physical exam, so she set up with the new doctor in our town. Although I really didn't care for doctor's visits, because I felt they were always looking to find something wrong, I wanted to humor my wife so I kept the 4:30 pm appointment. "Ugh!" I thought. "Now that I'm fifty, he's gonna insist on that damn prostate exam." I checked in with the receptionist. I sat for about ten minutes before the nurse called my name. I followed her back to the office, and she handed me a gown, telling me to remove all my clothes and slip into it. I felt a bit awkward, but I did. Soon there was a knock on the door and in walked Dr. Davis. The doctor extended his hand and said, "You can call me Scott." We shook hands and the doctor sat down. He looked over my records and then asked routine questions. Sleeping all right? Eating all right? Are you and your wife sexually active?" "Uh, yes," I stammered. Wanting to set a more relaxed atmosphere, the doctor replied, "But not enough?" We both laughed. "Any erectile problem?" asked Scott. I blushed a little and replied, "Once in a while."

The doctor began his exam. Blood pressure, heart, breathing—all the standard stuff. After taking some blood, the doctor asked me to stand up. I did so, while holding the back of my gown closed, which made the doctor laugh, "No need to be modest. We're all boys here." I tried to relax as the doctor ran his hands along my spine, and I tingled. Scott told me to get up on the table, when there was a knock on the door. It was the nurse asking if he needed her. He told her he didn't and asked her to lock the door on her way out. Scott turned back to me and said, "Untie the gown and remove it!" I did. The doctor came over and stood next to me, pushing, prodding, and poking me. I was feeling embarrassed, lying naked in front of him like that, but I reasoned, repeating over and over in my head, that this was normal. "I'm going to look for any skin abnormalities now." The doctor began lightly gliding his finger tips on my body. I had a tingle down below, and then, when the doctor circled my nipples with his fingertips, I began to get erect. "Very nice," said Scott. "You didn't seem to have any trouble getting hard." I blushed, since I couldn't believe I had gotten erect with a man touching me. Reading my mind, Scott added, "It's not out of the ordinary for a man to become erect during an exam."

With that, Scott reached down and began to roll my balls in his hand. My firmness increased, and I didn't know what to do. "They feel very normal," commented Scott," "a bit swollen. When was the last time you had an orgasm, Mike?" I think it's been nearly two weeks," I answered. "Do you masturbate, Mike?" asked the doctor. Once again, my erection stiffened as the doctor lightly caressed my balls. I blushed, "Well, once in a while. It's been a while with my wife, you know? Like a dry spell." We both chuckled. The doctor then removed his hand from my balls and lightly caressed my hard penis. My erection jumped in the doctor's hand. I began to wonder if this was normal; if this was ethical. But maybe it was routine now. "Good erectile response," commented Scott, still remaining extremely professional and serious. As though he could hear what was going on in my mind, Scott reassured me, "Mike, it is very normal for a man and even a woman to become aroused during an exam. The body just feels pleasure whether it's from someone of the opposite sex or the same sex. Sometimes, a man will get even more aroused when he's being examined by a male doctor because it is so taboo. But pleasure is pleasure, you know? Whether you get it from a woman or another man." I nodded in agreement. While the doctor talked, he kept lightly caressing my erection.

"This can't be normal. Can it?" I thought. Scott continued, "Just because you're married and enjoy the touch of another man doesn't mean you're gay. It simply means you enjoy pleasure from whoever your partner is." I was surprised with the word 'partner' but decided not to make a big thing out of it. After all, Scott was a professional, right? And he just needed to do his job. With that, the doctor raised stirrups on either side of the exam table and told me to put my feet up in them. I did as I was told, still surprised at how hard I was. The doctor lowered the end of the exam table. I felt so exposed, so vulnerable. Then I heard the snap of rubber gloves and knew what was coming next. I felt a lubed finger begin to gently press against my anus. I relaxed and was surprised at how easily the doctor's finger went in. I lay there and felt the doctor moving his finger inside of me. "I'm checking your prostate right now," he said. And while all of my past experiences with prostate exams had been painful, this one definitely felt different. It was definitely not painful and, in fact, it felt good. So good that my erection became even firmer, and a small drop of clear liquid leaked out at the tip of my cock. I felt embarrassed and even more so when I noticed Scott looking at the clear drop. Again, said the doctor in a very medical, reassuring voice, "Very normal. Just relax." I then felt the doctor's finger wrap themselves around my cock. A finger in my anus and a hand on my cock, and I was definitely aroused. "This shouldn't be happening. I love my wife. I love her breasts, her nice rounded ass, and her pussy. Why am I aroused by what this doctor is doing?" I wondered. It was wrong, wasn't it?

The finger in my anus began to feel warm and very arousing. I was trying to fight the feeling when I caught the doctor's eye. Scott smiled and whispered, "It's perfectly all right. Very normal and very natural." I relaxed and, as the pleasure grew, I began to give into it. I closed my eyes and let the feeling build within me, when the doctor suddenly stopped and withdrew his finger. I moaned, thinking it was over. The next thing I knew, I felt something larger, thicker, and longer than the doctor's finger pushing against my anus. I opened my eyes and was startled to find Scott sliding his own erection into my tight anus. I was about to say something when I was overwhelmed by the pleasure. This had to be wrong but, oh, it felt good. The doctor kept pushing slowly and gently, as he asked, "How does that feel, Mike?" I didn't know what to say. I moaned and looked away. "Are you okay?" asked Scott, as his pulsating erection throbbed inside me. "Oh God, yes," was all I could say. As the doctor began moving his hips, slowly pulling out, not wanting to force me to do anything I wasn't comfortable with, he nonetheless grabbed on to my erection and started stroking it. I was amazed at how good it all felt. I couldn't believe the pleasure I could derive from another man. The feelings were so intense. I suddenly turned to Scott as I felt him pulling out and, when the doctor caught my eyes, he understood that he was welcome to keep going. We smiled at each other in consent as both our cocks popped up to full attention. We then shut our eyes and enjoyed the moment. The doctor had a nice rhythm going with his thrusting cock and hand moving up and down my erection. He began increasing his pace and was now moaning. Suddenly, Scott stiffened and his hips quickly moved in and out of me as fast as humanly possible. His cum splashed inside my anus. He began slowing down and just held on to my legs until his erection slipped out of my anus. Before I could move, the doctor bent over and took my cock into his mouth. The warmth of his hot oral cavity almost threw me over the edge. When Scott's head started bobbing up and down and his hand started playing with my balls, I was sure I was going to lose it.

I was getting so close and wanted to let the doctor know. "Not much longer, doc. Mmmm... I... oh, I'm going to cum." Instead of pulling away, Scott increased his pace and, a few moments later, I felt it. I hit that perfect moment, and it was the most intense pleasure I'd ever felt. My hot cum shot out into the waiting doctor's mouth. I spewed one long string of cum after another until I was completely empty. The doctor pulled his mouth off my slowly deflating cock, patted his patient on the thigh and whispered, "Just relax."

The doctor cleaned himself up and put his pants back on. Then he pulled up the end of the table and gently lowered my legs as he brought the stirrups down. He went to the sink and brought a warm, wet washcloth over to clean me up. "I'm happy to report you're in good health, Mike. Why don't you get dressed and, if you want to come back next week, we can check out the results of your blood work and give you another workup." I sat up, catching his breath, and looked at Scott before saying, "That sounds great." I got dressed and walked out of the doctor's office with a very different perspective on prostate exams. Yes, this really did happen, and I'm happy to report I still get exams from him to this day.

Many years ago I belonged to a naturist group. We would meet at a member's home and after undressing we would have a social meeting without any sexual activity. Sex while at a member's home during a meeting was not allowed and anyone participating would be asked to leave. I was sharing a love seat with another older member. I was about twenty-four, and he was in his fifties. He was a strong man, and he kept staring at me as we listened and talked about a possible camping trip to the Kettle, a place in northern Wisconsin.

The man next to me, Stan was his name, invited me to his house after the meeting. It got late, so we decided to meet the following Tuesday. When Tuesday arrived, I drove to his house in a northwest suburb and parked in the parking lot across the street as he had told me. It seemed as if there were no lights on in his house. I went up to the door and had a last-minute indecision, but before turning around I rang the bell. Stan answered the door, pants, shirt and tie, dressed like he was having company. He invited me in and asked me to remove my shoes. Without my shoes, I was led into his living room which had a white fluffy rug. We sat for a while, talked, and had refreshments when he raised the subject of our conversation at the earlier meeting, which was about spanking. He asked if I would be interested in a spanking scene with him.

I told him that I had some reservations, but that I trusted him enough to say a tentative yes. He then turned on the TV and started a film about some spanking scenes. It took awhile, but I began to realize that all the subjects were young and that Stan was the spanker. After a few minutes, maybe ten or fifteen, he asked me to stand and undress but to leave on my underwear. I stripped, and then he directed me to go to the room along the hall and to wait inside for him. I did, but very nervously. The room was a small bedroom with a bed, a chair, and a small bureau. He had told me to stand in the far corner facing the wall. I did and started to get scared, wondering what I had gotten into. When he came into the room, he had not changed his clothes. He sat in the chair and instructed me lay across his legs. When I had settled in, he rubbed his hand over my briefs-covered ass and said he would keep it gentle for the beginning, and if all went well and we agreed, he would continue. That's when he slapped my ass with his first stroke. It was a firm stroke but something that I had felt before from my father, so it was bearable.

After about ten swats, he rubbed my ass again and asked how I was doing. I told him I was okay. He asked if it was hard enough. I said I was doing okay. So he continued. He had me count the swats from then on. We started over at zero and when he got to fifty, he asked the same questions again, while rubbing my ass. I said I was okay. He then pushed my briefs off my ass and down my legs. Then he continued as I counted. The swats were harder now, or so they felt. And as we progressed, they seemed even harder or my ass was getting more sore. When he stopped again at 100 swats, he checked my ass and asked the questions, but then he added did I want harder swats. I answered yes. He continued another fifty, and then he switched to a paddle and did another fifty in hard swats that made me wince. When he had gotten to the 200 mark, he told me to stand in the corner and face the wall. He told me that when I could handle it to come to him in the living room. When I got there, he offered me a refreshment, gave me a tissue to wipe my eyes, and asked if I needed to go to the bathroom. Then he told me to get dressed. We talked about my experience, as I sipped on the cold water.

I dressed, and he told me to return for another spanking in a week at the same time. He told me that at the end of each session, I was to hug him and thank him for the time and lessons I had learned. Over the next weeks, we graduated to more strokes and harder with more paddle work. Then he told me to get up on the bed and lay face down with my ass on the top edge of a tall wedge which had to be ten or twelve inches high. He spanked me by hand and paddle, and then asked if I had ever been spanked with a belt. I said no, and he told me he was going to do ten swats but they would not be really hard. I agreed, and he gave me swats that felt like my ass was on fire. Like they had come from hell.

It went on between the two of us for over one year, with spankings every Thursday night. One week, he even offered to restrain me. Since the beatings I was already getting were so bad, I said no, being afraid that if I could not stop him my ass would be ground meat. It stopped when he moved to Arizona. By the time he left, I looked forward to the beatings. If I left at the end of a session and could still sit in my car and drive without pain, I thought it was a wasted session and would tell him so. I was up to 600 swats by hand and paddle and up to twenty with the strap. If you have never done long, slow, hard spankings, you won't fully appreciate the pleasure I felt from them. A long, slow, hard spanking that is filled with pain and makes you cry almost uncontrollably can be cathartic.

It started out as a normal work day, though there were some forecasts of a storm moving in. I car-pooled to work with my neighbor and soon was buried in a work project. Around noon, I noticed some of my co-workers putting on their coats and leaving. I asked, "What's going on?" They told me a huge snowstorm was moving in, over a foot of new snow already, schools were closing, and driving was discouraged. I went to a window, and all I could see was a white wall of snow blowing around like crazy. I called my carpool neighbor and there was no answer. All my fellow workers were leaving, and I turned on the radio to learn that public transportation had also shut down. Soon I realized I was all alone, and was mighty concerned. I walked through the building, out of the office area, and into the assembly plant. It looked like everyone there had left too, but then I noticed that Mike was still there. We talked a bit. It turned out he was stuck with no car. He had car-pooled with a buddy and was also getting no answer to his calls.

Mike is a hot man, about thirty, 6'4" and really strong. Not a body builder, but a solid hunk of a man. We figured we were simply stuck there, maybe even for the night. At least there was a machine for sandwiches and stuff, and I had some decent coffee in my office. So we moved into my office and sat facing each other. Mike said, "This storm sure sucks!" I was looking at the bulge in his jeans and decided to risk it. I said, "Yep, this storm sucks, but a suck isn't always a bad thing." His face lit up, and he grabbed onto his crotch, saying, "Yeah, but my girlfriend doesn't like to suck dick." I grabbed my crotch and said, "Some people just don't know what a dick is for! And it looks like you've got a big one." Mike replied, "I sure could use a blowjob, but I ain't gay. Does it make me gay if I have a guy suck my dick?" I assured him it didn't—a mouth is a mouth, after all. So he stood up, loosened his belt and pulled down his jeans as he moved over in front of me. He was going commando, so there it was, dangling in front of me. I didn't pull out a ruler, but I'm guessing it was a good eight inches or more, and was getting good and stiff. I licked the slit a bit, and he let out a big moan. Then he grabbed my head and said, "Suck me like a bitch!"

No problem there! I took him deep into my throat and let him do the pumping. He seemed to like being in control. With one last big thrust, he yelled and let loose a big load of cum. I counted at least seven spurts as he sprayed the back of my throat. "Wow, that was cool," he said as he pulled out. "So, you like being my bitch?" he asked. "I think I'm in heaven," I answered, still savoring that big load, "and I sure hope we can do that again!" "No problem there," Mike said, as he pulled his jeans back up. And sure enough, we were stuck there until the next morning when the streets had finally been cleared. And he whipped out his dick for another round in the middle of the night. We both got a little sleep on a couple of couches in the reception area until the place opened again for business in the morning. My co-workers greeted me with words like, "It must have been hell being stuck here all night." "Well, we made the best of a hard situation," I answered. Nobody caught the double meaning in that, and Mike and I found many times in the next year to have some private time in a little store room. We were good buddies in that store room, but we never talked and hardly even exchanged pleasantries in the rest of our work places. It was a very special thing for Mike and me until he moved away. If by any chance he reads this, I hope he knows what a special man and memory he is!

A number of years ago, I made a visit for the first time to New York City. Can't remember exactly how or where it happened, but I met and started talking to a black guy. I was enthralled by this guy who was short and not very good-looking—spitting image of Sammy Davis, Jr.—but what a personality! I agreed to have dinner with him and went to his apartment so he could change his clothing. When he undressed in front of me, what I saw between his legs floored me, about a ten incher, soft and THICK.

Slut that I am, I immediately started to play to see what it would be fully erect! Ended up in bed with his trying to fit that immense cock into my almost virgin hole. Hurt like hell, but after the pain subsided, I was in Heaven. He fucked like a mad man, SO GOOD that I almost passed out! Don't know how long I was out, but when I regained my senses, he was still fucking my poor ass. I asked him if he was close to cumming and he replied he was working on his SECOND LOAD!!! Needless to say, we never made it to dinner. Never had such an experience again.

I had a rather quiet and routine sexual life when I was active. I do remember one unexpected encounter in my early fifties. I was out having brunch on a Saturday with a friend. The restaurant had an enclosed patio that extended out onto the sidewalk. I sat facing the street, so I could see everyone that walked by. Towards the end of the meal, I noticed this kid that walked back and forth at least a half dozen times. And he always seemed to be staring at me. After a while, my friend noticed my distraction and he too, would turn around and observe the kid when I mentioned that he was back. He confirmed that he was definitely checking me out.

The kid was a cute, dirty blond, probably late teens to early twenties—very nicely built and showing a nice package. We raised our glasses to him in a toast as he passed one time. I was, of course, flattered but never figured it would go further. I was luckily able to park right in front of the restaurant. When we left and got to the car, the kid was about a quarter block away and walking back towards us. As he was approaching, my friend said he obviously wanted me. When he reached us, we said hello to one another, and I simply asked him if he would like to take a short ride and get to know me better. He readily agreed! I gave my keys to my friend, and the two of us got into the back seat.

We drove off, and I told my friend to just drive around. In no time, the kid had my belt undone, zipper down, and my cock hardening in his mouth. After a few minutes of his enjoying me, I told him I wanted a mouthful too. He dutifully lowered his pants completely to his knees, and I bent down and started sucking his cock. In no time, I had the pleasure of a more than adequate load from him. He then went back to my cock for a while, and I jacked off and fed him my load. I invited him to come with us for more, but he declined, saying he was already late in meeting a group of his friends. We drove him back to the block where we met him, and he was on his way.

Duet

As we slowly drove around in downtown traffic, it probably wasn't difficult for anyone passing by us to figure out what was going on. I got into the front seat and we proceeded home—me with a very enjoyable taste in my mouth and a VERY fond memory.

So, more years ago then I care to think about, I worked for Younkers Department Store. I worked in a number of their locations. At one point, I worked in their downtown store, in one of the corporate offices. I would get tired of lunching with the others in my department—we usually met in the department head's office, ate lunch, and listened to him pontificate. Often, I would decide to go out for lunch, maybe shop, maybe just walk around in the downtown skywalk system. Just to get out of the building.

One day, I was shopping in the Metro area of the store. This was basically the basement part of the store but had some cool stuff. I forget what I was looking at, but I noticed this man looking at me. He was what I would call classic Greek looking—black hair, dark skin, heavy bread line, and thick build. As I shopped, I kept seeing him standing just opposite me, always in my sight line. He was hot, great round ass, big chest, and a fountain of black hair pouring out of his shirt collar.

Since I was on my lunch hour and in my own work place, I was a bit nervous about cruising. At the same time, I found myself really turned on that this guy was cruising me. In fact, my dick was swelling each time I looked at him. I was standing in the "china" area, acting like I was looking at a table setting. He moved to the other side of the table and basically laid his bulge on the table in plain view. I was impressed and now pretty much hard as rock. I watched as he adjusted his bulge for me. The back of his hand and what I could see of his arm were covered in course black hair. His dick was now pointing up and straining his slacks. I looked him in the face, and he made a head gesture to follow him.

Next thing I know I am walking behind this hot man, watching his bubble ass move under his slacks. I wanted to reach out and feel those mounds of ass cheek. He went into the restroom, and I followed. It was a tiny men's room—sink, two urinals, one stall. He stood at a urinal. I stood at the other one. There was only a small divider between the urinals. I wondered why it was even there. I could easily see over it. He was rubbing his hard-on through his slacks, so I did the same to mine, a bit worried that the precum I could feel oozing out my dick would make a very noticeable wet spot on my slacks. He unzipped his slacks and pulled out his dick. It was a beautiful, thick, uncut cock surrounded by curly black hair. "Nice," I said. He asked if he could see mine. Seeing mine was not nearly as big as his, I unzipped and pulled out my very hard cock. My cock is very average, about seven inches, cut, with a slight curve upward, but it gets really hard, and believe me, it was hard and oozing precum. Now, I love uncut dicks. Love the look, the feel, the taste, everything about them, so I was in a trance as I watched him pull his foreskin back and forth over the thick head of his cock. He asked if I liked what I saw and I said, "Fuck, yeah." He reached over and took hold of my hard-on. "Damn, buddy, your dick is so fucking hard," he said. I reached over and ran my hand over his ass. It was quite an ass. I could not believe it, here I was on my lunch hour, feeling up a hot Greek's bubble butt as he stroked my hard-on.

And then, bang, the restroom door flies open. We both immediately took the 'we're just two guys pissing stance', and our new visitor stopped, as if waiting to see if we were going to leave the urinals soon. I'm thinking, "There's a fucking toilet in the stall, for fuck sake." My Greek friend stuffs his dick back in his pants, zips up, and goes to wash his hands. I do my best to get my hard dick back in my pants as our visitor steps up to the urinal, unzips, and starts to piss. By the time I get zipped up, my Greek buddy has exited the bathroom, and I'm thinking, "Shit."

I exit the bathroom thinking, oh well, it was hot while it lasted and decide to head back to my office. Then I see Mr. Greek God on the stairs. He is sort of half walking, half waiting. He sees me and makes the 'follow me' head gesture again. I'm thinking where could he possibly be leading me. I follow his hot ass up two flights of stairs, wishing he was naked. He goes into the skywalk system, busy with the lunch crowd, and I try my best to keep up. He leads me into one of the many connected buildings and down a short hallway. I see a Men's restroom sign and now know where we are headed.

This is a larger, much more modern bathroom. Once inside, Mr. Hot Greek turns and takes me in his arms. I feel his huge chest and arms. He definitely works out. I reach around and grab his ass. Damn, it is so nice. Our dicks are hard again as we kiss and grind our crotches into each other. We separate just enough so I can look down at our crotches. Yup, two big, old wet spots. We unzip each other's slacks and take out our dicks. This is the first I have felt his. It is about the same length as mine, but much thicker, by almost twice. And that foreskin! So soft, so wonderful. I stuck my finger up under the skin and he moaned. I needed better access; I wanted to see, to feel his balls, his pubic hair, his ass. I undid his belt and slacks, as he undid mine. My mind was racing. We were in a public bathroom and had almost been caught not five minutes earlier in another public bathroom.

With our slacks undone, we played with each other's balls. Mine are not all that big, but his were like hard-boiled eggs in a black fur-covered loose sack. I reached up under his shirt and felt a forest of coarse hair across large pecs. I found a nipple and pinched it. He said, "Jesus, you know how to push my buttons." "It's easy when I'm working with such a hot man," I said. He leaned in, and we kissed long and deep. As we kissed, I reached around and felt his naked ass cheek. Covered in black hair and oh so nice. As my fingers moved into his ass crack, the hair got thicker. "Fuck," I said, "You have one hell of a hot ass to go with that dick and body."

He smiled, bent down, and took my raging hard-on in his mouth. While he sucked my dick, I found his asshole, buried in a deep thicket of hair. I wet my finger and pressed it on his asshole. He moved his ass in such a way that I know he wanted me to finger fuck him. With a little more spit, and a little pressure, I had my finger buried deep in Mr. Hot Greek's ass. He moaned with a mouth full of my dick. I was so close, so fucking close to cumming. I didn't know if that was what he wanted or not, for me to cum in his mouth or not. He sucked my dick and rode my finger like there was no tomorrow. "I am so close buddy," I heard myself saying. He stopped sucking my dick, stood up, and said, "Me too baby."

"I'd love to have your beautiful dick in my ass," he said, as he stroked my dick. I fingered his asshole and grabbed his dick. He put one foot up on the edge of a urinal, which allowed me to stick my finger further up his hairy ass. We stroked each other's dicks and kissed again. I could not last any longer and said I was cumming. Before I could react, he started to cum. His first shot landed right on my dick head. I don't know how he did that, but a perfect hit, which of course, sent me over the edge. We shot cum all over each other's dicks. We kissed again, sucking each other's tongue deep into our mouths as we caught our breath. I slowly pulled my finger out of his tight hole.

We stood there for a minute, looking at each other, at our cum-covered dicks. He took my hand and raised it to his mouth. He put my finger, the one that had just been deep up his ass, in his mouth and sucked it. "I want to eat that hot ass of yours," I said. "Only if you'll fuck it after," he replied with a devilish grin. "It would be my pleasure," I answered, "but now, I really need to get back to work. Sorry." "I know," he said, "I'm going to get yelled at too. But it was worth it." We both laughed and grabbed paper towels to mop up the cum that was stuck to our pubic hairs. We had barely gotten ourselves somewhat cleaned up and pants pulled up when the bathroom door swung open. A rather large, older man entered, grunted at us and disappeared in a stall. Mr. Hot Greek pointed at the floor. I looked and saw that our visitor had stepped in a puddle of cum and tracked it into the stall. We stifled a laugh, kissed, and exited the bathroom. Once in the skywalk, Mr. Hot Greek hurried off his way, and I went my way. We didn't exchange names, numbers, nothing—not sure why, just in a hurry maybe, or maybe, deep down, we both knew that this was a one-time encounter. Nevertheless, I had a smile the rest of the afternoon, and I did think about shopping on my lunch hour again the next day.

I had been with several men but this time it was amazing. We met online and then visited at a bar. He enjoyed role play, so we agreed that he would be the doctor, and I would be the patient.

I came to his house three days later. We played the parts well. He led me to his bedroom and told me to undress down to my shorts. He told me that sometimes a patient will see an instrument and will get upset, so he put a blindfold on me. He then proceeded to tie my hands over my head to make sure I did not accidentally hurt myself during the exam. I was excited and a bit fearful, but the next thing I knew he was gently caressing my nipples. It felt amazing. He continued to caress and then leaned over and licked my nipples. I had a nice tent in my shorts. He then slid my shorts off, and I lay naked in front of him. It was embarrassing, erotic, and a bit nerve wracking—all rolled into one. He began to examine my cock and balls. My cock was rock hard. He stroked me for a while, and when I neared orgasm he stopped. The frustration was strong. He then took an instrument that was a wheel with little barbs on it and ran it all over my body. I was twitching with excitement. He then went back to playing with my cock.

Soon, a large drop of precum appeared on my cock. He told me it was a very normal response. As I neared cumming, he stopped again and this time put nipple clamps on me. It stung but only seemed to make my erection and desire even stronger. He went back to playing with my cock, and then ran his finger across the tip. He told me to open my mouth; I did. He put his finger in my mouth covered with my precum. He told me to suck his finger clean. I did as was told. He then stroked my cock and stopped to tie my feet down. Now I was really aroused and still frightened.

I heard him doing something but was unable to see. I was not sure what it was. He then said to open my mouth, which I did, and then I felt his mouth cover mine and his tongue entered me. I was a bit shocked at first but then kissed him back. The next thing I knew he had placed a vibrator in my love hole. He turned it on and began stroking me. I was in heaven. It felt so wonderful. The feelings of pleasure were overwhelming. I just totally let go and enjoyed. I felt his mouth take my cock into his mouth. His head bobbed up and down until I moaned. He told me it was OK to cum and his mouth went back over my cock.

In short order, I came. It was one of the most, if not the most intense orgasms I have ever had. My hips lifted, and my feet strained against the rope. My toes curled and I moaned. Soon, I was drained. He moved and then I felt his mouth on mine. I kissed him, and he then delivered my cum into my mouth. I was surprised, but it was hot. It had a mild salty flavor and other than that no real taste. We kissed for a while and then he got up. He came back with a warm, soapy wash cloth and cleaned me up. He untied my bonds and told me just to relax. I lay there, and he cuddled up next to me. It felt so nice just to lie there with the two of us just gently stroking each other. It was heavenly. My next appointment is tomorrow.

I met this man, a Mexican about mid-thirties, and we started meeting and making out in the bedroom of his house. We would kiss, hug, feel, lick, bite and just enjoy each other's company. One day as we played, he told me he wanted to fuck me, something I knew would one day come up and wasn't sure if I was ready for anal penetration due to my history with anal sex with an uncle when I was a teen. My uncle was big and long and hurt me badly. But the second time he asked, I agreed if he would use a condom and lots and lots of lube. I watched him put on a condom, and then he lubed it so much that it was dripping off the condom. He turned me onto my belly, positioned himself, and slowly began to move his condom covered, fully lubed cock into my ass. He got about half in and then rammed it the rest of the way. It hurt for a bit, but then felt good. And penetration of my ass became a regular part of our playtime.

One day, I asked him to turn on his computer. I found my way to my emails and opened up a couple, showing him some of the pictures. He saw one of a guy bent over the arm of a sofa and decided we should try that position. It was great. Then he saw another and another and we tried them in turn. Some worked well for us, others didn't, but we had fun experimenting. Even the one of a guy pissing in the mouth of the other got a try.

I mentioned that my lover was Mexican because when he gets really fully excited and aroused he talks in Spanish, and I don't know a word he is saying, but the enthusiasm makes me quiver.

I used to a have a buddy I would meet up with on a regular basis. He liked it when men would meet him at his place of work, an upscale furniture showroom in a prestigious part of Los Angeles. Large, picture windows faced the busy street, and the furniture and wall partitions were organized in such a manner that one could see all the inside—but only if they were looking directly for something specific. I would park in the back and enter in through the rear door. Drummond, or daddy I liked to call him, would lead me in, back to where the beds were kept. A large, metal, four poster was usually the bed of choice. Sometimes, he would order me to strip buck naked; other times he would slowly undress me. Either one got me hard as rock and ready to play.

Daddy was about 6'1", blond hair now shaved bald, a lean, olive-skinned body, and a truly wonderful dick. Daddy liked to tie me up in various positions. Sometimes he would string me up, arms over my head, and tease my body with his hands, his tongue, his cock. Other times, he'd maneuver me into different positions, like a pretzel. Or he would tie me to the metal bed, spread eagle, and I would do his bidding. I had a very tight asshole, and had trouble taking any cock up my tight, fair-skinned ass, until daddy showed me what poppers were. The first real time I ever had my cherry popped was in the furniture showroom. He gave me a couple of hits, and then slowly eased his massive member into my cavern while I lay on my side tied up. It's didn't hurt at all! In fact, it was incredible, and I wanted him to go harder, deeper. My uncut dick was dripping precum the entire time. The excitement of being tied up and the slim possibility that someone from the street might see us was absolutely erotic and had me moaning like a bitch.

Before he finished, daddy pulled out and shot his tasty load all over my face and lips. I lost it right then, and my cum shot out, drenching me in my man-juice. I lay back, spent entirely in his arms. Daddy said I was a good boy, and he sent me on his way.

We met many times in that furniture store, with many more hot encounters, until the store was forced to relocate to another place. I still walk by the old facade, its empty windows mirroring back to me the hot and sinful times we had together. I close my eyes, and I can still feel his hard, daddy-dick inside me, making my tight hole insatiably hungry for cock.

A year ago, June 11, I'm on Scruff. I'm out running a few errands and this Latin guy hits me up. He's in town a couple days and wants to fuck. I'm always horny, so I invite him to come over, and I haul ass to get home. Fifteen minutes later, he's standing in my kitchen with his tongue down my throat and my hands down the front of his pants. I can't believe the size of his cock, fucking massive! We head straight to the bed. I can't wait to bury that monster meat down my throat. After some serious cock sucking, he can't stand it, flips me over, and mounts up. I'm in heaven; he's hitting my hole balls deep. This man knows how to push all the right buttons. He flips me on my back and mounts up again, the look on his face as he's burying his cock in me is so intense! Then it hits. He unloads his cum in my fuckhole. I haven't begun to have enough. He rolls over on his back, breathing hard, trying to catch is breath, and I start going down on his cock again.

He gave me five loads that morning—easily the hottest experience of my life. Afterwards, we cuddled and kissed and relaxed awhile. Really kind of bonded, if that's possible. As he's leaving, we trade numbers. He tells me he's headed back up north, but will be moving back here soon. I told him I wanted to date him. We're both a couple of whores, so he's like, "Date, who dates?" As the days go by, we're texting and talking on the phone, kind of getting to know one another. A month later, he's living in my house. We agreed almost immediately, in the first week of having met, that we didn't want to share the intimacy we have outside our relationship. It's been eleven months, three days, and nineteen minutes since we made that agreement. We've been monogamous. First time in my life. I'm forty-nine-years old. Still a fucking whore, but now with just one man. He still knows how to push my buttons. It's not always as intense as those first months, but it's amazing. As it happens, he's an amazing man. Initially swept off my feet by the incredible sex, he's kept me by his side because of his sweet demeanor, compassion, unconditional love, and loyalty. I met the man of my dreams that day. We're engaged to be married.

Duet

When I was twenty-one I moved from Chicago to LA. It was 1977, pants were tight, and men showed. I went out legally for one of the first times in my tight cords, and tight, double-knit, button down shirt. I was a free baller, and my pants left very little to the imagination. Thinking about it now, WOW we had balls. I met a British man who was a ballet dancer. He was the epitome of the dark-haired guy in Tom of Finland drawings.

But this man was suave and worldly, and so very handsome. Just talking to him made my heart pound. I was so freaking turned on, and my bulge only got bigger. This man was my perfect type, he was 6'1", very tall for a dancer, short crew cut, and wore a beanie similar to early Ringo Starr. He wore tight, bell bottom blue jeans that hugged his ass perfectly, and he also left nothing to the imagination showing through the thin jeans. I excused myself to pee, was in a stall, and he came barging in. At first I was scared, and he whipped his dick so fast, I almost passed out. Man, it wasn't hard, and he was already showing ten inches. He flopped and growled, "You like dick?" with a thick cockney accent. His demeanor completely different than when we were flirting at the bar.

I went down like a trooper on this incredible thick and meaty and perfect uncut slab. His balls were the size of a healthy lemon. A bar official came in and banged on stall door to clear out. We cleaned up, exited the rear of the bar, and went back to the motel he was renting in Santa Monica. Went back there and sucked and licked and did a 69 with rhythm and such young love for this older hunk of a dancer. His dick topped out at eleven and was more than I could handle without my jaw hurting. At one point, we both fell asleep—he with his dick in my mouth.

When we came, there was so much jizz from both of us that we cracked up, because literally it was for ten seconds like fire hoses, and dick snot all over the motel room. We again cracked up because there was cum that had managed to fly twenty feet. After sex, he told me that he was in a dance troupe that was on tour, and he probably wouldn't see me again since he was leaving in three days. This set me for the rest of life, because I have never had one so big ever again—almost never, that is.

The eighteen months I lived at the beach was one of my most sexually active times. I had a roommate and friends that, at first, thought I was straight, though the facts slowly came out. I never had sex with my roommate, Scott, but I saw his long cock on numerous occasions. Small guy, long, curly brown hair, hairy chest with a pleasure trail that went down to his long cock. I could understand why he was such a hit with the ladies because I did see his cock hard once or twice.

It was morning; he was in bed. There was one phone in the kitchen. I was up, phone rang, it was for Scott. I knocked on his door and told him it was for him. He came out, naked, with a raging, morning woody! I so wanted to get on my knees and service his cock, but I didn't. He talked on the phone for a while, but his cock didn't get soft. I was sitting on the couch, trying to watch TV but was fixated on his hard cock. He noticed I was looking but didn't turn away, nor did he make his phone call short. He finally hung up. He walked over towards me, scratching his balls and playing with his hard cock. Not covering his stiff cock, he said, "Sorry about my wood," and laughed, "just woke up!"

Watching TV, we discussed what was happening that day. He never stopped playing with his balls or making his hard cock slap on his thigh. Then, after about ten minutes, he returned to his room, and after he dressed, went to breakfast. Maybe he was waiting for me to make a move? Maybe he wanted his boner serviced? Maybe by then he knew I was servicing the Marines in the front apartment? I will probably never know? The cock that got away!

I woke early. The sun was just beginning to filter light to the quiet bedroom. I wondered if I was crazy, a married man, spending the night with Carlos, the man I had just met a day earlier but felt I'd known forever. I loved being to able open my heart and be understood by such a powerful Latin bad-boy, and he loved being able to have the respect and a meaningful conversation with an all-American, grownup boy.

Having kicked the sheets off earlier, I had full view of his muscular body, his stunning thick ass, and thighs. As he stirred and opened his eyes, he smiled when he saw me watching him. He grabbed my hand and pulled me down toward him, his lips parting to give me butterfly kisses on my mouth, face, and neck.

He whispered in my ear, "You trust me, don't you?" My response was as much moan as it was a "Yes." "Then keep your eyes closed, I have a surprise for you." I felt him slide away from me in bed and heard his feet—his gorgeous brown feet with the high arches and shapely toes that I had kissed and sucked the night before—cross the floor until I heard a closet door open.

A moment later, I could sense his kneeling over me. "Open your eyes," he said. I looked up. He was kneeling between my legs. His posture wasn't the only thing that was erect. His thick, shaved penis was at full attention, straining against a wide, studded, leather cock ring. His bulging pecs were straining too, against a leather harness with wide straps that still allowed the dark brown circles of his nipples to peek through. His powerful position over me excited me.

I am a submissive man. I like my lovers to get a whiff of my testosterone and try to prove that they have more. I'll give them a run for their money, but I want to lose. I knew Carlos was a man, a man with the testosterone that could take my ass, wear it out, and leave it dripping with the result of the explosion of those testosterone filled balls. I expected him to lean in and begin to make me his bitch. That's not what he did. He took me off guard when he began to caress and kiss me tenderly.

He covered my eyes with a black leather blindfold, whispering that he knew what I wanted and that he would make love to me his way. He held my chin and forced his tongue into my mouth. I willingly accepted it and sucked his tongue until he pulled it back. He held my chin harder as I returned the favor, sliding into his mouth. He held it and started to chew on my tongue. His other hand dropped to my chest. He grabbed my pec hard. He released my tongue and took my nipple into his mouth, swirling his tongue broadly around, and then started to nibble. As he pinched my other nipple with his finger, he twisted it and squeezed, hard enough and long enough for me to arch my back. The pain was really pretty mild but it made me tingle. Then a pause, and I felt a new sensation, more pain, but the kind that stimulates me.

I couldn't see it then but later learned that one of Carlos's surprises was a large leather glove, kind of like an oven mit, with the palm side covered in small, sharp, metal spikes, hundreds of little sharp pricklers that he ran over my belly. The sensation was crazy, especially not knowing what was causing it. He dragged his hand up my sides and grabbed my pits, causing sharp pain. I knew he was heading for my nipples, and the anticipation made my hips start to writhe. The first stroke across my nips was so intense I cried out. The pain was driving me crazy as he gently pinched and rolled my nipples between the spiked fingers of the glove. Next, he gently stroked the inside of my thighs. I was rock hard, picturing from behind the leather mask what was next. His sharp finger scraped my hole and moved up between my legs as he grabbed my balls. My hips lifted, and I screamed out in pleasure. He kneaded my balls, and I moaned over and over with every squeeze. He grabbed the shaft of my cock, and I was literally crying when he put his mouth on the head my dick. The contrast of feelings on my penis was overwhelming. He squeezed with his spiked hand and twirled his tongue around my dickhead. In one motion, he released his grip and slid my dick to the back of his throat. Now my cock was gripped again, but with the wet warmth of his throat muscles I spasmed and shot my load. He swallowed every drop without releasing his grip.

Apparently there is no rest when Carlos makes love. He grabbed my chin again and said, "There's more, we're not done." I heard a small metal chain and first my left and then my right nipples were in clamps. He tightened them, paused, caressed my pecs and pits, pulling at the soft, blond hair under my arms. He tightened them again, and I squirmed again when he pulled the hair in my pits. I was hard again. He tightened the clamps again, and I simply moaned.

He started fingering my hole with menthol warming lube. I then felt a vibrator teasing my ass. He slid it in. The vibrations on my prostate were making me quiver, and he gently pulled the chain connected to my nips. The combination of pain at my chest and pleasure in my ass was perfection. I couldn't help myself; I was moaning and writhing my hips. Without another word, his hard-as-stone manhood slid into my warm, pink hole. He groaned as he pushed balls deep, burying that studded cock ring into the soft flesh of my ass which surrounded my hole. I grabbed the leather harness and pulled him toward me. He rocked his hips, pushing just a little deeper in me each time. I know his dick was warm from the lube. He whispered in my ear, "Your hole is mine."

Still with balls deep in my ass, Carlos pulled back, and he began to stroke. In and out, getting harder and harder with each stroke. He pounded me, and pounded me some more. He was sweating a lot. His sweat began to drip on my crotch and my belly. It hurt, and I wanted him to stop. Yet, I didn't want him to stop because I knew that at some point in taking a beating like this from a man with Carlos's stamina that I would stop hating him and the tears in my eyes would soon be from ecstasy instead of pain. His stamina took me there. Every time he slammed my ass, I could feel it up into my belly. I never wanted anything more than to continue this rough intimacy. We were loud. We yelled—lost in passion. Then the verbal was gone, and Carlos just screamed like an animal as he jerked his giant, brown cock out of my pink hole. He jerked forward as a fountain of rich, white cream sprayed like a fire hose across my belly, my chest, and all the way up to my face.

"Get back inside me," I pleaded, and he re-entered me. He collapsed on my chest, exhausted. I squeezed my muscles and could feel his penis shrinking inside me. Covered in our sweat and cum, we just lay in each other arms. Not talking. Just extending the moment of intimacy. We didn't want it to end.

He gently pulled the blindfold off me, "You're a hell of a man to take a beating like that," he whispered. "You want more like that?" I just continued to stare into his eyes and nodded yes. He slapped me gently on the cheek, "Come here, I want to show you something before I make you breakfast." He gave a little tug on the chain attached to the nipple clamps still attached to my now red nips.

I followed him to the extra walk-in closet. We stepped in, and my eyes opened wide. It was like stepping into a mini-adult bookstore. On hangers were leather harnesses, chaps, jocks, some rubber, some Lycra, some spandex. Shelves had dildos of every size, material, and color. There were more clamps, cock rings of every description, ball splitters, and weights. Things I'm not sure what they were with cords and plugs, even spare batteries. I turned and looked at him. He grinned, "Don't worry, plenty of poppers in the fridge." I laughed, "I'm like a kid in a candy store." Carlos nodded, "I know what you mean, I told you I worked for a while in an adult bookstore. I've got some favorites." He kissed me, "Be my lover, we'll see what your favorites are."

My extremely well hung black stud and I have a tradition of getting together about once a year when I am in Texas. Not only is he hung big and long, he is a really very nice guy not to mention a terrific lover. This last time when I arrived at his place, he was wearing a robe and mentioned that he still had to take a shower. First, we had ourselves some wine, and then he went off to take his shower. We got naked and moved to his bed. Since he had just showered, I already knew that I was about to do something I had never done with him before. You see, he is very anal-oriented, like me, and loves for me to pump up my bionic cock and stick it up his fuck hole while he jacks off. Our usual routine is that I will fuck him for a while, and then he will fuck me for a while. For the finale, I will really fuck him while he jacks off. Our record was once when I fucked him three times while he jacked off and spewed cum all over himself all three times.

However, this time was different. I started playing with and sucking his cock, causing him to grow to gigantic proportions. I practiced deep-throating him, but I don't think I am very good at it because his cock is so long. Yet, to listen to his moans and groans he is very happy with what I can do. I eventually got down to sucking on his balls and that really got him going as well. Then, since he had just showered, I went further down to his fuck hole and started licking that sensitive place that all men have but so many are afraid to admit. My stud went crazy, and the more he yelled the more I licked, and I tell you, I enjoyed doing it as much as he seemed to enjoy its being done.

The next step was for him to fuck me, which I did to myself as he lay back and let me impale myself onto his long cock. It took awhile but I got most of it in. I still wonder why the last inch hits something inside me that makes it uncomfortable, but what I do get in feels wonderful. I am thankful that I can experience this feeling. He lets me stay like that for as long as I want while he jacks my cock.

Our finale for this session was my fucking him until he was about to cum and then some intense fucking as he shot off onto his beautiful body. I was able to taste and lick off some of that delicious man nectar. We had a good time.

My wife and a co-worker friend of hers started to get together sometimes after their workdays. Her husband was a state trooper, a total hot stud. We went to a Christmas party together, and when the women went off to chat with other co-workers, he and I sat and enjoyed some cocktails. I said I needed to take a piss and went off to the men's room. It was a large banquet hall so it had a large men's room with a row of five urinals and with toilets in booths on the opposite wall. I was standing in the middle urinal. I always take the one in the middle, so the chances are pretty good I can get a look at any guy who comes in to piss on either side of me.

Sure enough, the door opened. I am enjoying a good piss and I glance over and it is the state trooper, who smiled and said he needed to take a piss as well. I could not wait to get a glance at his cock. He slid his zipper down, reached into his pants, and pulled his cock out. Average size, soft, circumcised, and he starts pissing. But the amazing thing was that he was clearly looking at my cock. I was still pissing as I sort of stood back a bit so he could get a good look. I am not circumcised, so when I piss I always slide my foreskin back off my cockhead. When I am finished pissing, as I was at that moment, I slowly slide my foreskin back and forth over my cockhead to get the last drop of piss out.

He looked in my eyes and said he'd never seen an uncircumcised cock. I smiled and said he could look as long as he liked. Then I stood back, acting like I was tucking my shirt back into my pants, but instead unfastened them and just let my cock hang in front of him. He asked what it felt like to have that foreskin. I said, "Well, I don't know what it feels like not to have it," and grinned. He was just staring at my cock, and I started getting some wood. I told him he was welcome to feel it and grinned. He reached over and started stroking it! I could not fucking believe it. I was now rock hard, and so was he. I reached over and stroked his rock hard cock as well. We both smiled, and I suggested that maybe we could get together sometime. He answered, "Yes, we have to!"

So, we finished the party, sitting at the table, our legs rubbing together the entire time. No one could see us, but it was so fucking hot. We made plans to meet up at an adult cinema that used to be fairly close to where we both lived. It's now closed and has been torn down. We met there, sat in the back of cinema, watching some hot group fucking scenes. Both of us took our cocks out and started stroking, and then stroking each other. He leaned over and said he wanted a taste of mine and started sucking my dick, working my foreskin up and down over my cockhead, licking, kissing, and stroking my rock hard manhood. I told him to slow down or I was going to cum. He said to go ahead; he wanted my cum. I started blasting my cum load and filled his mouth. He was moaning and licking and swallowing every drop of it. Then, as my hard-on started to soften, he continued to suck and lick on my cock, sliding my foreskin all the way off my cockhead and licking every drop off and swallowing all of it! Fuck it was hot. That began a great time of our getting together for some mutual cock sucking and shooting lots of cum loads together!

On my birthday in 1985, I went to the bar and got a pleasant feeling from the liquor and coke that I was drinking. I waited a long time, hoping that someone would come along who would want me to take him home. But no one came, so about 9:00 pm I started home. I was driving down the interstate when I saw a young man with no shirt on, hitchhiking. There was no way I could resist that, so I stopped and picked him up. He told me he was coming back to Ft. Riley from southern Missouri after a visit with his young wife and child. Apparently, he did not have money for a vehicle and hitchhiked all the way. So I asked him if he got much sex in the military. He was spooked and said that he wanted to get out. I said fine but we had to wait for an exit or he would be arrested for being on the Interstate. We drove a few minutes, and then I said it was too bad he wanted to get out because I would have taken him all the way home, about 100 miles. He sat there a few seconds and said that his asshole only went one direction. I said, "Is that the only limitation?" He said OK. So, I took him to a package store and got him a six pack of beer.

We drove about twenty-five miles before I got off the interstate and drove on a federal highway. I saw a nice field and we moved into it. I reached over, unbuttoned his shorts, and began to rub his hot body. I sucked on his tits and nibbled his ear while I was playing with his soft cock. I then got down and started sucking on him. As I was sucking, I reached my finger down and began to diddle his hole, not going in, just touching it. He was not getting hard, but I was still sucking. Finally, I lay back over against the driver's side of the car. He reached over, pulled my shorts down, and started sucking me. Now, he knew what he was doing.

Before he had gone on too long, I was shooting into his mouth. I took some of the cum and told him to turn around. At first he refused, but then he did. I stuck the cum up his butt and played around getting him really hot. I got on my knees and stuck my still hard cock deep inside him and fucked that sergeant good. I played with him for the next sixty miles and when I got him to Ft. Riley, I let him out. Years later, when Desert Storm began, I prayed that my soldier boy would be safe.

FIRST TIME

I passed Mr. P's house every day on the way to and from school. It was really a mansion by small town Iowa standards, white clapboard, three floors with a large, wrap-around porch. The style made it look almost

First Time

like a southern plantation, but with a Midwestern flare. A wrought-iron fence kept out stray dogs and unwanted guests from the extensive grounds. Mr. P lived with his mother, an old woman almost ninety; he was in his mid 50s. He and his mother had converted their large house into an old folks' home, an affordable alternative for the elderly with limited means in the 1960s. Mr. P's house was just down the street and a block over from my house, also in the better part of town.

As I would walk past after classes in the afternoon, I would see a row of old men and women, seated in white wicker rockers, oblivious to the world around them. Some read; others just stared, wondering where their youth had gone. No one took much notice of me. Sometimes Mr. P would be on the porch or in the yard, always ready with a "Hi there, Phil" or a "Come in sometime and I'll show you my French collection." Mr. P knew I was a French student and loved all things French. Sometimes he would tease me and say to me, "You need to get longer pants, those are getting high-water; you must be growing too fast." He was acquainted with my parents, but when they spoke of him at all, it was in whispered tones and always to question why after all these years and with so much money he never married. I confess I liked him, and didn't see any harm in him at all. He just seemed trapped in this small town, a man with wealth, taste, and style surrounded by decrepitude, decay, and death, somehow dedicated to taking care of people who were on their way out.

One autumn day when I was sixteen, I took the usual route home and saw Mr. P out in the yard, raking leaves. Handsome if somewhat faded in a 1930s sort of fashion, he looked dapper in a straw hat, cardigan, and the perennial white shirt and khakis. He was, after all, a gentleman. He seemed old to me, naturally, but not so old as to find nothing attractive about him. After our usual greetings and small talk, he hemmed a bit, and then asked, "Do you have some time to look at those French books and magazines?" I had nothing pressing to do, and it would be hours yet before anyone would be home at my house.

"Sure, why not?" I said, heading to the gate in the iron fence. Mr. P opened it for me, and I walked onto the front porch, giving a greeting to the old people seated there. Most of them ignored me, but a few returned my salutation, and then went back to their musings. Old Mr. W, a family friend, winked at me and doffed his hat as I walked by. The porch radio was rather loud, with the hits of the 1940s big bands booming out fox trots and hits very well known to the old ones listening, or pretending to listen. Once inside, I was impressed with the vast rooms, the heavy carpets and hangings

First Time

and carved wood paneling. Good quality Louis XV reproduction was interspersed with walkers and wheelchairs. He guided me into his office, which faced onto the front of the house. Windows opened onto the porch in full view of the rockers. A gentle breeze pushed the large, lace under-curtains into the room at intervals, and the fall wind rattled the leaves outside.

The room was large, with big, comfortable, leather chairs and a great desk, piled high with photographs, books, and magazines of all sorts. The lights were off, but a small desk lamp illuminated a portion of the desk. Mr. P guided me to that spot and told me to look at what he'd gathered and he'd be back in a moment. He then slipped out the door, leaving it slightly ajar. I glanced down at his "French collection," composed mostly of books, a few old "Paris Match" magazines and some of no particular interest to me. But one item did catch my eye and held my attention. There on the desk, laid out in full view, was a French magazine opened to a page of gay male pornography. I had to blink to see if it were indeed real. Photo after photo of naked men and boys, with rounded asses, finely chiseled faces, and chests and… penises, fully exposed and not concealed behind a pillar or loin cloth. They were beautiful, profound, naughty, miraculous, and riveting. I turned the pages to find more and more images, each more titillating than the next. My cock was rock hard in moments, pushing off to the right and extending my pocket in an obvious way. "Glad you like what you see!" came a voice from the door.

Mr. P had returned, entered, and had obviously been watching for some time. He quietly shut the door. A click told me we were quite alone and locked away. There was no point in denying it. The erection in my trousers was apparent and beginning to show a life of its own. I was speechless, not really knowing what to say. Had he laid this trap for me? Was he going to tell my parents? Or was something else afoot? Should I run or should I wait and see? I was exceptionally young and very naïve. And very horny. This just might be a possibility for something special. "I guess I can't hide it," I said, thrusting my hips forward and showing my bulging erection to its best advantage. I looked him evenly in the eye. God, I hoped he wanted to suck me off. This whole scenario had all the earmarks of a set-up job. He was too gentle to be a monster. His eyes were riveted to my dick. His own hard-on was beginning to show in his slacks. He advanced carefully into the room, coming up behind me at the desk and bending into my ear. In a whisper, he told me, "You can go if you like; I can open the door and you can go. Nobody's holding you. I won't force anything on you. It's only if you want to."

First Time

I was still unable to say much. I nodded an assent. He must have known he could trust me; somehow it was apparent in our rudimentary exchanges that this is exactly what I wanted and needed. My gaze drifted from the page of pornographic images to my own throbbing erection pushing out the cloth of my pants, and then out across the room to the open windows and the old people rocking on the front porch. I raised my head as if to indicate my concern about being overheard or discovered. "Never mind them. Most of them are deaf, anyway," he whispered. "Are you sure you want to stay?" Again, I nodded in consent. I swallowed hard and my heart was pounding. Slowly, he thrust his pelvis forward up against my ass. I felt a good-sized dick brushing up against my ass. He wrapped his arms around me and caressed my neck, my shoulders, my chest, and then went further down. He traced the outline of my hard-on with his fingers, rubbing as he went along the length.

"Hmmm...big boy for such a little guy. Very hot. Shall I ease your constriction a bit? Your pants seem rather tight." He moved his hands to my belt, loosening it, then unhooked and unzipped my fly. His left hand rubbed my flat stomach while the right dove between my pants and my underwear. The sensation of his hand on my covered cock was incredible. I stiffened even more. He groped my shaft through the cotton of my briefs while I moaned softly in appreciation. I pushed my ass against his hard cock. He groaned in response. "Thanks," he said, kissing my ear and neck very softly, "but this is about you." With that he used both his hands to draw down my pants and underwear. My hard cock sprang out, and my balls fell loose. He pulled pants and underwear all down to my knees. I felt terribly exposed but also deliciously vulnerable. With experienced hands he felt my ass, feeling the roundness of my young buttocks and the crevice of my crack.

"Beautiful," he murmured. I'd never heard those words to describe any part of me before. It had the desired effect of relaxing me entirely and giving myself into his passion. The exploring hands then circled around to my genitals, the left hand fondling my balls and the right grabbing my cock and slowly stroking the shaft. My knees buckled a bit, but I righted myself, as I didn't want to miss a bit of his ministering. He seemed to know instinctively that ball play was new to me and squeezed and rubbed them between his fingers with relish. My response was exactly what he wanted. My breaths came in rapid gasps. He stroked my cock with a firm grip, as if he knew that's exactly how I jerked myself off. He soon moved his left hand to my hard-on as well, stroking with both hands up and down vigorously.

"Nice, big cock, just perfect. I like how your balls slap my hands as I wank

First Time

you." I'd not heard the word "wank" before in regard to masturbation. Although I was a bit self-conscious of the noise my cock and balls were making from the jack off session, I simply didn't care after a few minutes. The old heads on the porch never turned, never seemed to hear the commotion. Lace curtains billowed, and the radio continued to cover us, thankfully. To this day, Duke Ellington or Glenn Miller can get me hard. All too soon, I knew the inevitable ejaculation was near. My breathing was so heavy I was almost choking.

"I think I'm going to come very soon," I managed to say. His stroking increased and he tightened his grip on my member. "Don't worry where your semen goes, just let it come," he said quietly. I looked down at the image on the page, a young man not much older than myself with a cock of comparable size. At that moment, my orgasm began. The first jet splashed onto the page. The second volley shot over the magazine and hit the desk lamp with a soft sizzling sound. A few more followed, sending milky trails onto the lamp shade, the desk, the magazine, and beyond. He didn't stop stroking after my last spasm, but continued the pace at first, then gently and slowly lessening the intensity for a few seconds. My cockhead was highly sensitive at that moment, but I didn't wince or pull away, but let the feeling drift over me of an incredible over abundance of stimulation.

From nowhere, Mr. P produced a towel, mopping up the semen with one hand but still holding me with the other and kissing my neck and hair. My labored breathing gradually returned to normal. My gaze was fixed on the back of old Mr. W's head on the porch, still rocking gently just a few feet away from what had just transpired. Frank Sinatra sang in the background. Mr. P held me for a short time, and then helped me pull up my trousers and adjust them. Gently, he refused any offer I made to reciprocate, reminding me that this was my time, and that he received wonderful images from me to savor for "later" as he put it, holding up the semen-soaked towel and sniffing it. I could not help but notice the large wet stain of precum on his otherwise pristine khakis. He asked twice if I were all right, and I answered in the affirmative. I was not a victim but fully aware of what he wanted and what I wanted. We both got something good from the encounter. It wasn't the last; there were a few others. I learned a great deal about gay love making from Mr. P, but it was usually rather furtive and often on the sly and always quick. A few months later, Mr. P and his mother sold the retirement home and left town; I was abroad going to school at the time and never heard at the time the exact reasons for this sudden departure. Nor did he ever write. Perhaps he knew all too well it might raise some questions. He was ever the protector, the guardian of the gay future.

First Time

I'll never forget those few encounters, as horrific as some may say they were between an under-aged boy and an older man. I learned the word "pederasty" a few months later and saw in so many texts how it was reviled. Years later, I learned of the way the Ancient Greek men taught their youths about life and sex and thought how really lucky I was to have been treated to that education by a caring, careful man. There was nothing of the prurient or disgusting in these "lessons" as far as I was concerned. I was glad of the attention. An older man with sophistication, breeding, and many fine qualities took an interest in me and helped me through a difficult time of getting to know my body and appreciating it. He was kind, generous and giving, teaching me things I needed to know. He never pressed his advantage and always gave me an out. It didn't matter to me if I were but one of many or the only one so treated to his special care. I later heard from someone in town that he was compromised in some way and had to leave quickly. A sad outcome for a lovely man.

I vividly remember my first orgasm, as most of us do. Shortly before my eleventh birthday, my genitals began to grow and my voice deepen. I wasn't sure what was going on, and naturally, my parents assumed I was "too young" for "The Talk" about maturation and the facts of life. By the age of twelve, I had pubic hair and a good-sized cock, although I hadn't a clue about masturbation or what was really happening. I just assumed I was like everyone else. When I went to the urinals to pee, however, those boys next to me would exclaim with a "That's so big!" or "You're as big as my older brother!" I think that put a permanent freeze on my ability to urinate in public, even today, well over fifty years later.

That year of my twelfth summer, I would occasionally mess around with my cousin, who was also my same age and size (and level of ignorance). This messing around amounted at this time to looking and fondling, because it felt good. Neither of us knew how to masturbate. Once I had to stop him touching me, since I felt certain I was going to urinate. But usually that feeling of wanting to shoot something out of my cock went away. In PE in middle school, I soon noticed in the showers that I had the only big long cock with pubic hair, and got teased, mostly because I was so small in body size and terribly skinny. In point of fact, I never remember my penis being as small and shriveled as some of the other boys' cocks.
One day in early September in seventh grade, I overheard a group of guys talking about jacking off. They said they couldn't wait to start, as they witnessed their older brothers doing "it" at night while in bed. "You rub

First Time

your cock like this!" said one of them, showing an up and down motion with the palm of his hand and fingers extended. "You rub your hard cock right near the head and piss slit, and sperm comes out after a while. It is supposed to feel really good; it's like fucking."

As luck would have it, that night I was totally alone in the house, both parents called away to meetings that would last well past nine o'clock. After they left, I rushed to finish my homework (always adroit) and then ran upstairs and lay down on my bed. Down came my jeans and my underpants. My hard cock sprang out and with a thud landed on my belly. Dutifully, I rubbed the head and shaft of my cock, just as the guys discussed earlier that day. The feeling was incredible. I noticed after a while the sensations would intensify, and my balls would contract up and become tighter and very sensitive. Several times I stopped, for fear of the piss that would come out if I went too far. Then I recalled the boy saying that sperm would come out. Did it come out mixed with piss? I didn't know, but I was determined to find out. This time I went to stand over the toilet and began the process again. I kept at it until a blissful dizziness filled my head. My cock was thickening against my hand, and I felt a spasm of pleasure hit me. At that exact moment, a gush of white liquid shot out of the head of my cock and hit the lid of the toilet in front of me. It was followed by several more shots, each building in pure pleasure, until after eight or nine such spasms, the flow of semen (as I soon learned it was) tapered off.

I was astounded. My knees buckled. I recall my breath coming in gasps and my whole body shuddering. The white liquid, still dripping from my cockhead, had a milky quality and had mostly fallen into the water in the bowl. Toilet paper cleaned off my cock and a quick flush got rid of the evidence. After about fifteen minutes, I returned to my room for round two. It was the same exquisite experience, only not as much cum the second time. It became a lifelong delightful ritual. I soon learned to wrap my hands around my cock and pump and that my balls would demand equal time of rubbing. The icing on the cake was to learn how to auto-fellate myself. The rest is blessed history, and a habit I enjoy intensely to this day.

I was kicked out of my closet back when I was in my middle teens in the late fifties. I had a neighbor who was home on leave from the Navy. His dress blues fit like skin and with the white boxers underneath hid nothing from my hungry eyes. I knew I was into men early on and was wishing I could find someone to experiment with. My neighbor was keeping

First Time

an eye on me while my parents were visiting my sick grandmother in the western part of Pennsylvania. Being in school at the time, I didn't want to travel with them.

After some sweet talking with my parents, I convinced them to let Jerry keep an eye on me. He was game, thinking he could use the time to lay his girlfriend in our house. The parents gone and with Jerry here, I set in motion my plan to get him. I figured if he stayed in my room I could make my move when he was sleeping. What helped me with my plan was his girlfriend not wanting him to screw her in my house with me there. She made out like hell, but never let Jerry get to second base. Poor guy had a bad case of blue balls I'm sure.

After getting tired of her not giving in, he convinced her it was late and that she should head home so her folks would not get on her case. Her gone, it meant just us two watching TV and checking out my dad's Playboy mags. I got Jerry a beer from the frig, and said I was going to take a shower. I asked Jerry if he could do me a favor and help me with a problem I was having.

I told him I was uncut and was having a problem sliding my skin back to properly clean my dick. He laughed and said sure he'd help. I'm in the shower and suddenly the curtain slides back and in steps Jerry. I almost passed out when I saw his dick. He was hung and thick. Not round, more of an oval with a dark purple mushroom head. I went down on my knees and put my mouth on his cock before he knew what hit him.

He leaned against the shower wall and spread his legs, giving me full access to his man meat. I was able to get only about a third of that beautiful cock in my mouth. I sucked and jerked his cock, and he gave me what I wanted, my first load of someone else's cum. By the time Jerry went back to his ship, I had given him what his girl wouldn't—my tight virgin ass.

The summer of 1969 was hot and eventful. At eighteen, I was fresh out of my last year in high school, pale, small-of-frame, a redhead, and freckled. I was no one's ideal, or so I thought. I was, at the very least, in good shape. My greatest gift was an oversized cock and balls, which my strong Irish Catholic upbringing had told me to leave entirely alone. I needed to earn some extra money for college, so I'd just landed a job with a local contractor as an apprentice carpenter to the company's chief framer. Three months of work lay ahead of me with a rather attractive new boss.

First Time

This Master Carpenter was named John. He was about forty, stocky, and well-built if a tad on the pudgy side, with an in-your-face attitude about most things. Although not particularly handsome, he had a something about him that made me curious when I first saw him. That impression was repelled the moment he opened his mouth. Rude, coarse, uneducated, foul-mouthed, and rather abrasive, he was especially suspicious of a college boy who looked too small to be of any real use to him. Yet on the job, he was very instructive, and helped me to quickly master the essentials of carpentry and framing. And yet all our conversations were peppered with expletives and sexual innuendoes.

At one point while I was holding a stud in place for him, he looked up at me, glanced at my crotch, and said, "I forget your name, but I'll just say 'Hey you with the ten inch dick,' or do you even know you have that much?" I was embarrassed and speechless. Of course, I was not ten inches. But, my cock always bulged in any kind of pant I wore, the looser the fit, the worse it seemed to be. I was so thin and narrow hipped that my genitals always looked too big for me. He just smiled at my discomfiture. That became my name to him: "Big Cock."

On one day in July when it was especially hot, we were working at an isolated house far out in the country. I was pretty much drenched in sweat when we stopped for lunch. I removed my shirt and hung it up to dry. John did the same. I noticed his good pecs, still apparent on a body covered with a strong down of sandy hair.

He said nothing to me when I sat down, but continued to drink his beer and stare at me. When he finished eating, John leaned back on a pile of boards and rubbed his crotch, saying he was especially horny today as his "old lady" never gave him any. So he decided he would jerk off. My heart was racing, and I was scared to death. "But you're married," I said "...don't you get...I mean...doesn't your wife...?" I began in a very naive fashion. He just smiled, shook his head, and told me I had a lot to learn about women and marriage, as he proceeded to unzip his fly and take out his cock. He was already hard, and I could see his large cockhead on a thick penis about five or six inches long. He moaned as he stroked, slowly going up and down the shaft and eventually lifting out his balls, which were large and hairy. He increased the pace of his jacking and slowly edged down his pants. Cock, balls, legs were all hot. Swallowing hard, I followed suit, undoing my belt, unzipping my jeans, and letting my cock spring out, hard and proud. I wrapped my right hand around my shaft and began pumping slowly at the base, so as not to come too quickly.

First Time

I soon kept pace with him and lowered my pants to my knees, exposing my whole cock and then my balls—low hangers, not huge, but of a decent size. John rose up and approached me, looking not at my eyes but at my cock. He began to instruct me in the art of giving head, telling me exactly what he wanted and expected. The only head I had ever given was to myself, being very flexible, but I figured that didn't count. As with carpentry, he was a good teacher, and I learned quickly. I also transferred what I had learned to do to myself during self-sucking episodes. Very soon he was moaning loudly. He gave an order and I would obey, even to the straying of my fingers into his rectum, which made him quiver visibly and made his knees buckle every time I explored his ass with my index finger or thumb.

John then began to lick my shaft with his tongue. Bit by bit, he covered every inch of my dick and eventually headed to my balls. He then took a beat before plunging his mouth down on my cock. I was panting with ecstasy as both his hands slid up and down the shaft, slathered with his saliva. He stopped and gave me a long look before he said, "I want you to fuck me…fuck me hard…NOW!"

He dove for his coat pocket and produced, among other items, a small bottle of lube. We both shed our clothes and kicked off our shoes, in spite of the nails and sawdust all about us. He greased up his ass hole, and then applied a healthy handful to my aching cock. He then assumed a position on all fours and told me roughly, "Fuck me!"

Somehow, instinct or my own imagination took over. I did indeed fuck him. Hard. Hot. Heavy. The sawdust clung to our bodies as we rolled about the plywood floor. We would pause now and then, and he breathlessly told me where to push harder or how to touch him to give him pleasure. He carefully guided me to find his prostate. That drove him into a frenzy of pleasure. Neither of us minded the sawdust. After a few more thrusts, he came, drizzling a thick, white flow from his cock. The sight of it made me come as well. My orgasm seemed to last forever as I pumped at least ten big spurts into his asshole. I disengaged from him and sat back on my haunches, my cock still rock hard and dripping semen.

John was panting, with his gaze still fixed on my cock. I glanced down to see my semen pouring out of his rectum and pooling on the floorboards. I smiled, feeling like a proud pupil who had learned his lesson well. My first experience was amazing.

First Time

I started late with men. My realization that I wanted man-sex evolved over a long time. When I was still working, I used to go to adult theaters when I traveled on business. After a while I realized I was more interested in the cocks than the pussies I was watching. I started going to adult bookstores and watching gay videos. Then I discovered chat rooms. My first was a guy I had been chatting with online for a long time. I had to go to his city on business. He came to my hotel. He was sixty-six and experienced. He immediately started kissing me and fondling me.

After a while we got naked and into bed. More kissing and foreplay. He had a hairy chest, which I love. I moved down and sucked my first cock at age fifty-nine. After I sucked awhile, he wanted to 69, so I got sucked by a man for the first time. Then he surprised me. He said my ass was the sexiest part of my body, and he rimmed me. I had never felt anything like that. It was sensational. Unfortunately, he found a young lover, and I never saw him again. Now, all you have to do to get me under your control is to rim my ass. It was a great introduction to male sex. I've not been able to get enough since then. I have discovered that I love most things sexual, just no rough stuff or scat. I discovered I love to be fucked, and I've never met a cock I didn't like.

Here's my story, describing my first time experimenting as a young gay man. Now I'm sixty-one, athletic, and a gay dad with three wonderful college grads, plus family and friends who could care less about my being gay.

I always had an attraction to other guys, but even though I went to an all-boys' boarding school before college where I was a student government leader, I never acted on any impulses, just kept my dick down, down, down in the shared gym and showers while lusting privately at all the gorgeous guys and swinging dicks I saw on a daily basis. I never once acted on any of those impulses, just whacked off mercilessly and gloriously at night in private. Ahhhh, to have the sex drive of youth!

Then I went to college in Washington, DC, where, for all intents and purposes, everyone saw only a straight, preppy jock with a nice head of dark red hair. Being a redhead, I of course suffered from heavy acne during my teenage years, so I never thought of myself as even handsome. Now that I look back, I realize I was—and, oh, what opportunities I might have had. But being also a guy who always wanted to have kids and be a damn good

First Time

dad, I guess it was a blessing in disguise. Otherwise, I'd have experienced incredible gay passion and lust—and then probably would have gone down the 1980s HIV route, with whatever THOSE consequences might have been.

Anyway, in college I rented and sort of ran a group house with friends from college, both sexes. One of them who came to live with us was Peter, an openly gay dancer who was also a friend from my boarding school. In college, I was in ROTC during the post-Viet Nam years and in great shape, and, as I said, lived an openly straight life to everyone who knew me, my housemates included. I didn't accept that I was gay until I was forty-six. One Saturday night, when no one else was there, my high school friend/housemate Peter and I got high and cooked a dinner, bbq-ing and playing with the cat that had decided we were a good house to live in, which is why she moved in with us. We all loved her because she was an outdoor cat, and in all three years we were there, she never once needed a litter box—and it never even occurred to us to have one in the house. Anyway, Peter and my conversation started to turn, with Peter telling me stories of some of his then very few M2M adventures, and I couldn't help but discreetly get hard as a rock. Peter was short, had a nice athletic, perfectly proportioned body, and we were very close friends.

Peter had been working out dancing and complained of muscle ache, so, heart in mouth, I casually said, "Lie down on your bed, and I'll give you a massage." Remember, it being a Saturday night, party night, there was no one else in the house, and it was around 10:00 pm. He gave me a quiet, almost wondering look and said simply, "That'd be great," and took off his shirt while keeping his shorts on.

So I started to massage his tight, V-shaped back. The more I massaged, the more I admired his bod and secretly kept thinking of how much I wanted to touch his dick—which would have been a first for me, and for us, of course. And the more I massaged, the more my hands moved down to his lower back and started brushing the top area of his little melon-like buns. His breathing got quiet and calmer while mine became heavier, with my heart racing and, as I massaged, my dick getting even harder, if that was even possible.
So, surprising myself, I heard my voice say—as if from some other body—"Turn over, Peter," which he, startled from a semi, dream-like state, did. And I could see that his dick in his shorts, a nice, stubby, five inches long, was as rigid as mine. His eyes were closed as I started to massage his chest and tight stomach, which is when he moaned ever so gently. And that's when I said, again in that same distant, other guy's voice as if not my own,

First Time

"Take off your shorts," which he did without saying a word. And then I couldn't help myself, and with a low groan, I grabbed his dick and gently started stroking it, marveling at its texture, softness and hardness combined, while inside my head there was a turmoil of screaming emotions—elation coupled with fear, wonder, and amazement at my own audacity. And I went down and started sucking his dick, all the time my inner self was screaming, "Look at you! OMG, you're sucking Peter's dick! And it's amazing!" But of course, it being 1975 and my first time ever, there was a conflicting subconscious emotion of "Oh, how gross."

At the same time as I was reveling and surprising myself in my actions, Peter moved his hand into my wide open shorts, pulled out my eight inch dick and, without any hesitation, started sucking it deep down his throat. Within seconds, I practically choked him with a huge load. I swear I just kept cumming and cumming and cumming—and he took every drop. But that's when my guilt immediately manifested itself along with disgust, and even though I knew I should reciprocate and in the back of my mind, wanted to, I simply couldn't. That other bold personality and voice disappeared, my dick wilted, and although Peter encouraged me to go to town, I begged off. Giving me a knowing and far more mature look then his nineteen years would have indicated, he pushed me down on my back, straddled me, and then jacked off on my chest while kissing me, which was also a first. And he came buckets too, sat up, stayed there and started quietly massaging his cum all over my chest.

As I said, Peter was and still is a great friend so he kept my confidence and no one in the house was the wiser, which, of course, over the next two to three years led to two more such encounters between us, with me being a bit more reciprocal, as I tried to accept these amazing M2M desires in myself. But I didn't accept myself completely and wholely until after having married, having three gorgeous kids, and turning forty-six. But here it is, forty-two years later, and I remember every detail as if it were yesterday.

Well, as a married guy who has a passion for all sex pleasure my story certainly would not bring any excitement to my fellow closeted friends. My first guy fun was my first sex. It was with a cousin who was about four years my senior. He introduced me before I was a teen. We would get naked, and he would try to do anal with my young hole. I do remember it hurt and was no fun for me but much for him as I now know. We broke it off when he started dating and never really had any guy fun after that. I, too, later married, and it was not until my early thirties did I have oral fun with guys I would meet in hotel saunas or gay friendly clubs. Anyway, not very exciting, but the enjoyment of both sex fun has been a choice of mine since preteen.

About ten years ago I was going through a divorce and a bit of a dry spell with the ladies. I happened to check out the personal ads on Craigslist, hoping to find someone to relieve my situation. I didn't set my search for anything in particular. I came across an ad looking for married men looking to experience an amazing BJ. Well, the soon-to-be ex wasn't much into sucking cock, so I thought I'd respond to this ad. BTW, it was posted by a male. I had never made any kind of physical contact with a guy before, so when he responded and we set up the meeting at his place, my heart was in my throat. I told him that too. He told me to relax and if at any point I was uncomfortable we would stop.

We went into his bedroom and got undressed. I lay back on the bed with my knees hanging over the edge. He knelt on the floor and slowly began to lick my cock and then my balls. This continued for a few minutes before he slipped the head of my now hard cock into his mouth, slowly working his mouth up and down my cock. After a bit, he asked me to move to the center of the bed so he could be more comfortable on the bed with me. I did, and he climbed onto the bed and his knees were on either side of my head. My God, there was a 7½" thick cock, hard and in my face! He asked if it bothered me?

I got very intrigued having someone else's manhood so close and told him, "No." He said that it was starting to drip precum earlier when he was on the floor so would I just want to wipe it off or try tasting it—if I was brave enough. Well, the dare was taken, and I licked the tip of his cock and tasted his precum. MMMM! This was nice! I popped the head in my mouth and tried doing what he was doing to me. He moaned and asked if I was sure I hadn't done this before. He did a nice load that almost filled my cupped hand. He looked at me and asked if I needed a towel. I said no again, and slurped it up! I've been enjoying men, cum, and hot sex ever since!

My first sex was after I left the small town I lived in to attend seminary. An older student took an interest in me, and I would visit his room frequently. We often discussed sex. I'd talk about my interest in men, and he talked about how bad it was to have that interest. After a while he did come on to me, and we ended up having sex together. It was my first time sucking and fucking. I was in heaven, even though the relationship never went beyond fuck-buddies, and lasted for only a short time.

My first day in college I was in class when I turned around and saw the most beautiful and handsome man I had ever seen in my life. I was speechless and maybe a little too shy to speak, so I turned back around and collected my thoughts. I was afraid I would never see him again unless I introduced myself to him, so before the end of class I turned around and spoke. I don't remember what he said, and I didn't even remember his name since I was looking into his beautiful blue eyes and time stopped.

When class was over, he stood up. I knew he was tall, but I was surprised that he was 6'5". I am 5'7" and felt so short as he towered over me. Anyway, I told him we should get together and check out the town, to which he agreed. That night, all I could think of was him and what was his name. Two days later, I went to class and there he sat in the same seat, and I also took the same seat in front of him. I spoke and asked his name again, to which he said it was David. I immediately thought he was as beautiful as the statue of Michelangelo's David and I never forgot his name again. We exchanged phone numbers, and I told David I would give him a call.

That night, I couldn't stand it and had to call him to see if he would like to go out for a hamburger. He said he was hungry and would love to. I was really in heaven at this point. I went to his dorm to pick him up, and we went to dinner and talked for about two hours. I did find out that he was dating a girl and would see her on the weekends. I was a little crushed, but I was so glad to have met the most beautiful man in the world, and now he knew me. At this point in my life, I had never done anything with a guy before.

A month went by and we saw each other from time to time for dinner. I told him I played golf and he wanted to learn—wow, another thing that would keep us together—and we really bonded as best friends. At night, we would go out on the dirt farm roads and drink beer and talk for hours. Since we both had to pee a lot, I would always go over to his side of the car to pee—I had to check him out.

First Time

This went on for the rest of the semester, and one night I told him that if he left his dick out I would suck it. I couldn't believe I said that since I had never sucked a dick before. The only thing I had done is circle jerks in high school. When we got back in the car, David said, "I left it out for you." I looked at him and said I had never done it before but I still wanted to suck his dick. He laughed. I leaned over and put the head of his dick in my mouth and gently sucked. I could taste the salt from his piss. I was so excited, and I had a boner that was throbbing. David said that if I didn't slow down he was going to cum. I looked up at him and asked, "What do you want to do?" He said it felt great, so I continued sucking. I was really in heaven, and all sorts of things were going through my mind. I couldn't wait to taste his cum. He shot a load that was so strong it hit the back of my throat, and my mouth was so full I couldn't swallow it fast enough.

I had been told that cum was salty and bitter, but his was like sweet pudding and tasted so good. Damn, I didn't know what was happening or what had just happened, but I knew this wasn't going to be the last time I sucked his dick. After lapping it up and licking his dick again, I told him that my balls were aching, and I had to jack off. I moved back over in my seat, opened my jeans, pushed them down to my ankles, and grabbed my cock, saying, "Would you jack me off?" David took my dick in his hand. It felt so strange to have someone else's hand on my dick, and it felt so different. I always used a full hand grip, and David just had a thumb and two fingers on it. He jacked my dick about ten times and I exploded. Cum went everywhere—on the dashboard, seat, all over my crotch, shirt and jeans. I had never shot that much cum before, and I had never been that excited either.

It's been several years since I thought of that night, but it is one I will never forget. This was the turning point when I knew I wanted to be with men. David and I remained friends for several years and enjoyed time together, but he ended up getting married to his high school sweetheart. He did tell me, "She doesn't suck cock as good as you."

My first sex was at a young age of thirteen. Skipped school with my good friend Jeff. We went to my house for the day. We sat and talked and looked at my dad's porn mags. I do not remember how it started, but Jeff and I ended up in my parents' bed, and I gave him a blowjob. This was my first time ever sucking cock. Jeff was Lebanese and Italian mixed, so he was olive-skinned and extremely good-looking. He was about 5'7" with an eight inch, gorgeous cock, which got totally hard as I sucked him.

First Time

For the first cock I ever sucked I was in heaven. It tasted so good, and I felt so comfortable doing it. I remember that he wanted to fuck me. I was unsure of it because I was a virgin at this time, but I ended up letting him fuck me and enjoyed it a lot.

He was gentle and went slow until my hole opened up to take his cock. I lay on my stomach as he entered me, slow at first, then he increased the tempo. I was moaning in pleasure and did not want it to stop. We fucked in this position for about twenty minutes until he came on my back. This was my first time, and I still remember it to this day, forty-two years later. Sadly, Jeff has passed away from AIDS. He left for NYC after we graduated from high school in 1980, and I found out about 1984 that he had passed away. I miss my friend, and I hope he got to do all he wanted before he died. I am now living with my partner of twenty years.

I didn't grow up in Idaho, just right here in LA, California. I was on the track team in high school and, like the typical story, we had a team closeness that every athlete can attest too. My FIRST man on man experience happened in the showers after practice. I had been checking out Vic for some time, and I saw that curly, blond hair, beautiful tight body, and of course a thick, suckable cock with low hanging balls. After practice one day, he stayed behind to pick up our racing cones and volunteered me to help him. By the time we got in the locker room, everyone was gone so we stripped and showered alone. He lathered up his sweet cock longer then usual and soon was semi-hard. He joked about "not getting any for a while." He asked me about my sexual experiences and was I "getting any?" Soon he was very hard and complaining that his balls were so full they were going to bust. He asked me if I had ever touched a man. I was game, so I said, "Yes, with the guys on my street."

He came over to me and took my cock in his hand. He was soapy, so it felt so good to be stroked. I then grabbed his cock and did the same. Soon we were kissing, and our bodies were grinding against each other. By then, our cocks were VERY hard and squeezed between us. He bent down and took my cock in his mouth. I had never been sucked before, so I came almost right away. Then my turn. Actually, I couldn't wait to get his cock in my mouth. I only sucked for about three minutes but to me it was like a life time. I knew then and there that I WANTED COCK! He blew his load and I instinctively SWALLOWED it! THAT blew his mind. I guess no guy before had ever swallowed his creamy load. Of course, we swore secrecy and never told our girlfriends. But we had a recurring bromance for the next four years.

I really found my sexual perfection in college, but my first male on male sexual encounter happened in high school. I was on the track team where there were numerous studs with equally hot cocks and balls. There were brothers, especially John and Ron. Ron had exceptional, low hanging balls, perfectly round with cum-filled orbs. But John had the beautiful cock, long and thick; both were uncut.

One afternoon, John and I helped the coach put away the equipment, so by the time we got to the showers, it was just him and me. John seemed to always be lathering his cock and balls in my direction but this afternoon it was exceptionally sensual. He put soap on his cock and balls, and then lathered up. This time, his cock seemed to grow in length. As his cock thickened and began to rise to the occasion, my cock was doing the same because what I saw was HOT!

We approached each other and began to soap each other's cocks. I swear I almost popped my load right there. This was the first time I had held a rock, hard cock! Our cocks were throbbing. He bent down and swallowed my average cock, felt DAMN good. Then I bent down and rapped my lips around his huge cock. We measured his cock on a different day, and he was an impressive eight-plus inches.

We sucked each other, taking turns—no anal sex, until later! We soaped each other's cocks until we blew our loads. Must say, John was an impressive cum blower. His cum shot in a huge arch; later I had the pleasure of feeling his cum shooting in my ass. Has anyone ever had the feeling of your sex partner shooting their cum in you and you actually feel it? AWESOME!

My first time was in New Orleans. I had never been with a man and to be truthful didn't think I wanted to be with a man. I was just about to graduate from college and had only jerked off. I went to the French Quarter and went to a porn show. I was surprised to find a bar in the theater; it wasn't much of a theater. After watching and getting hotter and hornier, I asked the bartender if he know where I could get a blowjob. I was ten or more years younger than he was, and cute. He asked if I wanted a man or a woman. I was trying to be cool and said, "A mouth is a mouth, doesn't matter." He told me to come around the bar and go to the back room where he unzipped my pants and out popped my hard as hell cock. He touched it, and I almost levitated. When he put his lips around the head, my knees buckled. He put his hands on my thighs and leaned me against the counter. Without thinking, I asked him if I could put his cock in my mouth. He was surprised, asked if I were gay, and I replied that I wasn't.

We switched places. Touching his belt and his zipper and his moist underwear was hot. He wasn't expecting it, and he wasn't hard but was big. I touched the tip of his cock with my tongue, and then slowly licked the top part of the shaft. Finally, I took the cockhead in my mouth. It was soft and not a turn on. We changed positions again, and he returned to sucking my hard has nails cock. It didn't take me long to shoot. I left happy, scared, worried. I left for NYC shortly after that and found the 2nd Ave Theater on 14th Street. I shot in a man's mouth and liked it. I decided I was bi and used that theater for man cock for quite a few years before I was actually able to bring someone home and suck and fuck on a bed.

I was next to the youngest, growing up in a family of eleven kids in a very small town. I had a lot of relatives living in the same town; they also had multiple kids with several about my age and several who were older. When we got old enough, we all went to work on my grandparents' farm. After a long day in the fields bailing hay or digging potatoes or whatever the job was, everyone went to my grandparents' house. Before eating dinner, we would go to the basement, strip out of the sweaty farm clothes, and take turns showering in groups of three or four people. There could be eight to twelve of us, all standing around naked, waiting for our turn in the shower. I was the youngest at the time, eight or nine years old, and the ages went up to guys in their forties. I wasn't sure what it all meant, but I knew I loved looking at all the swinging dicks that were visible. I always made it a point to be one of the last to take a shower so that I could see them for as long as possible.

When I was around ten, my next oldest brother and I started sharing a bedroom with bunk beds. It was during this time that he started playing with my dick in the middle of the night. I would wake up to find that he had pulled my underwear down below my knees and was stroking my dick and playing with my balls. Initially, I pretended to sleep through his play sessions. But after a while, I got curious about why he was doing this. One night, I woke up during his playing and asked him why he was playing with me and where he had learned to do it. He said he had learned it from my oldest brother, who had been playing with him for the past couple years. He asked me if I enjoyed it. I said, "Yes" and told him to keep doing it any time he liked. I never asked if I could play with him, however. Not really sure why I didn't, but I know I didn't.

My oldest brother is eighteen years older than me. He had been in the Air Force and came back home to live after his discharge. He was a very handsome and sexy man, and I had seen him naked in our grandparents' shower and in the shower in our own basement many, many times. He had his own bedroom next to the one I occupied. After about six months of my brother playing with my dick every night, I was either very curious or very horny or both; I got up the nerve to go to my oldest brothers bedroom in the middle of the night. I woke him up and asked him if he would play with my dick like my other brother had been doing. He certainly was surprised by the request. He just looked at me, and asked if I was sure of what I was asking. After I gave a very firm yes reply, he pulled back the blankets of his bed and invited me in.

Over the next ten years that we slept together, I learned everything I know about having sex with another man. He was a very gentle and patient lover. He never forced me to do anything. I was always asking him to show me more. It was a most amazing time in my life. It ended when I left home to join the Air Force when I was twenty. I always wanted it to resume, but I never had the nerve to ask him until I was around forty-five (he would have been sixty-three then, but still a very handsome man). Sadly, he said he didn't think it was a good idea so we never got back together. At the age of eighty, he died from Alzheimer's. I miss him dearly every day and often think about what could have been if he had been willing to let me back into his life and his bed. To this day, no one in my family knows of the special relationship we shared.

Here's a true story about my first fuck buddy, the taking of my cherry, and how I came to prefer being bottom. I am a very shy guy and never make the first move. I am 6'2", 205 pounds with broad shoulders and nice pecs. I came out before AIDS and had not been out long when I went into a bar hoping to hook up. A nice looking guy bought me a beer. We struck up a conversation, and then headed back to my place to have some

First Time

fun. While I had not been out that long, I usually was the top. I attribute that to my large build but always had the mindset of being versatile.

Brad had different plans about who would be topping. After hearing much coaxing, I allowed him to enter me. He had a very wide and thick banana cock that curved upward. It took quite a bit of time just to take him inside me. He was very patient and incredibly rock hard. After all, he did realize that he was taking my cherry. He took me on my back with my legs over his shoulders. He lay very prone on me and controlled me completely, which I surprisingly enjoyed. After he was fully inserted, I had to wiggle off him because of the pain—a few months later, I learned about the beauty of using poppers. He eased back into me and started mini-stroking. The pain eventually gave way to pleasure. I told him that I was ready and he became a driven man. He hit me with hard, long, power strokes that, in spite of what I feared, felt incredibly pleasurable. I kept a full hard-on throughout the entire ordeal and had to be careful touching myself once the turbo-fucking started so that I did not cum too quickly.

Seriously, Brad was like the energizer bunny! I later realized how hot the sex was when I recalled that his sweat would drip off his face onto mine. If he withdrew too far and his cock popped out of me, he would try to find my hole using his hips only. He supported himself on top of me with his hands and arms and was sometimes successful. I usually had to take hold of his penis and guide it to my well-used hole. As soon as it was at the mark, he would bury himself in me, and the fuck machine would be back in full swing.

I studied his face as he was fucking me and will never forget the look as he seeded me deep. After a few times of getting together and after I insisted, he finally let me fuck him. I have a very thick, seven inch cock, so he had a look of complete pain on his face after inserting just an inch or so. I said, "You hate this, don't you?" When he nodded yes, I withdrew. It was at that moment that I became his total bottom. In fact, I have had a preference for bottoming ever since. We got together several times, and he always fucked me in the same position where he had me completely submissive to him and his desires. Fond memories!

I was very young and lived next to a farm in Lancaster County PA. The farmer—blond, muscled and thirty-three years old—was a hot MF, especially in the summer when he would ride his tractor plowing the fields shirtless. Buzzed my nuts!! In late September, I was up visiting, as often as I could, just to be near him. We were in the drying barn. At that time tobacco was a huge crop in that neck of the woods. He was up in the rafters hanging the tobacco when he said, "I'll give you a quarter if you give me a blowjob." HOLYFUCKINGSHIT I thought. FUCK YEAH. So he said, "Close the barn doors," which I did as fast as I could. When I turned around, he was on the barn floor with his pants and underwear pulled down, exposing a HUGE COCK and BALLS. Since this was the first cock and balls I had seen might have influenced my perception. I only remember asking, "How does your wife take all of this?" Unfortunately, I didn't suck him to completion. It was never mentioned again even though I kept attempting to initiate another session. I moved away after high school, and never saw him again. But, being the first, he still buzzes my nuts.

It was the summer between my first and second year of college. I was working construction as an unskilled laborer for a plumbing company. We were working at a high-rise apartment building. One of the buildings was already completed and had tenants. One day, the foreman sent me over to one of the apartments to fix a leak in a bathroom vanity.

I was six feet tall, 178 pounds with dark hair and eyes, and in pretty good shape for working construction all summer. The man who greeted me was a gentleman in his mid-forties. Trim, nice looking, and very cordial. He showed me to the bathroom, and I got down on my back under the sink. As I was looking for the leak, I felt his hand on my thigh. I didn't know what to do. I was afraid if I got mad at him I might lose my job and yet at the same time I got hard. He kept caressing me, and all the time I'm thinking this is crazy. I've got a girl friend, yet this guy is really turning me on.

I finally finished and slid out from underneath the sink. There was a nice bulge in my pants. The man smiled at me and said, "You are a handsome young man, and I'd like to thank you for fixing my sink." I said it wasn't necessary, and he moved forward and said, "Why don't you just relax and let's enjoy. No need to rush back. The foreman knows you are here." With that, he kissed me. I kind of froze again, but the bulge in my pants was pressing hard. When he licked my lips, I just opened my mouth. He then lifted my t-shirt over my head. He reached up and caressed my nipples. I melted. I closed my eyes and let everything else go.

First Time

I felt him take my hand and lead me to his bed. He undressed me, and I climbed naked onto his bed. He then undressed and snuggled up next to me. He kissed me, and then lay back on his side and just drifted his finger tips all over my body. I was rock hard. He leaned back to kiss me, and I felt his cock press into the back of my hand. I wasn't sure what to do or how to do it, but I took hold of his cock and began to stroke it. He sighed softly into my mouth as we kissed. Then he kissed my neck and chest and spent lots of time on my nipples. He was lightly caressing my back, and he moaned and told me how good it felt. As he licked my nipples, my chest, and my arm pits, he gently pulled my legs apart and lightly caressed that area just behind my balls and in front of my ass hole. No one had ever touched me there before. It was simply amazing. Words cannot describe how good that felt.

He would caress me down there, then play with my balls, then stroke my cock. He alternated between the three areas, and I have never felt anything so wonderful. Finally, he kissed his way down to my cock and began to suck on it. This was the first time anyone had sucked my cock, and I was amazed at how wonderful it felt.

He slid his body around and there was his cock right in front of me. I kissed the tip and ran my tongue around the head. He moaned, so I kept it up. I then took his cock in my mouth and did to him what he had done to me. I was getting close to cumming when I took my mouth off his cock and told him I was going to cum. He looked at me and said, "I want to drink you down."

I went back to sucking his cock. Soon I felt it. It was the most intensive orgasm I have ever had in my life. My head and shoulders along with my legs came up off the bed as I shot my load into his mouth. I was breathless, and when I went to reach for his cock he pushed my hand away and said, "You just rest." He turned around and came up next to me. He cradled me in his arms and told me to relax. I did. After a while he cleaned me up, he dressed me, and I headed back to work, but not before he asked me to come back later that evening. I told him I would be back for sure. But that is another story.

GLORY HOLE

I masturbated early on. Who didn't? This adventure was scary for me. I was sixteen years old and was on a fishing trip with my mom and brother. I had to use the washroom. I was peeing and there was a hole in the wall. I didn't know what a glory hole was. So this guy put his finger through, and I didn't know what to do. He bent down and said put your cock through the hole, and I got my first blowjob. I shot so hard my legs buckled under me. I got out of there so fast since I didn't want to see him.

On the way home, I came three times without touching myself. When we got home, I told my brother what happened. That was the beginning of our playing around until I was nineteen and we quit. It was great. We are both married now and never even talk about what we did as kids.

Here is an experience that was a game changer for me. In the late 80s I was a twenty-something, horny, married guy that wasn't getting enough at home. At that time, I had a sales territory that required me to travel several days a week, during which time I would stay overnight in one of a dozen or so small cities and towns in the North East. After a few months on the job, I had created a mental map of what I believed to be all the adult video arcades and XXX movie theatres in my service area. Initially, I visited these adult establishments for the thrill of watching, masturbating, and cumming to really hot porn in an attempt to relieve some of my pent-up sexual energy.

As time went on, my desire to visit these adult establishments intensified until I rarely drove through a populated area without stopping to wank out a heavy load in a porn shop or movie house. I came to realize that certain booths had glory holes. The thought of having my cock played with by another guy began to tantalize my imagination.

It is still emotionally challenging to recall that I was so insecure at that age that I actually had to force myself against my Roman Catholic religious indoctrination to summon up the courage to slide my rock-hard, uncut penis through a menacing hole into the adjoining booth. Inevitably, the desires of the flesh won, and I actually began to derive more and more pleasure from my anonymous sex partners. At first, the mere fondling touch of a man's hand on my penis was enough to make me ejaculate. Prematurely at first, but fortunately my time duration expanded with frequent practice.

As time went on, I discovered that in a few arcades, one or more of the remote booths, usually at the end of the corridor, had especially large glory holes. I recall frequenting these booths with the anticipation that my

Glory Hole

anonymous partner would simultaneously fondle my balls while he jacked me off.

Back in those early experimental days, I was so nervous that if someone attempted anything more than simply touching my penis and balls I was thrown into flight or fight and my immediate response was to flee the premise in fear.

Gradually, my curiosity and my desire for more intimate physical contact enabled me to progress from simple touch and fondling, and I began to seek out more intense stimulation. It was about this time that I received my first anonymous glory hole blow-job. This guy was great, and he will always hold a fond place in my memory.

As I recall, he began by stroking my uncut cock. I was really enjoying his attention when I noticed that his other hand was coming through the lower part of the oversized glory hole. Acting in primal response, my knees bent slightly, my legs spread further apart, and my pelvis arched forward so as to make it easier for him to reach and play with my ball sack while he masturbated my shaft. I was totally absorbed in the tactile pleasures I was receiving when suddenly I felt as if I was experiencing the most intensely pleasurable fuck I ever had. I surmised in an instant, that without so much as missing a stroke, he had deftly replaced his stroking hand with his warm, moist, mouth and throat.

Up until then, I had never experienced anything so sensually delicious. To my astonishment, instead of fleeing in fear, my pelvis pounded against the gaping hole in the wall, plunging my raging hard-on deep into my mysterious lover's ravenous mouth. He clutched at my nut sack, pulling me closer and tighter into his glory hole framed lips which hungrily devoured every inch I could thrust into them. In a matter of seconds, my bent-kneed legs began to quiver, and I recall wishing to no avail that I could somehow hold back my eminent ejaculation and savor these new, exotic, and intensely delicious pleasures of the flesh that I was experiencing for the first time.

Banging my pubis bone against the wall, I came, and came; and he took it all. My legs shook with the short spasms of passion, and I wanted him to have all I could give him and more. We stayed connected while he knowingly held me in his warm mouth as I transitioned through the 'please don't move' moment, to 'Oh My Fucking God,' what kind of erogenous pleasures did I just experience.

He was patient with me and let me make the first move. Reaching down between my still quivering legs, I appreciatively took his still clenched hand off of my victorious, albeit passion-bruised, balls. I held his hand for a moment before giving him a solid, manly squeeze, a silent attempt to convey my sincere appreciation for his selfless gifts of incredible pleasure. By now, my cock had begun to soften, and I could feel him gently working my cockhead with his tongue, softly sucking the last drop of cum from it before reluctantly surrendering his command over it.

Despite the fact, or just maybe because my balls and leg muscles ached in a really good way for more than a day afterward, that intimate first anonymous, blowjob gift remains one of my favorite sensual memories and one that still brings me joy-filled pleasure.

I had already accumulated a few years of cruising the department store restrooms. I went to about four different store restrooms on a regular basis, this time it was Jordan Marsh. I did the routine. I tapped my foot. If there was a glory hole, I made use of it. This one particular time, I stuck my head down to look underneath the stall wall. Then I stuck my cock thru the glory hole, and this mid-twenties, light brown-haired man went down on my junk so nicely. I think, up until then, I never had felt THAT good from a blowjob. This guy knew how to make me squirm without ever having meeting me.

I finally went into his stall. I thought this guy was something else when he added his hand to the job. He really worked with his mouth, so strong yet gentle. His shirt was unbuttoned with his tie hanging down on the outside of both his pecs. His chest hair was perfect over his pecs, down his middle and down to the Sweetness. I would soon learn that this would be my next addiction. I blew a fierce hot load. He gave me his number, told me where he worked, and suggested I should stop by anytime after four since he would be alone then. Needless to say, shortly thereafter I was meeting him quite often.

It always would start with his sweet mouth and that damn knowing hand that soon wandered to my ass cheeks. He'd massage my hole, and then put me on my hands and knees, feeding my teenage ass with his throbbing cock. It would only last about fifteen minutes, a HOT fifteen minutes with his grabbing my shoulders and pulling my ass all the way down to his balls and pubic hair. I can still remember how that felt. I can still remember his cock

Glory Hole

in me, how his pubes felt against my ass, and how his whole body felt all over me.

While most of my exploits are considered tame to me, there is one that I think was pretty hot. I attended a college that had glory holes in two buildings that I know of. I worked in the costume shop of the theatre at the college for work study for a semester, so I got the fittings on all the hot, musical theatre guys. There was one guy that was gorgeous, and very straight.

I used to buzz by one of the glory holes after work. One day, I was waiting for some action, and a guy entered the next stall. He peeked at me and said he wanted my big cock. Naturally, I obliged, and got a nice suck. I asked to suck his and really went to work on it. He pulls out and asks for mine again. It feels different this time, and I hear him saying, "Jesus you're thick." His ass was riding my cock through the glory hole. I thought that only happened in porn movies. He asked me to let him know when I was coming so he could get the load. I obliged, and he slid his head under the stall wall, and I shot in his mouth. It was that "straight" theatre guy, and he let me eat his creamy cum! The scene never repeated, and he acted like he didn't know who I was the next time we met.

The first time I saw a glory hole was on the campus of the community college where I went to take the SAT test. It was a Saturday, so other than the people taking the test, there were not many people on campus. I finished the test before time was up, turned in my exam, and left the testing room. As I headed to the parking lot, I saw the men's room sign, deciding it would be better to relieve myself before the drive home, so in I went. There was a line of urinals next to several stalls. I went to the urinals and unzipped. There was some graffiti on the wall about getting a BJ with an arrow pointing to the stalls. As I looked at the stall, I noticed a small hole about crotch level, perfect for looking at a cock in the urinal.

I was excited and getting hard just thinking about seeing a cock. I went into the stall to see what it might be like to watch. In the stall, there was more graffiti, and on the side opposite the stalls, a hole in the wooden, dividing wall, stuffed with toilet paper. As I sat there, dick in hand, thinking about what had happened in this stall, I heard the door to the restroom open. I froze. I waited with breath held as the footsteps came closer. I could see

Glory Hole

the shadow of someone standing in front of the urinal on the other side of the wall. I heard the zipper and clothes being rearranged. My heart started to beat faster. I looked through that small hole and saw a semi-hard cock and two beautiful, big balls hanging over the top of white briefs. I sat mesmerized as he relieved himself, my cock in my hand, his hand on his cock. He finished up, put his beautiful cock away, zipped up, and left.

That time, I was too scared and excited to do anything—that time. I plan to go back to that men's room while taking some classes at night.

I'm married, so I understand down low. I'm slutty, so I understand that every man has physical needs that must be met. And I'm a giver, so I understand that the big box home improvement store near my office is a good place to serve down low men who have needs. This store has a reputation with many repeat, even daily, guys stepping into the toilet stalls for release. I expect that favorable reviews on the Squirt site help keep business steady at the glory hole in the last two stalls that kind of turn around a corner, giving a little extra privacy.

I was there just around an hour recently, and can safely say I set a personal record—seven men—a variety of ages, shapes, and sizes. All of them entered with their balls full of cum and left with those same balls drained of the sweet juice that I craved in my throat, on my face, and up my ass.

Customer number one, I'd done before. Hispanic guy, smooth, tats on muscular veiny arms. Very little pubes on that nice, muscular V below is six-pack. Already erect, he was seven inches of slender smooth cock and small tight balls. I immediately took him all the way to the back of my throat. He did the silent moan and relaxed. I used my hand on his long, slippery cock with just the head in my mouth. Up and down and swirling both my hand and my mouth, he shot his load on to my face. I like to leave the drips and runs of white cream on my face for my next glory hole friend.

Number two. Older guy in work clothes too. Limp when he unzipped, he gave me a challenge I like, softly touching and caressing his saggy dick with my hands. As he began to slowly harden, I cupped his junk with both hands and fed his head into my warm mouth, rolling my tongue around the head as he got harder and harder. Stiff now, I sucked him all the way in and began to slide my throat up and down on his now six inches. The harder he got, the more he squirmed until he shot his load—too soon—in my mouth. I held

Glory Hole

him for a minute, but he pulled out. Since he was still oozing that last bit of cream on his tip, I flicked it with my tongue and he pulled back through the glory hole.

Three, four, and five were about the same—Latin, tradesmen, on their way to one job or another. Coming into the stall, wanting to release their pent-up urges. Maybe straight, maybe gay, it didn't matter. What mattered was they wanted a warm wet place to dump their load, and then get on with their day. These guys all have the same body type. Muscular arms and backs from hard work, but somehow soft bellies from eating too much crap. But each of them presented me with a hard cock and full balls that I expertly softened and drained.

Number six, I had also done before. The first time he came in I was initially concerned because he was wearing an orange apron over his clothes—he worked at the store! I thought he would throw me out, but instead he pulled up the apron and pulled down his pants. I could tell he was a good guy because he stood back and was touching himself but also put a finger on the glory hole, indicating he wanted my dick. I was happy to oblige this sweet all-American boy type. And he, with some considerable talent, sucked me dry. I always figure how a guy sucks is an indication of how he wants to be sucked. In this case, quickly, intensely, with tight lips and force. Apron-boy came fast. His load was thick and salty. Awesome.

My customer number seven was worth the wait. Smallish guy, probably 5'6", dark hair. Wearing a brown delivery uniform. Muscular, very muscular, the kind of muscular that is usually compensating for something, like a small penis. Nothing could be further from the truth. He dropped his baggy uniform pants to his ankles and pulled his underwear down to his knees. It was at least nine inches, probably more, and thick. It took only a few strokes with his own hand and there were precum drops on the thick, brown head of his dick. Years of practice have made me talented, but we all know there are sometimes limits to what we can do without gagging. I gagged. I gagged bad. But it was worth it, first as he moaned with every stroke, and then deep down as I took it all. Then it was really worth it as he spasmmed huge mouthfuls of cum into and on me.

Like I said, I'm slutty and secretly have sex with men, so glory hole sex suits me just fine. As I departed and walked through the appliances on my way out of the store, an all-American boy-next-door type wearing an orange apron approached me and asked if I needed any help. Winking at him, I just smiled and said, "Maybe next time." For sure!

GROUP

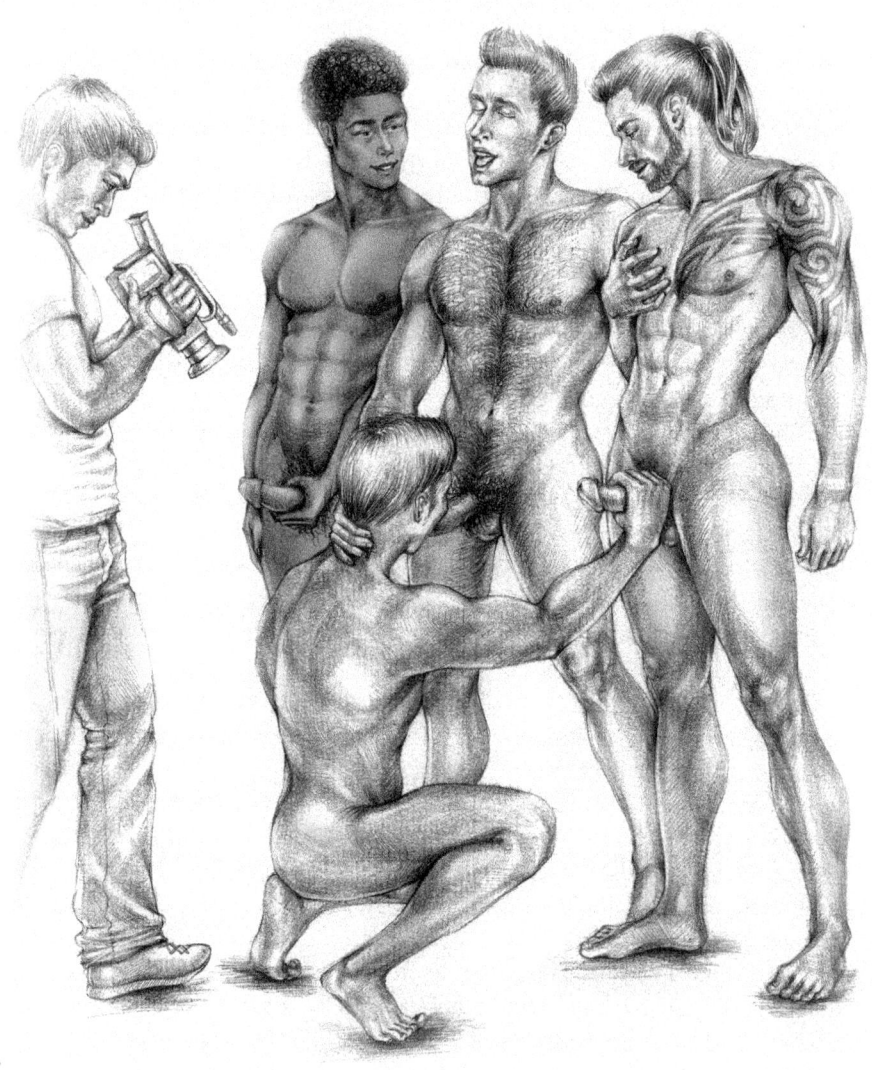

When I finally came out to my friends in New York in the mid-1970s, they were delighted and decided to introduce me to the NY gay scene. We had a late dinner, about 9:00 pm, took a brief nap, and then prepped ourselves for a night on the town. They instructed me to wear a t-shirt, tight jeans, and black leather shoes, definitely no sandals or sneakers and hung a chain around my neck that held a small black vial of real poppers, the original kind that you actually popped, promising me that one sniff would send me to the moon.

About midnight we took off for a night of adventure. I quickly learned that the most active gay bars could always be found in seedy, poorly lighted warehouse districts, on "the wrong side of the tracks." Our first stop was The Anvil, located in the meatpacking district. After entering the dimly lit and smoke-filled bar, the first thing I saw and heard was a row of three naked men spread out on the bar being fisted! A large stage at one end allowed customers to watch paid performers fisting, occasionally with members of the audience. The damp and musty basement with near pitch-black, darkened caverns and passageways was strewn with groaning naked men, some of them lying in stagnant puddles of water that had leaked from pipes overhead. An occasional rat scampered by. I was so shocked, I vowed never to return. But, of course, I did.

Later, we walked a few blocks to The Spike, a notorious leather bar with men in harnesses, tit rings and clamps, leather chaps, and some sporting Prince Alberts. Everything was painted black. The room was heavy with smoke. Behind a black curtain was a small, dark room, so dark that you could barely make out where to walk. Stumbling over a couple of writhing, naked bodies, my shoes sticking to the floor, I slowly inched my way to a side wall. As my eyes dilated, I saw several couples fucking, a few men down on their knees and sucking. Everyone had their shirts off and most had dropped their jeans. When I pulled up my pants after about half an hour, I discovered that my wallet was missing, my driver's license, credit cards and money were gone. That's when I learned never to take a wallet when I planned a night out and always to stuff my money and keys down one of my socks, where it was nearly impossible to be stolen. This same place that housed such heavy sex on Saturday night, just a few hours later hosted a lavish Sunday brunch, featuring luscious eggs benedict and warm camaraderie.

And then there was the Mineshaft. Gritty, dirty, the epitome of sleaze, it was probably the most popular and notorious gay club in history. Customers were encouraged to check all their clothes and stroll about naked or in a jock. Behind a partition there was an entire wall of men kneeling in front of glory holes, servicing whatever passed through. Downstairs, you could choose to perform in the re-creation of a jail cell, the back of a truck, or lie down in a sling and wait for a fucker to walk by. The most infamous room held a bathtub where men could lie down and take turns being pissed on.

Undoubtedly, the most frightening and dangerous place was the abandoned warehouse district along the crumbling piers of the Hudson River, especially the rotting wooden structure of Pier 48. With no lighting to help as I stumbled along, tripping over broken floor boards and empty beer bottles, bumping into hidden walls and naked men, and being groped by strangers I could not see, I was occasionally satisfied with the adventure. More often, I fled after a few minutes, fearing what I was getting into.

I am a member of a local nudist park, Indian Hills Nudist Camp, in Lacombe, Louisiana. For the most part, the park is pretty straight, but every now and then, bi folks like me sneak in! It's a well-known fact that at the end of the nature trails, guys gather for M2M fun. Occasionally, a couple will venture back and put on a good show for anyone there, but generally it's all guys.

It was a warm spring day, and I visited the park by myself. I sat by the pool to admire some of the eye candy, but there wasn't a lot there that day. Several extremely overweight women whom I did not enjoy seeing nude. I decided to walk to the back of the trail to see if anyone was there. It's about a quarter mile walk down a grassy path and at the end are a few benches, a slant board, a couple of chairs, a lounge chair, and a large mirror for anyone who wants to see what they're doing.

As luck would have it, there were three guys there already. Two were sitting on a bench and one was jacking himself off while the other watched. A third guy was laying on his belly, with his ass up in the air. His hole looked like it had already been used a couple of times. One of the bench guys motioned me over and wanted to suck me, so I gladly obliged. I stood on the bench with my legs on either side of him so as to put my cock right in his face. I held onto a branch to steady myself while he gave me a fantastic blowjob. All the while, the guy on his belly was laying there, looking like he was asleep.

I got sucked for a nice long time and was sporting a rock hard cock. The guy who was jacking himself shot a nice load while watching me getting sucked, long and sloppy. When I felt like I was getting close to cumming, I pulled my cock out of the guy's mouth and stepped down off the bench. I walked a few steps to the guy on his belly and slid my wet, hard cock into that hole that looked like it was just waiting to get filled. It didn't take but a few thrusts until I shot a very impressive load. I pulled out just far enough to see my cum filling his hole, and then I pushed back in to finish the task. He obviously was not sleeping because he was moaning with delight from the time I pushed my cock in his ass until I got soft and pulled it out.

The other two guys loved watching, and when the last drop fell off my cock, the three of us picked up our towels and walked back toward the pool. The bottom that I just fucked stayed there, still with his ass up in the air, I guess waiting for the next guy to come along. I showered and got dressed, then I drove home, quite satisfied with my visit to Indian Hills.

Several years ago I would occasionally get some playtime with "the Master." He lived on what used to be a small agricultural farm that contained several small buildings. Once arrangements were made for me to visit, he would decide on what was going to happen. I would text him when I was five minutes away, and I would receive instructions.

On this day, I received my normal set of instructions. I parked in the normal spot, slid the door open, walked into the first building, and closed the door. Once inside, I had two minutes to get ready. I had to strip naked. There was a leather hood lying there for me to put on. Once I had it on, I could see nothing. I had to stand there; I'm completely naked, with my hands behind my back, and waiting. Within a few minutes, I would hear a door open and the master would walk in. He would walk in behind me and place his cock and balls in my hand to hold. He would use the straps and completely enclose the hood from the back and tie it.

He would then lead me into another building. He would decide where I was to be, and I would stand there until he was ready for me. Upon his command, I would kneel down and he would be sitting in a chair in front of me. There was a zipper across my mouth, and he would unzip it. He would guide my head forward until his cock was in my mouth. While I am sucking on his cock, suddenly there was a hand on my ass. There had never been anyone else in the room with us before, at least not that I knew of. He lubed up my hole, and then began to fuck me.

The master directed him on how to proceed with pace, depth, tempo, etc. My focus was on the cock in my mouth while enjoying having my ass worked over good. With the hood on, what I could hear was very limited. Things seemed to get quiet for a while. Suddenly, he withdraws from my ass. I feel hot streams of cum splattering all over my back. At the same instant, my mouth is filled with the Master's hot, sweet, man juice.

I remain on all fours with the Master's softening cock in my mouth. The new guy uses a hose and washes me. The Master orders me to stand, and the other guy completely dries me off with a towel. I am in my normal position as the Master walks behind me and places his cock and balls back in my hands. He leads me back to the initial room where I started. He unties the hood and tells me to wait one minute before removing the hood, dressing, and leaving. I do as commanded or know I will never be invited back again.

Years ago when I lived in the WDC area, I was a member of a group called JOE (Jack Off Enthusiasts). They met on a regular schedule. When you arrived at the meeting location, you were given a big black trash bag to hold all your clothes, securing it with a name tag. Then you just walked around or stood and watched the sights until you saw something you liked or someone found you. Anything oral was permissible—absolutely no anal play was allowed.

Most of the participants were not exactly my type. On occasion though, there was this one guy with a really nice body that would attend. I played with him on several occasions when we were both at the same meeting. On about our fourth time, he stood up from sucking me, quietly told me he lived just a couple of blocks away, and asked if I would like to go home with him.

Of course, I did! It took us very little time to get to his place. Upon entering his apartment, he quickly stripped, and then undressed me. He led me to the living room and had me sit on the sofa, saying he would be right back. He went to his bedroom and returned with lube.

After some hot kissing and sucking, he lubed me up and impaled himself. He told me he loved to get fucked and would normally be still horny after a JOE meeting, even if he came more than once. He would come home and use a dildo to get off again. After some play on the sofa, we went to his bedroom to extend the fun for a while. I was always glad when I went to a JOE meeting and he was there. After some tit and cock work at the meeting, it was always home and straight to his bed to eat his ass and stuff it.

Group

I recently read a story of a JO club, where no anal was allowed. Jogged my memory of the hottest club I'd ever attended, with anal delight part of the deal. Called Bear Naked Chicago, met every couple of months, hosted by a retired dude in his nice, older brick home with the entrance facing a forest preserve, which allowed privacy from neighbors. Volunteers at the door checked the registration, collecting $20, which included pop and snacks (BYOB). On a slow night, fifty guys, on a busy night, 100, all ages, many bears, all oozing.

Clothes in a bag upstairs, with the action in the basement—several rooms, low ceiling, octopus furnace, pipes along the walls, a make-shift community shower with room for buddies—but it was just heaven for us fuckers! Five slings, with fuckees taking turns. Since most are bottoms and I'm a top with an ever-hard, my dance card was ALWAYS full. And at the far end, in the dark, coal cellar, was the busiest orgy room on the planet, including a mattress and dozens of hungry mouths and asses. I swapped phone numbers with some of the regulars for future workouts.

Alas, Paradise Lost. Seems that the street parking was chocked on certain nights, so the neighbors bitched. The city lodged a cease-and-desist with the dude. Fuck!!! Bear Naked Chicago still exists, but now alternates in the back room of a couple gay bars, guessing without slings or shower. Ah, what a loss for us hornies.

Just back from a hotel sex party and quality prime beef of those attending. There were six of us. At first, everyone kind of sampled what was available, but two of them paired up. That left four of us to figure out what to do. OMG, I love their imaginations. Setting the picture: No. 1, a thirty-year-old, nice build, nice cock, average-sized. Not all that much into sucking but did love to be sucked. No. 2, a young bear, maybe fiftyish with nice equipment. Had seen me at an earlier party, topping an occasional bottom. He really wanted to be fucked but not in front of the others. Eventually, he let me have his load, which was massive. I love the feeling of a cock pulsating in my mouth as it unloads.

No. 3, probably fiftyish also, shaved head, massive cock with a head hard and ready to get in my mouth. He was versatile, really worked the thirty-year-old and me together and he didn't want to cum yet. No. 4, me, a seventy-six-year-old with an eight inch hard-on, thanks to Viagra. No. 3 and No. 4 (me) soaked him with our cum after he had sucked us for about fifteen minutes. Fun to shoot together. After coming down from an ejaculation high, I asked him if he wanted me to take his load. No argument there. He also had A+ equipment and a head that filled my mouth. Again, I was reminded how great it is to feel a loaded cock discharge and fill my mouth. I've become such a cum whore I can't believe it. I'm pretty sure I'll be there again in ten days. Life is a ball, just suck on two of them.

One year, for New Year's Eve, I got invited to an all-men's gay kilt party. Never having attended before, I wasn't sure what to expect. Most of the evening was like any other fancy party with men chatting, enjoying good food and drink. Then, one of the two hosts pulled me into a side room. He said he needed to make sure I had worn the kilt properly. And by properly, I mean with no underwear. He moved his hand up my leg, until he was caressing my naked, hairy balls.

I had worn the kilt correctly, with nothing underneath. He rubbed my nuts until my cock was rock hard and throbbing. He lifted up the blue plaid of the kilt, my fuck tool nearly slapping him in the face. His thick lips began to move along my shaft, causing precum to drip out of the slit. He enveloped by cock, sucking slowly at first, and then picking up a little speed.

It was at that moment his husband came in. He was an older, daddy type. He smiled and watched his partner suck on my uncut cock. Then he got behind me, dropped to his knees, and began to lick my ass. I could feel his tongue edging closer and closer to my butt crack. His tongue then entered me. He was tongue-fucking me with an intense velocity. And his man was continuing his expert cocksucking skills. Without warning, I couldn't take it anymore, and I shot my massive load down the host's throat. The sound I made was like a Scottish battle cry.

Some of my cum dripped from the corners of his mouth, and he pulled me close, giving me some of my semen back. It tasted so good. Then his partner stood up, turned me around, and kissed me passionately, tasting my asshole on his lips and tongue. I spent the rest of the party with a big smile on my face, spent and satisfied with the unexpected servicing from my two hosts.

I'm a bottom, and I had been without sex for a year or so. I wanted it but was concerned about guys just wanting to hit and go. I wanted someone to loosen me up again. I finally met this guy who was nicely hung, and sane and mature enough to know I needed warming up. He was gentle until I adjusted, and then we went at it hard and heavy. The next time he visited he brought a friend, not as hung but still really nice. They tag teamed me, and then my friend asked me if I wanted to try double penetration. I absolutely did.

It had been a fantasy of mine even before I knew it was possible. I sat on my friend, and his buddy came up from behind. Before I knew it, we were moving like a well-oiled machine. I had to keep kissing my friend underneath me to keep from getting really loud. It only lasted a few minutes, but I wanted to do this to completion. I want this every day!

My friend, K, and I met last year. We were introduced over the internet by mutual friends. I was heading for Thanksgiving to our mutual friends about 500+ miles. They wondered if I would mind if they asked their friend K if he wanted to ride along.

It turned out that K already had reservations to fly to visit his own family, but we decided we would enjoy meeting before we each took off. I was dating a guy who was a total bottom. The more dick and cum he had up his ass, the happier my friend was. K said he is very versatile, going both ways either top or bottom. The trouble is we all lived an hour and a half in different directions. The three of us were to meet at a private men's club, membership-only place, that has either booths for private play or a general meeting play area with several couches while a gay flick plays in a continual loop on the screen.

K was running late, and it's a little hard to find the unmarked private men's club. My boyfriend went looking for sex while I stayed near the front entry to meet K and help direct him to find the unmarked club.

I am a total top and love rimming. A not bad-looking guy, definitely a bottom, kept cruising me as I waited. Then K arrived. I found my friend and we went into the general play area. We spent a few minutes getting to know each other. There already were several men in that general play area. My friend removed his pants and bent over the couch. I stripped, started eating his ass, and immediately crawled on board for a good fuck. I was concerned that K would feel left out, so I looked around. Others were eying K. I asked K if he wanted his turn, he said sure. K dropped his jeans and immediately had his hard dick up my friend's ass. He suggested I use the opportunity to check his out. First, I ate K's gorgeous ass, then I tried my turn entering K's ass. I am short legged, so I was having to stand on my tip toes to keep a good rocking motion going. Too soon I started to get cramps in my toes, so I had to back out.

About that time, the guy who had been cruising me earlier entered the room. He saw I was naked, gave me the eye, stripped down himself, and lay on another couch with his legs in the air, showing his puckered ass. I couldn't resist, so I went over and started eating my third ass of the afternoon. Since I was very ready myself, I started to enter this third ass. Just as I entered, the guy climaxed. He shot his load over his head and past the arm of the couch against which his head was resting. His cum was hitting the floor, wasted!

I still had not climaxed, so I looked over at the other couch only to see K still fucking my friend, but someone taller than me now had his dick plowing away where mine had been in K's. The scene was very exciting to watch. Then the guy in the rear apparently was climaxing in K's ass, and K definitely was climaxing in my friend's. I quickly bent down and was able to catch a little of my friend's cum as he unloaded without touching his own dick at all.

After they all came, the three of us went out to eat. We had a good time talking and getting to know about each other. K is very nice looking with a nice personality. We all hinted we wanted to meet again. K and I emailed a few more times. But I was seeing the other friend at the time, so we never made plans again to meet.

Six months later, my friend and I were no longer seeing each other. I enjoy male nudist opportunities. Several weeks ago, as I was entering an area of a men's nudist camp play area along wooded trails, I recognized K coming off the trails. It turns out we know several more mutual acquaintances that he was with that day. We only had an opportunity to talk a little that day. I asked if it was ok if I contacted him again. It turns out that K's present job seldom gives him two days off together. Tomorrow is one of those rare times, so K is driving to visit me. He has already said he wants to be topped several times on his day off. I know where my tongue and dick will be after he arrives.

I was from a rural NW Missouri family with eight kids. My parents were a hardcore, white, guy father, and an understanding, open-hearted mother. She instilled a strong ethic in how to live in society and how to live with fellow humans. Basically, enjoy life and sex, but don't bring children into the world for me to raise. So four of us boys did just that. We boys all learned about sex from each other. Good, equal sex. No brutish, macho sex. Lot's of trolling around the house looking for a horny brother.

When my older brother got back from the Army and I was in junior high, he got horny, and liked to trade BJs with his younger brothers. As time went by, I had to convince him to play around. He was well endowed and loved to cuddle, kiss, suck, and get sucked. My younger brother and I generally ended up in the same bed in the household, and would play around and sleep together. My oldest brother was another horny guy. We played around a little when he would come home from college. Later, when I was in high school, his wife had to be away all summer attending an ailing mother, so I stayed with him. Wow, did we have a lot of good sex. He had a long term relationship until he passed away.

Finally, I went to college. Since I didn't have my regular playmates, I trolled the park and bus depot toilets. Lots of horny men in the Midwest back in the late 60s. Then, after college, I knew I needed to get out of the Midwest and moved to northern California for a taste of the hippy/craftsman thing, This brought me my life's art, and meeting a man to be with for the rest of his life. Now I go to motel/house parties and small group sex parties. Even here in California I live in a suburban/agricultural area on the north Coast. Always looking for a connection on the social media. Nowadays, people who remember me and my partner's house parties over the past two decades, drop by. Life brings us what we need.

Sometime around 1988-1990 I did temporary assignments around the country, for thirteen to twenty-six weeks at a time. I was in Denver for a long assignment and was staying in an apartment in downtown Cherry Creek. I use to frequently visit the park up near the botanical garden. I had a large 4X4 pickup and would cruise the park. One afternoon, a thuggish looking guy hollered, "Sexy Truck." I replied, "Try the driver," and proceeded around the park and back close to the spot where the comments were made. I parked and sat there for just a few minutes when the individual came over. Really a ragged looking, long haired freak, skinny as a rail, but appeared to be clean and smelled fresh. His name was Vito, short for Victorio.

Group

We chatted for a bit, and then he got in the truck, and we went to my apartment where it got really hot. He was mostly hairless except for his head, with hair long and shaggy, and he had an equipment package to make you scared. It was as big around as a soda can and more than eleven inches long. He was Italian and lived up to the term Italian Stallion. We played around in the kitchen and living room for a bit. It was difficult trying to get him into me, so the bedroom was the playpen of choice. Lots of lube was taken along. He tried to fuck me for about forty minutes. It was a painful process, but I wanted him badly, and he wanted me even worse, I think. After about fifty minutes, he pushed thru my anal ring, and we lay there for a few minutes before he started to advance into me. At about the hour mark, he had it all in me and was eager to pump me up. It was painful, but oh so pleasurable to receive his ministrations. He fucked me raw, both figuratively and literally. No condoms, lots of lube, and just intense pleasure. Somewhere about forty minutes after breaking my anal hole he went berserk with his fucking, moaning, and pounding me into the mattress. I was screaming; I am a noisy fuck. He hit my magic spot twice that I can recall, and I creamed all over the bed. He wasted none of his fluids, and I had it all in me for a long time. He stayed in me and got hard again for round two. It was a sloppy, noisy time, but it was so intense and good. My ass was raw from the first fucking and worse after the second. He was good at what he did.

We laid together cuddling and kissing, and having some oral relief. We ended up in the shower where he fucked his goodness into me again. It was still a problem entering me but not near as difficult as the first time. I ended up taking him back to the park, and we both agreed to get together again. He had my phone number, knew where I lived, and I had his number. It took about a week for my ass to get well, and I called him. He came over to my place, and we started in the living room and kitchen. We fucked on the couch, the coffee table, and the floor. He filled me with his love fluids, but it was the same problem getting into me as the first time. We both were flying on the love and adrenaline. I can vividly remember our couplings. Such intensity and vigor. He spent the night, and I was awakened three times with his fucking me deep and long.

He was immensely talented with that eleven-plus inch dick and could hit spots I never know existed. I stayed in Denver for six months, and he was over at my place at least twice a week. I could never get enough of his loving dick and guess he was the same with my ass and loving. He wanted me to stay and work in Denver, wanted us to become a couple, but I was afraid to make that commitment. I did miss him when I left, or at least I missed his enormous dick and his ability to use it to make me weak and beg for more.

Sometimes, we would go out to drink, eat, and socialize with folks we met in the bars and with some that he knew from being a resident of Denver. One time, five of us were at a steak house in downtown Denver. We sat in a booth at the back of the restaurant, out of the way of the majority of diners. The booth was crowded, so I basically sat on Vito's lap. We got a bit carried away. They cut a hole in my pants. Vito had his dick out of his fly, and I was sitting on it. Oh man, what a feeling—an absolutely thrilling sensation. Rich, the waiter, took our order without incident. He brought the order out when it was ready, and then very nicely told us we couldn't do what we were doing. We, of course, denied any impropriety. We said if you are that open come by my place, and we can see if we did anything wrong. We gave him my number and address. He called the next afternoon, and I told him to come over after 4:00 pm if he was free. He said he was, and I immediately called Vito. Vito came over about 3:45 pm, and we had a hot and heavy session before Rich arrived so we were ready when he showed up.

He was a nice guy, ready to play and totally afraid of Vito's dick. We prepped him well, orally and manually with foreplay. I fucked him first since I was not as impressive as Vito. When Vito was ready to ride the boy, I started sucking him, and he was hot to trot. Vito pushed into him with some protestations from him to stop—it hurt, he couldn't take it—but we were ready to do the boy some good. He finally got it inside him, and he was very excited. I sucked two loads out of him, or rather Vito fucked two loads out of him that I took and swallowed. He was overjoyed at the experience; he had been fucked before but never with anything that big or with a threesome. He came back three times over the next month or so, and he fucked me a couple of times. He loved my sucking him and Vito pounding the hell out of him.

Vito was so very hurt when I left Denver that I thought he was going to chase my car down the street. The only thing he ever asked for was a Christmas tree, which I gladly bought for him. About three months after I left, I had a letter from one of his friends. Vito had passed away due to Pneumo Cysti Pneumonia. I get weepy to this day that I wasn't there for him when he passed away. I had no idea that he was positive, and now, even many years later, I remain negative. What a loving friend and time to have in my memory.

Group

I remember a time when I was thirty, when I was a complete pig. Usually a top, I do consider myself versatile. I do have a daddy, Chuck. Something about him just makes me melt, and I can't say no to him. I have tried, but I truly cannot find it in me to say no. At the time, we lived about fifteen minutes apart from one another, and I used to pass his neighborhood on the way home from work. One day he messaged me and asked—told—me to stop by on my way home. I figured it was just a usual time of his being horny and wanting to get off in my ass or mouth. That day, I was particularly busy in the evening, but he wouldn't let me say no.

Fast forward, I arrive. He greeted me shirtless, with a huge bear hug and a kiss and told me to follow him. Naturally, I followed, and he led me to the basement. While he was holding my hand, I started to get that feeling in my ass that knew I was about to get plowed—and good! When we got to the basement, I looked over and saw a boy, about nineteen years old, on his hands and knees in a jockstrap scrubbing the floor. Chuck introduced me to him as his house servant. Said he comes to clean his house twice a week. This certainly got my bone twitching, watching this young boy paying no attention to anyone but the floor he was cleaning—his beautiful ass in the air, perfectly delicious looking, waiting for someone to touch it. I walked over to him, since I thought I could touch him, but Chuck said, "No, he is not why I wanted you to come over."

He led me to the couch, told me to strip naked as he took off his pants. Chuck was not particularly huge, but his manhood was meaty and always pointing to the stars. I leaned forward to take his manhood in my mouth when he stopped me. I was shocked, but he looked at me and asked if I liked presents. Confused but intrigued, I said, "Of course." Then he snapped his fingers, literally, and the cleaning boy popped up and walked out of the room. Shortly after, he walked back in, holding the hand of a 6'3" twenty-five-year-old with a swimmer's build, perfectly hairy, and blindfolded. Chuck motioned for the cleaner to kneel in front of me and whispered to me, "Don't say a word. He has no idea who I have here." I nodded. This boy leaned forward and found my cock with his mouth. He gently licked my sack and shaft until I was precumming. He started moaning, and I reached down to touch his beautiful ass. Feeling his hole, I realized he still had jizz all around his opening, which means he'd already been plowed, most likely recently. I looked at Chuck, and he said, "This boy has been a present for many people today. He is a cum whore, a TRUE cum whore, and your load is going to be his last today." With that, the boy stood up, and Chuck directed him to get on all fours. I didn't waste any time; I got up and walked

Group

to him, knelt down, and licked his hole. I wanted to taste the other cum all over his hole and see how deep it went into his guts. It was delicious, salty and sweet, and ready for more.

I then proceeded to tease his hole with my cock. Chuck said, "Just ram it, don't be gentle." You don't have to tell me twice, so in one motion I put my cock deep inside this boy, and he let out a huge moan, the kind that changes a man's voice back to puberty for a split second. The kind that lets you know what he is, a cum whore. I banged this kid to oblivion. He was screaming in ecstasy. Chuck asked to join but knew I wasn't giving up his ass any time soon, so he did what any daddy would do. He got behind me and teased my hole with his cockhead. Chuck was a huge precummer—the king you might say. Though my fast thrusts into this whore were not jiving with Chuck's attempts at fucking me at the same time, he finally found the rhythm, and Chuck went in me. We found a groove that sent me over the edge, and I was getting close to cumming, both of us thrusting our entire bear weight into this kid who was already cum drenched. I finally let out a moan, as did Chuck, and we both came in seconds of each other. Feeling my guts fill with daddy's cum and my release into a whore sent spasms of pleasure down my spine. We just stayed put, him in me and me in him for what seemed like a very long time.

Then daddy whispered, "Good boy," and pulled out. I followed suit, and the kid just stayed on all fours. The cleaning boy came over, knelt down in front of daddy, and took his cock into his mouth. I looked a bit shocked and he said, "The boy is here to clean everything," and gave me a wink. Then the cleaning boy came over to me and started the same. I looked at Chuck and winked. He knew what I wanted and said, "Go ahead boy, your birthday is coming up." So, I picked this kid up and put him in front of the cum whore and banged the cleaner right in front of the whore, who was still blind folded. I made them kiss and tongue each other's bodies. When finally I was ready to cum again, daddy was standing in front of me jerking off. I took his cock into my mouth, and he came down my throat. I decided the cum whore needed some more attention, so I bent down and kissed him, sending Chuck's cum into his mouth and he grunted.

I decided to cum on the cum whore's face, and after I did, the cleaning boy licked his face fully. This was his job after all, to clean. When I went to the bathroom, the cum whore took his blindfold off and thanked me for his breeding. He was so handsome, and I was in love. I slipped him my card and headed out for the evening. It was one of the best times I have ever had with daddy, though there were many great times! Shortly after I got in my car, I received a text from the cum whore that read, "Don't drive too far; I want to talk to you. Don't tell daddy." I agreed, told him where I was parked, and about five minutes later a car pulled up. He asked me if I would ever do that again to him and, of course, I said YEAH! He said, "Good and climbed into my car." That's a story for another time though. Happy cumming!

I was working out of town a couple of weeks ago. A fuckbuddy of mine, Ryan, lived not far away, so we arranged a play date. The day he was coming to my hotel, he texted me and asked if it would be alright if he brought a friend with him. Of course, I agreed. When they got there, the friend, Bill, turned out to be a thirty-one-year-old hottie! I'm sixty-three and Ryan is fifty-six.

In less than a minute, we were all naked and had a dicks in our mouths. While Ryan was sucking Bill, I started eating Ryan's ass, like a man starved! Bill said he wanted to watch me fuck Ryan and asked if I minded his taking a video with my phone. I loved the idea! Soon I was balls deep in Ryan, and Bill was filming the action from all angles. Bill got behind me and was filming a close up of my ass and cock going in and out of Ryan. He must have liked the view, because I felt his tongue licking my balls and moving up to my hole. I leaned into Ryan and held still while Bill proceeded to ravage my hole with his tongue. After a few minutes, he resumed filming, and I resumed plowing. It wasn't long before I felt Bill's cock rubbing up and down my crack, looking for an entry. He found my hole, and he worked his cock deep in my ass. We soon got in sync, and I was sliding into Ryan, and then backing up on Bill. I was in heaven!

We fucked like that for a while, then Bill wanted to fuck Ryan while being filmed. So I sat on Ryan's face, and he ate my ass while I filmed Bill's cock going in and out of Ryan's ass. The scene was so hot. I knew I was about to explode, so I gave Bill the phone, and I spun around and shoved my cock into Ryan's mouth, shooting a huge load down his throat. That brought both Bill and Ryan over the edge! Both shooting at the same time, on Ryan's chest, which I greedily licked up, and then kissed both of them to share their cum. I would say a good time was had by all! And I have the video, which I've jacked off to many times already.

When I first came out it was when I went to a real estate school with my brother, who was also gay. One night he went out while I stayed in our two-bed hotel room. Later that night, he came in with a cute, young hottie, probably a college student. I was sort of asleep but woke up to see the cutie eyeing me in my bed, so I knew he wanted me too. Sure enough, he had sex with my brother who then went to sleep. And then he comes over to my bed to ride my cock for a while. Well, he stayed in bed with me for more morning fun before my brother had to take him back to campus! Everybody was happy and satisfied to say the least!

Recently, I had another first. I was invited to an all male orgy at a private residence, and I accepted. It was through a friend of mine who went to this monthly orgy and was able to get me invited while I was visiting him. I had no idea what to expect, so I quizzed my friend extensively as we drove to the place. As soon as I walked through the door, I spotted the man I wanted to have sex with. He was looking at me and promptly invited me to sit beside him while we waited for others to arrive before getting naked. I am white, and the man I sat beside was black, one of my favorite colors! Blacks have always turned me on, especially to be their bottom. I am a confirmed bisexual with a penile implant giving both sexes the fucking they need.

There were a little over twenty guys attending. When the host announced that we could begin, everyone took off their clothes and started picking partners or just roaming around. The only bedroom had a king-sized bed and there must have been twelve guys on and around the bed doing all sorts of sexual things. I watched, and when my new friend saw me, he motioned me over to him. We began kissing and fondling before I sank to my knees and started licking and sucking his magnificent cock. Evidently, my new friend was a popular participant as others were working on him as well. Finally, he led me to the bed, and we found a place where I could lean over while he gently inserted himself into me. He fucked me for many minutes, and then stopped because it was early in the orgy and neither he nor I wanted to have a finale within the first few minutes; so we parted.

I do not know what I did after that, but later we hooked up again and really went at the kissing, nipple play, and cock sucking, to the point that I leaned over the bed and the fucking commenced again. After a while, we found more room on the bed, so I crawled on the bed and turned over so we could fuck face to face. Later, he flipped me over, and I ended up with my head on someone's foot—but that seemed kind of natural at an orgy. I got royally fucked and loved every moment of it, especially the moment of his orgasm.

Although I was at an orgy, I really did not participate once I met this handsome black man. I left town shortly after but we are in contact by email, and I am invited to stop by his place whenever I am in town.

A buddy who had been fucking me periodically found another lover. He's the kind of guy that has only one man at a time. Even though he had a new fuckbud, we stayed in touch via email. I was surprised when he invited me to a golfing weekend with his buddy. His buddy had a camper permanently parked by a lake. I accepted and joined them. Once in the camper, we were always naked. His fuck bud is a nice guy, so we got along very well. At one point, we got on the bed, and I started sucking my old buddy. He was lying down. I was on my knees between his legs. I felt his new buddy get behind me and rub his cock against my butt. I reached behind me and guided him to my hungry hole. He slipped in and started fucking me. I was in heaven. This was something I had fantasized about. We had a couple other good sessions that weekend, but being spit roasted was the highlight for me. Oh yeah, we did play a round of golf.

I am eighty years young and still enjoy an active sex life. I love to be naked with men who also like being naked. Age does not matter, size does not matter. The only thing that matters is a willingness to romp and roll and have fun. Over the years, I have had many men to enjoy; some I remember vividly and some not so much. But it seems I have enjoyed them all, one way or another.

My first sexual experience was with my brother with whom I shared a bed. I was about eight, and he was a big man of sixteen or seventeen and had a cock that at the time was the biggest I had ever seen. I had seen our father's cock and my brother was larger than he was. Anyway, one night he caught me stroking my cock and asked if I had ever wanted to feel his. I said yes and he let me stroke his cock. The next time he asked me to suck his cock, and sometime later he asked if I wanted him to show me how men have sex. He told me what he was going to do, and then did it. Oh boy, was that great or what? It hurt like hell, but when he finally got in me it felt very grown up and great. And then he did it often. I got to like it more and more.

My second partner was an uncle. I was in his bed and naked and he came home from a date, drunk and horny. I guess his lady had not let him fuck her. And in the middle of the night he awoke, grabbed me, and fucked my ass. I don't think he knew it was me and not his lady. He was bigger than my brother, and he stretched my ass even more. It hurt, but I fell in love with anal fucking. I like that even more than sucking.

The next partner I remember was Tommy, a boy I knew from school. He came to my house after school. No one was home, so he stripped and showed me his long and thin weenie. He asked me to suck it, but I told him to go fuck himself. He fucked me instead.

Over the years, I have had many a cock up my ass, and I can't remember one I did not like. My current boyfriend has a cock that is almost nine inches when erect and about five or six inches around. He likes to fill me up with what I call tons of cum and gallons of pee. I love his pee enemas. They were something new in our relationship when he proposed we get married. We didn't, but he is a very needy boy of about twenty-seven who wants and takes me for a sexual ride every time he comes over, which is about three or four times a week. He has stayed the night, but because of his job as a nurse at a hospital he has to get up and leave early.

I love sex. I love the kissing with lots of tongue, the touching, playing with my nipples, and rubbing our bodies together. I love when he plays with my cock and balls and ass. I just love cumming. I am eighty and he is twenty-seven, and we love each other with a lot of passion.

I was the middle son of my father's five boys and three girls. Growing up in mid-20th century, midwestern farm country brought some of us boys together in fun ways. It was so much easier to play around with my brothers than trying to find playmates out in the country. I learned what I know about sex from them, as opposed to those folks who were horny, good-looking, and living in an urban environment. With the help of the thinly available print porn of that era, we had a pretty good inspiration to try stuff.

Two of my brothers took the straight trajectory and got married in due time—even after we had been playing around for years. My mother always said she didn't care about us having sex, but let us know not to expect her to take care of any children out of wedlock. We would turn the boys' room into a mini-orgy of brotherly love, sucking cock, chewing nipples, teasing the horniest one by stroking dick, just out of reach.

College started and those who would got married. A decade later, three of us either divorced or just found a good man to love. I came out here to California in the early 70s for "Peace and free love" in the gay-lib times. Then my younger brother, and the love of my life, moved out here. We played around some, but he found the love of his life, and I kept on living the California artist dream. Did have a lot of sex in San Francisco in the 70s-90s, but always lived in the country. Did meet the man of my dreams. Life went on, but I will always remember those times the folks were gone, and two brothers were home alone, fucking.

There's a gay nudist camp about fifty miles from where I live, and a buddy and I decided to check it out. Very nice being naked, lounging around the pool with a couple hundred other naked guys, all types, all races, all ages. After we checked in and set up our camp, we went "sight seeing"—the glory hole, "training" area for the BDSM crowd, and so on. But the thing that caught our attention was the relatively secluded hot tub. We made the rounds, dropped in on a couple of parties, and walked the notorious trails. About midnight, we decided it was time to check out that hot tub. Surprisingly, we were the only two there. After soaking for a few minutes, my buddy started playing with my cock, and pretty soon I had a raging hard-on. We were alone, so I sat on the edge of the tub, and he started chowing down on my cock.

I must have closed my eyes, lost in the pleasure. When I opened them, there was another couple watching the action. They were a daddy/son pair like me and my buddy. The daddy said they'd been enjoying watching for a couple of minutes, and did we mind if they joined us. Of course, I said yes, but I did slip back into the water. My buddy kept on fondling me, and I could tell the other daddy was getting the same treatment. After a while, I thought, "What the hell?" I got back on the edge of the tub and pulled my buddy's head to my waiting dick. A split second later, the other daddy did likewise. This definitely upped my horniness, and pretty soon I turned my buddy around and started fucking him. The other guys must have been turned on because the daddy flipped his boy over and started fucking him too. Me and the other daddy locked eyes while pounding away. Pretty soon, he winked and said, "Wanna swap for a while?" and I said sure. We swapped bottoms and kept on getting on with it. This went on for what seemed like hours, but I'm sure it was really just a few minutes. We swapped back, and each of us unloaded in our boys' butts. Never saw either one of them the rest of the weekend, but man that had to be the hottest sex I ever had.

I enjoy porn in general but really love man on man porn. The thought of two men or more being together, sharing love/sex in tender moments in a world where men are taught not to show emotions. This act either of love or lust is needed in our lives to survive and to me the human male touch is very important. I learn many things watching man on man sex films and get ideas for things I haven't tried or can improve on. Seeing a man take a load and swallow it makes me want that load on my lips and throat also. I often wish I could jump into the screen and kiss that man's lips just for that sweet and salty flavor. There are times when my precum starts to flow, and I really get that need I love so much, a man. When I finally do, I want to try the things I saw in the film to fill the desires that make my heart flutter. There have been times that after seeing a male three-way, I have to find two guys to use me in the ways that two guys can with another man. I know I will be filled at both ends and enjoy the feeling of cum sliding down my legs. If all goes well and if they are up to it, I will let them change positions to do it again and send me to the clouds again. I love this and find out it was better than the film because the air in my room is filled with the smells of men, you know, that musty sweet smell of hot sex. Damn, I wish I could bottle and sell it to other men. What a job that would be, mixing business and pleasure for a little profit.

I make a yearly 1200 mile drive to visit a friend who had several strokes years ago. He has lived in a facility for physically or mentally challenged persons for nearly twenty years. I usually spend three nights in a hotel nearby during the visit.

I belong to Silverdaddies, where I list my itinerary in the travelers section. Last year no one contacted me. This year I had plenty of messages. Two days before starting my drive, I received a message from a younger man from a town about an hour away from my friend's. His interest seemed genuine. We exchanged a few pictures and then phone numbers. He called to finalize plans to meet. In the conversation, he confirmed what I suspected from his profile. He was into manly scents. He requested that I not use deodorant the day we were to meet because he loves licking strong armpits. I am uncircumcised, so I asked if he would prefer I not wash there also. He was so happy.

That night, I took only a quick shower before sleeping. The next morning, I finished packing, dressed for travel, drove much of the way, spending the night at two different rest stops and sleeping in the car. This was July, so both times I woke up sweating. Early the next day, I arrived at my friend's room. Some years back, an employee at the facility had hooked up a system where he could record from two different DVD players. This had recently been dismantled by a worthless cable person. I spent the morning pulling all the equipment connection and starting from scratch and getting everything set up with three DVD player/recorders. Everything was very dusty along the walls of the room. By the time I could check into my hotel, I was easily smelling myself.

As soon as I was in my room, I sent a text to the younger man from the nearby town. I napped till he arrived. After I let him in, we started making love. He loved bathing me with his marvelous tongue. He spent hours licking my armpits, under my foreskin, and eating my ass. I was enjoying all of him since I also have a roaming tongue. We both were great kissers. I did spend a good time fucking his great ass before we ended the nearly four hour session with a nice 69 blowjob of each other.

Two days later, another man was scheduled for play time. It was ok, but I was nowhere as turned on as I had been with the first visitor. I did not cum. The first day visitor and I had sent text messages several times after our session. He had already said he would be interested in returning if I was available. Even though it was late, he made the trip back. This time, we were even more wild, including my feeding him a nice load of piss. The evening climaxed when he gave me one of the greatest combination jack off/blowjobs/body massage I can remember receiving. Tremendous all-body climax as he swallowed my cum. I was screaming so loud, I expected the persons from adjoining rooms to call the front desk.

We are keeping in touch and hope to spend several days together when I make the trip to check on my friend next year.

How I became a porn addict: I had my first taste of porn when I was in my early teens in the 60s. My dad always hid some paperback books in the bathroom cabinet with some pretty provocative subjects. Once I found them, I was off and running—and shooting a load almost every visit. I had to be careful, however, as not to soil the pages, a tough job with young spunk. After high school and a couple of years of junior college, I ran away from home and got a factory job. I now had my own place to live and my own stash of reading material. Plus a move from straight to a bit more male-oriented subjects. I preferred the book form of porn because the movie stuff was way too expensive for my budget.

After turning twenty-one, the bars were my porn, real live sex. I could have a different story every night and sometimes even be the star. Then someone turned me on to a dirty movie theater where I could watch porn and maybe even get a blowjob at the same time, maybe even swallow some myself after the movies started to repeat. Today, I like it all. With the internet as my partner, I can almost always find what I'm in the mood to view or read if the real stuff is not available—from videos to pics to stories, all just a click away.

Nice thing about being gay in the military, I went to bathhouses all around the world. I was at the Pentagon for five years and had a black live-in lover who bred me daily. When his cousin visited, I had twice the pleasure. We went to bathhouses in Philadelphia and tasted a lot of black dick, and then went to a gay resort in the Florida Keys that catered to blacks and their white boy toys, which I was. He'd watch guys breed me after that and when he came, the cum would run down my legs and make a pool in the grass. He said twenty-five black guys had my ass, and I enjoyed the hell out of it. Needed help to walk the next day, but damn fun!

This story brought back memories of my college days. This was in the early 80s. AIDS was just coming into the light, and a lot of guys enjoyed fucking guys and getting their cocks sucked—all the time considering themselves straight.

My initiation into our fraternity house at that time was to be "the cum dump" for about 75 guys. This was before the whiny little bitches took the fun out of it.

The night of our final initiation was to be downstairs in the basement and basically be the "adult male" entertainment for the drunk guys, when their tight ass g/f's said no! There were four pledges downstairs, and we were instructed to service the guys sexually—their choice and my total pleasure.

I think I gave about thirty or more blowjobs and got fucked more than twenty times. I got fucked so much I had warm, creamy cum streaming down my legs; my ass was full. I sucked and/or got fucked by most of the football team, the basketball team, and most of the water polo team. Big cocks, OMG cocks, average cocks, but very few small cocks. Most of those studs were hung. They were young and horny, so they pretty much all had good-sized loads. Some came back for seconds, I drained those studs!

Some of those studs remembered me and became my regulars over the years. We ALL did our duty, and we ALL got pledged.

MARRIED, DIVORCED

This happened just last night. NOT A LIE, true story here. I was driving the long drive between one city and another. Bored with nothing on the radio and no one to chat with. Since it was late, I turned to an online app for entertainment. Much to my delight, a faceless pic popped up and messaged me, "Stop by and blow me, you won't be disappointed." With no pics exchanged and only enough information to obtain an address, parking instructions, and how to enter the home, I thought, "What the hell."

I arrived, parked where I was told, and entered the garage from the side door, as instructed. The place was pitch dark. I instantly got that nervous feeling, but I stayed. I'm so happy I did. From the corner, I heard a voice, deep manly voice much like Barry White. He said, "You ready?" I replied with, "Yes Sir." After being called a "good boy," he instructed me to strip off all my clothing and to get down on my knees, using my clothes as cushion. I complied, still nervous, but this time with a raging hard-on.

He walked over to me in the dark, placed both his hands on either side of my head, pointed my face up to him, and said, "I hope you like huge cock." Before I could reply, the largest cock I had ever seen, felt, tasted, or dreamed about slapped me across the face. A little laughter from him as this caught me off guard, and I yelped a bit. From there, he gave me instructions on how to please him. He told me to run my tongue all around the head of his cock and to place the head on my tongue, keeping my mouth open. This nine-plus inch cock was filling my wide open mouth, and I started to get cock hungry—that moment when you can only think about bouncing your head up and down on the cock, pleasing the daddy it is attached to while he relaxes and instructs.

Finally, he let me start sucking him my way, so I took the cock as far as I could, but it was huge. Then he said he would take over. With his hands still on my head, he started to face fuck me. The pain of this huge dick thrusting in and out of my mouth was pure joy. After about five minutes of repeated mouth abuse, he finally pulled out and said, "I need to see you, but I need to know if you can be trusted to be quiet." I, of course said, "Yes, Sir."

He stood me up, placed a blindfold on me, and guided me through to some steps. Fortunately, he didn't cover my eyes completely, so I cheated and could see some of where I was going, which was the kitchen of his home. Once there, he put me on my knees again and whispered in my ear, "If I hear a peep out of you I'm going to beat you senseless." This made me extremely nervous. But he started working his cock in my mouth again, and he started breathing louder and getting more intense with his thrusting. I could feel his cock swell.

Just then I heard a woman's voice, "Marcus, what are you doing?" His wife was calling from upstairs, "Are you coming to bed soon?" Holy shit! I lost my hard-on, and I didn't want to make any noise. This didn't bother or stir him at all. He kept thrusting his cock into me, making me his mouth bitch as he answered her, "Just going to make some popcorn, you go back to bed and I'll be up in a few." She replied, " ok."

After the coast was clear, he stood me up and told me, "Good boy, now you get what you really want." He bent me over the counter of the sink and put his cockhead on my hole. Covering my mouth, he said, "Ready for this?" I shook my head up and down, he lubed my hole, and slowly pressed further and further into my hole. The pain was intense, but I didn't allow my emotions to show. The head and more was now in me. I wanted it all, so I started to thrust my ass back to him with tears in my eyes, but I knew it would be exhilarating once he was all the way in.

After about four pumps of his bare cock fully in my ass, he grabbed my shoulder with one hand, keeping the other over my mouth and moaning quietly as he filled my hole with cum. The pure ecstasy he was feeling was evident in his body convulsing nonstop until he finally pulled out.

Once he was done with me and recovered, he whispered, "Now that I know you can be trusted, I will have you back for more. You're a good bottom whore and I want to use you when I can." I said, "Absolutely." He guided me back to the garage, told me to leave the blindfold on the steps, said that I should get dressed and leave. As he was closing the door, I heard his wife coming down the steps, saying, "Babe, we don't have popcorn, what are you really doing?"

He texted me this morning and said he fucked his wife last night with my ass juice still on his cock. I'm going back tonight!

Bi Married guy here who was not very aggressive and was somewhat shy and nervous and clueless on many topics when it came to man sex. Was online looking and reading posts when a post from a guy struck me as being special, so I responded. We seemed to hit it off online, similar likes, no pic exchange because I was married. We decided to meet in a parking lot of a strip mall in my town. Got there, hopped into his front seat, chatted for thirty minutes, and then he invited me over. I found out he lived about a half mile away from me, on the same street. I didn't want to have my vehicle seen at his house, so I rode with him, leaving my truck at the parking lot.

Walked into a beautiful house. We kissed in the kitchen for a good while, and then went to his bedroom. Tons of foreplay, touching, kissing, ass playing. He put a rubber on, and I didn't stop him. He was rough and knew what he wanted. This was the first time for me, so afterwards I was sore, but loved being fucked by a former Marine. Two real men in bed. Got to visit this fine masculine man a dozen or so times after that. We eventually drifted apart, and then he moved away. I will never forget him.

It was a bright and beautiful autumn day, filled with warmth and sunshine. The countryside was ablaze with color as the trees and foliage were changing color in preparation for winter. We planned to take advantage of the warm weather and spend some quality M2M time in the remote recesses of the Wisconsin woods. It was quite a hike back into the woods where we knew that we would not be interrupted—or so we thought. The spot that we chose was secluded, peaceful, and private. I brought a large stadium blanket that we laid on the crinkling leaves. We were very comfortable, at peace with nature surrounding us everywhere. The sunlight danced off the leaves in prisms of intense color while the wind was warm and gentle. It was a perfect day.

We feasted on some sumptuous wine and hors d'oeuvres that my married friend made at home. He was a delightful gourmet chef. As we enjoyed our outdoor ambiance, we shared our masculine passion, bold and beautiful.

He was a tall, handsome man who fashioned an adorable handlebar mustache. His chest was strong and smooth, and he loved nipple play. So I stimulated his nips until he was moaning with pleasure. As I worked my mouth and tongue down his treasure trail, he was oozing with tasty precum that glistened like lube.

Although he was happily married to a wonderful woman, he enjoyed genuine intimacy with another man. At those times, he was a man's man. His sculpted body was strong, smooth, and sexy. It yearned for some deep-throat, oral ecstasy, so I did not disappoint. I made it my mission to drain him CUMpletely. As I deep-throated his impressive seven-plus, uncut tool, his body convulsed in rhythmic spasms of forceful fantasy. At that point, he was MY man, that dick belonged to me, and soon it would feed me this wonderful, white-hot, lava load of cum. It was a healthy protein load that I feasted on as his orgasm exploded like a fucking fountain of cum in a volcanic eruption. It was oral bliss for both of us.

Married, Divorced

I gave him a chance to rest, relax, and reload, so we could enjoy the intensity of a second volcanic explosion, when much to our surprise we realized that we were being watched. The eyes that intently studied us and our masculine scent were the eyes of two bucks—male deer. We began to study them as intently as they studied us. We didn't dare move so as not to spook them. But here we were, two men having sex in nature as two bucks watched us. Were they entertained by our invasion of their natural setting? Did they relate to sex between two males? We didn't know what to think but we sat in stunned silence as the four of us studied each other. It was truly a significant emotional event in my life. Later, we enjoyed the intensity of a second orgasm, never to forget what preceded it.

This summer I was contacted by a man from a neighboring town whose profile I had never seen before. His profile was very limited in information, usually the sign of a married man. He was interested in visiting me. We had messaged occasionally for about two weeks. He explained he could not visit because he had family staying with him.

Then one morning, he asked if I was free for an early afternoon visit. I said yes. He showed up as scheduled. When he came through the door, I was very pleased. The words Greek God would be putting him down. Late thirties and over six feet tall, very tan, and muscles everywhere. Great looking, nice smile, perfect male specimen. He also had an unbelievable dick. My medium length of seven-plus inches was at least two inches shorter than his, and its girth appeared double mine.

We were soon naked and romantically kissing and exploring each other on my bed. I am not a bottom, and I wondered if I could get more than the head of his dick in my mouth. I really wanted to make him happy. His body language definitely said, "Come fuck me," but what my finger found were extremely strong, tight sphincter muscles. I feared I would never penetrate anything that tight.

I explained my concern. He said it was no problem. He asked me to lie on my back with my hard penis extended skyward. He lubed my dick and his own ass. Then standing over me facing forward, he bent his knees and started sitting on my dick. In no time, he was sitting totally impaled on my dick. Then he started to ride it up and down. I got in sync with his motion so my movements extended the thrusts to their absolute fullness. I then reached forward and started masturbating that gorgeous dick in perfect rhythm to our thrusts. We were playing our own symphony of pleasure.

We were communicating in grunts and heavy breathing. All of a sudden, he moved his hand forward. I knew without being told. He replaced mine with his, and on the fifth stroke of his hand that dick became Mt. Vesuvius, spraying the most gorgeous, warm, white lava, completely covering my chest, neck, and chin. I did not think anyone could deliver that much semen in one explosion. He had to retrieve towels and washcloths from my bath since I would have left a sticky trail had I tried.

In our post-sex discussion, I learned he was married to another man but his daughter was visiting during her summer vacation. His lover was intimidated and was concerned that she would hear their lovemaking. I said I would gladly meet his needs again if his partner wouldn't.

I am happily married to a wonderful woman, long-term marriage, first and only wife. We are sexually active on a daily basis. What she does not know but may suspect is that she is responsible for my sexual attraction to other men.

Ever wonder why so many posts by men on sexual meeting sites are from men wanting to give a blowjob to another man? For myself, it is because of the visible pleasure my wife shows when using her mouth on me, bringing me to climax, softly sucking as she hears my growls of pleasure, my cry of orgasmic relief, relaxing sighs, and feels my cock go limp in her mouth. Fuck. Who wouldn't want to experience that?

That began my search for a "blowjob buddy." Craigslist isn't all bad. I posted a real desire to exchange sexual favors with another guy. Out of all the trash replies I did receive one that was an intelligent response. We met three times, at a McDonald's and twice at a bookstore. Worked out little details like, please, no cologne. We agreed to meet at a no-tell motel, $20 for two hours. We set a day and time. I would arrive first, pay, and then call with the cabin number.

Blowjobs are not easy. Over time and with repeated practice I began to experience the pleasures of giving. And I came to appreciate the pleasures of worshipping a hard, sexually ready and eager cock. When sucked in, one-by-one, loose hanging testicles fit nicely in the mouth. These are the testicles of another man, a man's loaded nuts, in my mouth. This is what it's like to pleasure a man. What a treat! The permutations are known—hand on the back of the head, fingers locked in head hair, fuck you with my mouth, getting my mouth fucked by you. Now it was me that heard the cry of pleasure, felt his cock go limp and savored that my tongue was lying in a pool of cum. It was an oasis of mutual, manly, sexual enjoyment in a world of platonic relationships.

People have their own likes. One of my blowjob buddy's was dirty talk, something I'd not done before. He loved when I narrated his actions. He loved hearing me praise his cock sucking, telling him how good his fucking little cunt-mouth felt, how he was going to get a mouthful of my cum as a reward for being such a good cocksucker. He would have made an obedient sub for a willing dom. He moaned a muffled sound of delighted agreement when I told him, "Don't swallow. After I'm done, spit it in your hand and I'll watch you jack off with it."

Good times, and I'm glad to have experienced the pleasure my wife has known.

The only time I have ever had any physical contact with another guy was during a threesome with my wife and a guy we met online and later had dinner with. He was curious about doing it with a couple, and I was secretly curious about being with a guy. I did get to suck him and tongue his balls real well. When he was ready to squirt, he pushed me away so he could finish himself just a couple seconds later. He did fuck my wife some prior to that, but he never worked up the nerve to reciprocate with me. All I know is that I realized that I liked sucking cock much better than eating pussy. That experience took it from the realm of fantasy to reality. I have wanted to do more with men ever since. Maybe one of these days.

I had my first encounter with a man. It was nothing big. He was my family doctor. During the course of my exam, he stroked me until I shot a load. I was ashamed and aroused all at the same time. Those of the same sex never did such things before. It sure was wrong.

I got married about ten years later but always in the back of my mind that exam stood out. The more M2M relations became prevalent and acceptable, the more I wondered what it would be like. I got on a local dating site and answered the ad of a man. We talked by phone several times, and finally I asked if I could meet him. His name was Joe. I got to his place, and Joe and I talked for about half an hour. Among the things he said was, "If you have sex with a man, it doesn't mean you are gay." He also said, "It is normal and natural for two men to have sex." He then said, "Who knows how to pleasure a man, better than another man."

I listened to all this, and he finally said, "I'm going back to my bedroom. I would love to have you join me, but if not, just let yourself out." He got up and left the room. I sat there for a few moments and started to leave, but then I reevaluated all that he had said and went back to his room. My plan was just to do some touching and to keep my clothes on. When I got back to his room, he was sitting on the end of the bed. He motioned for me to sit next to him. He began to massage my neck and shoulders. No big deal I thought. I became very relaxed, and his touch felt very good. He massaged my arms, and I was comfortable with that. Soon he reached around and began to massage my chest. It felt good, and I became more relaxed with each passing second.

It was then I noticed his touch changed to light caresses. He began caressing my nipples through my shirt. I sighed and thought no big deal. His hands unbuttoned my shirt, and he caressed my nipples with his fingertips. It felt wonderful, and I thought as long as I keep my shirt on I will be fine. He kept it up until I finally laid my head back on his shoulder. His touches were amazing. My face was facing his, and he leaned down and we kissed. I felt his tongue, and my mouth opened to receive him. It's just a kiss, I thought. My shirt was then pulled down and off my body. I still had my pants on so I'm OK, I thought.

We kissed and he played with my nipples. I was now lying on the bed, and he was kissing and licking my nipples. I moaned, and when he touched the front of my pants, I didn't know what to do. But as long as I have my pants on, I'm OK. He moved his hand up and down the front of my pants and said, "Why don't I loosen your pants. It must be uncomfortable in there." I nodded my approval, and he unzipped and unsnapped my pants. We kissed, and I felt his fingertips lightly caressing my erection through my shorts. In a few moments, he was sliding my pants off. I was lying there with a raging erection in my underpants. We kissed, and soon he had the tip of my cock out and pinned back against my stomach by the elastic waistband of my shorts. He lightly caressed that area as we kissed. It felt amazing. When he began to slide my shorts off, I helped him.

In a moment, I was naked. Then he undressed, and we kissed, our naked bodies rubbing up against each other. Erections pressed up against each other. He kissed his way down my body and began to kiss the tip of my cock. Before I could think of what was going on, he flipped around, and now I was facing his erection. He kissed my cock, and I in turn kissed his. He then kissed and licked my balls, and I returned the favor. He began to suck my cock, and I began to suck his. I had never felt so close to anyone in my whole life. It was normal and natural just as he had said. We sucked and moaned. It felt so delicious. Soon, I was getting close to cumming. I opened my mouth and said I was getting close. He looked at me and said, "I swallow."

He then went back to sucking. I moaned, and in a few minutes I was cumming, pumping my creamy load into his mouth. He sucked and licked, and then I heard him say, "I'm close." I kept stroking and said, "I swallow too." I wanted to give him the same pleasure he gave me. He bucked and shot his load in my mouth. I swallowed the creamy, sticky, slightly salty mixture. He turned around; we kissed, tasting our cum on each other's lips. We both cuddled and drifted off to sleep. We woke up about half an hour later and talked, and then I dressed and left. It was amazing and everything he said was true. I so enjoy being with my wife and with a man. The best of both worlds.

He started cruising me a couple weeks ago. Hot, hunky profile. Can't join my parties since he's married and might meet someone he knows. Being an ex-Boy Scout, I finally decided to help him out at his house. Have to admit, I'm way too old to break in these newbies. Bless them though, since we were all there in the beginning, married and hungry for man sex. He was not at all relaxed, perhaps thinking she might return at any moment. He was so up tight, with almost no experience in sex play. Sitting on my dick, he unloads on my chest, and then immediately disappears to the bathroom, leaving me to jerk my load—so typical. I'm out the door in thirty minutes.

I'd like to think he had a good time, but truth be told, I'd rather be at Walmart. I recall my many past parties that would go for hours, from fireplace to dinner table, to sling, to hot tub, back to sling, and great chat and laugh with buddies, sometimes thirty guys. Couple times fifty hornies in my basement many years ago, but that's another story. I still host occasionally, mostly smaller groups—hard to give up the good times. But thankful to say, been there, done that.

A couple of years ago my house burned down. Electrical fire during an ice storm. During the months of construction following, I made weekly, sometimes daily visits on my lunch hour to see the progress and tell them what I wanted for flooring, tile, fixtures, and so on. During that time, I got to know a couple of the workers involved. One of them was Richard, the tile man, and his helper, who I later learned was his son. I teased him about the quality of his work as my dad had been a tile setter himself and taught me the trade. While I had been talking to him, I had noticed his very large basket and tight ass filling out his jeans. For a man his age, I'd say around fifty or so, he was amazingly built and still had a great body.

Toward the end of the job, I drove to the nearly completed house and met Richard and his son working on the last of the stoop in front of the fireplace. I started touring the house and heard Richard tell his son to head back to the shop and grab more of the sealer they were using on the slate tiles. The construction manager and the insurance guy had shown up, and we did what we needed to do. They left, and I was hanging around taking pictures to show the people back at my office the progress being made. As everyone was leaving, I noticed Richard still working on the fireplace, putting in the last couple of tiles. He was on his left knee with his right leg up, foot flat on the floor.

Because of the way he was positioned, I could see his crotch, which had been a sight of major interest to me since I first met him. As I finished up what I was doing, I came back into the living room, and Richard was now down on both knees, back on his haunches with his crotch in full view. And I do mean Full View. He had pulled his cock and balls out of his jeans, and they were hanging quite nicely right there in front of me. Cut and about four inches, looking to be about a quarter hard already with a Prince Albert piercing. He grinned when he saw I had seen him and asked if I liked what I saw. I said, "Oh yeah," and walked over to him. As I did, he raised up and reached up for the front of my slacks, rubbing and starting to unzip me. He said he had thought I might be open to this and since this was the last time he'd be there he better do something about it.

After he got my fly open and my cock and balls in the air he went down to the root and started an amazing blowjob, jacking his cock all the while. Now

Married, Divorced

I'm not all that large but damn he was obviously well versed in the art of cock sucking. After about two minutes of this I thought I was gonna cum, so I pulled back and reached for his armpits to raise him up so I could get a taste too. By that time, he was about eight inches long and not too thick, but starting to drip and lube up. I took as much of him as I could, not being used to a ring on the end of it, and proceeded to show him just how much I love a hard cock and good set of nice balls. As I was sucking, he said his wife didn't know how to suck cock for shit and that he loved what I was doing to his dick, but he needed some more himself. So we both shucked our pants and lay down in a classic 69.

Now here we are in my unfinished living room, going down on each other like there is no tomorrow, in full view of anyone who could walk in, and neither of us cared a damn. Since I love to eat ass as well, I was working my way back, when he groaned and raised one leg and let me dive in face first. Well, I got his very hairy ass as wet as I could and told him I'd really like to fuck him. He said he was hoping I'd say that. He got up and walked over to his tool bag, brought out a tube of KY, and proceeded to cover my dick and his ass with lube. Said he had come prepared, just in case.

Well we did it, with him on his knees, leaning on the newly tiled fire place seat. He was tight and hot and very sweet, and he was no stranger to making a dick feel real good inside him. I never last all that long when I'm fucking so after a minute or two I told him we needed to either slow down or stop. He said, "No, keep going, but I want you to come in my mouth." So I picked up some speed and started really slamming him. When I was just about to pop, I pulled out, and he turned and took my dick in his mouth and swallowed everything I had to give. I actually had to pull away at one point, it was so intense.

Well, I'm not one to leave a man hanging, so to speak, so I got down on all fours and took his cock into my mouth again to finish him off. As I was doing that, his hand was sliding down my back to feel my butt and hole. I asked him if he wanted inside and he said, "Hell, yes!" So we switched positions with me on my back, head in the fire place, and him lubing me up. Up to that point I'd never been fucked with a dick that had a ring on it. Let me tell you, it's a whole new sensation, one I heartily recommend! He asked me if I liked it, and I said, "Oh hell, yes!" He said his wife loved the ring too, which is why he'd gotten it. Well, all good things have to come to an end and he was doing his damnedest to get me to cum again. Long, sweet, deep strokes with a whole bunch of rabbit punches in between. I told him I wanted to taste him too, so when he was ready he pulled out and shot in my mouth. A very heavy, tasty load too!

After we had both calmed down a bit and were starting to get dressed, I asked if he played with guys as much as I thought he did. He said as much as possible, but still loved his wife. But she just didn't know how to suck dick at all or how to fuck him when he needed it. So he goes elsewhere. This was the first time, or so he said, that he'd ever done it on a job site or with a client. I said I was glad to have been his first in that regard and if he ever wanted another round to call me. Just as I was leaving, his son drove up, and I quickly asked if they had ever played together. He said no, but he thought his son just might have the same tastes. He'd noticed a sign or two.

Since then, Richard and I have played a couple of times, and it's always a flip fuck kinda day. Hot man. I keep trying to get his son involved, but that's another story.

I'm quite proud to claim that I was a fucking STUD in my youth! Most of the time it was just a circle jerk because we didn't know what the fuck we were doing. But there were a few times when I explored my manhood and graduated from my adolescence. The few times that I got to seriously suck and fuck, we were covered in CUM. It was FUCKING GREAT!

Unfortunately, we all went on to marry but we never forgot our adolescence. Two of us from the group are now happily divorced. In April, I went home to Wisconsin to visit friends. The other divorced guy and I picked up one of our married friends for the weekend, got a nice hotel room, and enjoyed marathon sex all fucking weekend.

It felt fucking GREAT! It was a WET and WILD weekend where we relived our youth and shared lava loads of CUM! When we delivered our married friend home, he returned fully fed and bred. That fucker took more dick and CUM than he had in years! After his return, he sent us an email thanking us for a wild and fun time.

He said that he fucked his wife like a farm animal that night, and she told him that he needed to get away with the boys more often! You suppose she knew? Her husband is a total fucking STUD who could satisfy anybody's needs. But that weekend, he was our personal CUM DUMP and he eagerly took EVERYTHING that we gave him.

Every married man should have that opportunity from time to time.

I am retired and married with very little personal time away from my wife, so having a fantastic source of pics keeps me horny and ready. With my spouse I am totally top. With my male lover, I am totally at his will and discretion. And he introduced me to M2M anal sex at this ripe age of seventy-seven. My lover is in his early thirties and sprouts constantly when we are together. I met him online at another group, and we texted for a while, about once a week, and then one day he suggested we meet. I agreed to breakfast, and he picked a restaurant about half way between us. We live about twenty minutes from each other. On the way to our first meet he texted me and suggested I come to his place instead. I hesitated only a moment and then agreed. He gave me his address and off I went.

When I got to his place he took me into his bedroom where we sat on his bed and talked. I discovered he had a roomer who had some physical problems and would not be interrupting or interacting with us. Then, after a short time, he said he wanted to fuck me. Now I had not been fucked since I was raped by an uncle when I was a pubescent boy. The memory was so great that I froze at the thought of being anally attacked again. He did not force me and said that if I said no then no it would be. We kissed and he groped me and turned my fires on. I finally said yes and he began to slowly undress me.

I froze, and he could not get his hard cock into me. He gave up and said it was okay and that we would try again next time. Next week turned out to be the next time. And the first thing he did was undress me. I suggested he use some lube, and after swabbing his cock and my ass he pushed hard and he was in. It hurt several different ways, but he went slowly, and finally he came inside me and flopped on me. When he slowly pulled out, I felt empty until I saw his bagful, and then I wanted more. He's plowed me every time we've met since, except for our breakfast dates.

It had been four years since I had had an encounter with a man. I was happily married when it happened, and it left me with feelings I couldn't understand. I felt it was wrong, yet at the same time I have never felt such intensity in lovemaking. I couldn't get over the fact that a man could give another man such pleasure. I tried to forget, to bury the feelings, but four years later I got online and met a man. We talked for several weeks, until he finally invited me over to his house.

I met him at his lovely home in the western suburbs. We chatted for a while, and he said several things which made sense. He told me he was gay but also said that just because you find pleasure with another man doesn't mean you are gay, but bi. He also told me, "Who knows how to please a man better than another man." He said that in some cultures men began their sexual lives with same-sex partners to learn about pleasure. He then invited me back to his bedroom. I felt at ease but a bit apprehensive at the same time. We got in his bed and talked for a bit before he leaned over and kissed me. I had never been kissed by another man, and the truth was it was very nice. He smiled at me and began to caress my chest and kissed me again.

This time our tongues slid into each other's mouths, and I got an instant erection. We kissed passionately for quite some time while he unbuttoned my shirt and began to caress my nipples. The pleasure made me melt, and I knew I would do whatever he wanted. He took off my shirt and kissed his way down and began to kiss and lick my nipples. All I could do was moan. He moved his hand down and felt the front of my pants. He whispered that the pants must be uncomfortable and suggested we take my pants off. We slid my pants and shorts down off my legs. He kissed the tip of my cock as he fondled my balls. He told me my cock was very handsome and loved my low hanging balls.

He then took off his clothes and we cuddled together. We kissed and made out like teenagers. He began to stroke my cock, and I reached down and began to stroke his. His cock jumped in my hand as I stroked him. I alternated playing with his balls and stroking his cock. We made out like this for a while, each taking turns playing with each other's bodies and making us both moan with desire.

He then told me to slide down a little on the bed. As I did, he inverted himself so as his head was at my groin and my head at his groin. He gently licked the tip of my cock, and I moaned. He closed his mouth around my cock and began a gentle sucking motion. I looked at his cock and leaned in. I placed a tentative kiss on his cock, and he sighed. I now wanted to give him as much pleasure as he was giving me. We sucked, licked, and kissed each other. With each moment, the intensity of pleasure grew. We were now both moaning with desire and passion, and I was nearing my climax.

I took my mouth away from his cock and told him I was going to cum. He stopped sucking for a moment and said, "Cum in my mouth." Then his mouth covered my cock again.

I knew if I was going to cum in his mouth it would be only right to have him cum in my mouth. As we both neared orgasm, we both began moving our hips, fucking each other's mouths. We went on, and then that exquisite moment hit me, that instant when the orgasm begins. The pleasure is so intense and you want it to last forever. You try to keep from cumming because you want the pleasure to go on and on. Then you let go. You moan with indescribable pleasure.

I had stopped sucking for a moment until my orgasm had subsided, and then returned to sucking my friend off. Soon he was overcome with his own orgasm, and for the first time I tasted a man's cum. It was thick, slightly salty, and I kept sucking and swallowing. I coaxed that last couple of drops out of his cock, and then we both rolled over on our backs resting. In a while, he moved back around, and we kissed. It was an amazing afternoon, and this would be only the first time that we met.

I hate the term "bucket list", but that does not change my nagging curiosity about same-sex sex. I had a cock sucking experience when younger and nothing since. So I wonder, what's it like to truly take the time, to relax and fully enjoy a hard cock. What's it like to keep my lips snugly around an orgasmic cock? What's it feel like when he's cumming? What's it like to have a mouthful of fresh cum? What's it taste like, how warm is it, is it slippery on the tongue? How much is there? Will I swallow, play with it, let it roll down my chin? What is it like to give that pleasure to another man?

Craigslist helped. Yet it takes lots of effort to be comfortable with my selection and to be the comfortable selection of a prospective partner. I narrowed it down to three guys. One seemed to be an alcoholic. Another had about 150 pounds more than his profile and was easy to reject just on credibility. I met the third guy at a McDonald's and again at a bookstore. We talked privately of our histories and desires. We agreed to meet for sex.

All married bi-men know the problems of arranging secretive meetings. I had no desire to upset my wife, cause her anguish, disappoint, or anger her. This effort had to deal with avoiding all of that. But I was driven and patient and successful. Eventually we met at a $20, no-tell motel. We both liked giving blowjobs and getting them. Gradually over time, we vamped it up by sending emails of scenes that we'd like to enact. I had emailed Bob, asking how he'd like to find me when he arrived. I was always at the motel first. He said naked, which differed from our usual of undressing together. My reply email just said that I'd give him directions after he was naked. So I was naked when he knocked, and I stood behind the door while opening it. Bob slipped into the room, and I went to the bed and lay down on my back, legs hanging over the edge, my hands caressing my cock and balls. On the other side of the bed was a wall covered with mirrored tiles.

Bob undressed and laid his clothes neatly on the corner desk. "Come over here and get yourself hard" was Bob's first directive to me. "Stand between my legs." I propped myself up with the pillows and watched as Bob's dick grew. He wasn't very big, but he always had a generous cum-load, pouring out contraction after contraction, making a big dripping mess wherever it landed. "You are a good little fucking cocksucker," he said. Positive reinforcement and very accurate. "You're going to suck me off." We both continued jacking. Bob wet a finger, circled a nipple, and gave a relaxing moan. I drooled in my hand, wrapped it around my cock, and continued pleasing myself. "I know what you want." We were both putting on a show. "Ok, cocksucker," Bob warned, still standing, tight against the bedside. I've got my legs, one on each side of Bob, draped over the edge, crotch at the bed's edge. "Lick your lips. Show me that wet, hungry cunt-mouth of yours. Cocksucker." He runs his tongue over his lips, licks his hand, and keeps stroking.

Then it was my time to give instructions. "I want you to jack off and cum all over my cock. Use my cock as your target. Give me all you've got. Cover me with cum," I insisted. Bob gives a grunt and stares down at my penis and testicles. My hands have stopped. "Cum on me. Make a sticky mess." He's too easy. Bob leans over to get a better aim. "When you're finished, you fucking, little, cunt-mouthed cocksucker, immediately drop to your knees. I'm going to finish in your mouth." That's all it took. A low growl and Bob's first shots hit their target. I watched as pump after pump covered me in lumpy-thick white jizz. It rolled off the sides and flowed down in the valley between my nuts and legs. "Now, fuck me with your mouth."

Bob dropped, and I stood. He hesitated, seemed to steel himself, and slid his mouth over me. Slick and snug, his lips flowed over every bulging vein and ridge to my cock's base. The slop on either side of me pressed against his face. Looking in the mirrors, I saw it dripping off his chin. "God damn you're a good cocksucker." And he was, and he truly enjoyed doing it. "This is what you want." Mouth full, he's not talking. He's tight on me, slippery, sucking with feeling and desire. "That's what you taste like." I finger off a lump on his cheek and run it across his nostrils. With a full mouth he's breathing hard through his nose. "Tongue-fuck me." I feel the tongue massage, and I grab handfuls of hair. Holding his head, I start with full-length, goal-oriented strokes. I'm building and controlling his head and fucking his mouth. "Get ready pussy-mouth. Fucking cumsucker."

Sometimes this happens. My cock will quickly swell by maybe five per cent to a satisfying fullness. Of course, Bob feels this and lets out an appreciative moan. I'm tight and ready, far past anything but my nut. "Here it is cumsucker. Don't swallow." Bob can make you feel like a god giving nectar. With his mouth plugged, he whimpers like a baby, sucks, tongues, and makes sounds of simple pleasure. He stays on me until finished. I pull out. My hands are still holding his hair, and I turn his head to look in the mirror. Quite a mess, as always. "Open your mouth and look at what I've given you. Damn you're a good cumsucker." He stares at the loads in his mouth and moves his tongue around, playing in the pool of cum.

Last thing I said: "Swallow."

I am vacationing in Florida for a couple of weeks and of course I check out the action on the Silverdaddies website. I am married, so my availability is limited to when my wife is out with her family. I make contact with a guy who is going to be returning up north in a few days. After a day or two of emails back and forth, we finally set something up at his place. When I arrive, the guy answers the door in nothing but his shorts and looks great, very tan, great body. He tells me another friend of his showed up and to follow him upstairs.

I get to the bedroom and see that there is a guy naked on the bed with his legs in the air, and the guy that I contacted immediately pulls his shorts down to reveal a magnificent, big, thick cock! John, the guy I was to meet, and I are both in our late sixties, and I would say the bottom was in his early forties, had an accent and skin coloring of someone from Honduras—a lot of the landscaping workers here are from there. John slips on a rubber and begins fucking the guy. I get undressed, and I am immediately behind John, my hands all over his hairy chest and his ass, as I am kissing his neck and ears. My cock is hard, and I am running it between John's ass cheeks. Soon

I fall to my knees, and I am trying to rim John the best I can while he is fucking the other guy. I am also pulling on his low hangers that he has clasped on a leather ball stretcher. John pulls out and slips a rubber onto a long, but slim dildo that he rams into the bottom's ass. He instructs me to get on the bed and over the bottom's head so that he can suck my hard-on while he is being rammed with the dildo. The bottom is moaning the entire time.

John wants me to fuck the bottom, but I tell him that would be a long shot since lately, when I put a condom on, I lose my hard-on. He wanted me to try it bareback, but I refused. So I slip the rubber on and low and behold, I was able to get my cock up that sweet, hot ass. I think it was partly due to the voyeuristic pleasure, plus this guy's ass was not real tight. My cock is on the thicker side, gets extremely hard, and has a big vein running along the top. Between the irritation of the condom and a real tight ass, it can be painful and unpleasant for me. So I worked up quite a sweat reaming and ramming this guy's asshole in every possible position until he had enough. John wanted us both to cum on his chest, and we obliged. John never shot his load. John, who posted his position as a top on Silverdaddies, asked me to come back the next morning so he could try sitting on my cock. However, I was not able to get away, and he left to go back north that afternoon.

I'm married to a woman who at the time this happened, knew nothing of my sexuality. I worked for a guy who I suspected was gay, but was never really sure. He wasn't married, and while I was working for him, he took in his "cousin" to live with him. I had met the cousin a couple of times while they were shopping or around the community where we live.

I admired my boss from the time he had come to work with my group. He was bald, tan, baby blue eyes, nice build, and hairy, everything I like in a guy. He knew I was married, but I think he suspected that I liked to play both ways. Anyway, after his dad died, he was clearing out a lot of his dad's things and mentioned that he was selling several items. I was interested in some of them and asked if I could check them out. Well, I went to his house, and during the time there I saw that he had a swimming pool. In conversation, I mentioned that I always wanted a pool because I loved to swim nude. He lived out in the country, and his place was huge and very private. With that, he said I was welcome to skinny dip if I wanted to because he and his cousin never wore clothes when they swam, and he knew how much they enjoyed it.

I didn't need a lot of coaxing, so I stripped right there, put my clothes on a lawn chair, and eased into the pool. I swam around for a while, enjoying the freedom I feel from swimming nude. After a little while, the cousin undressed and got into the pool with me. My boss stayed clothed and sat on the side, just talking and watching. The cousin was a small man, but had a cock on him the size of a race horse, even when he was soft. After swimming and talking, I couldn't resist telling him how endowed I thought he was and that he must make some people very happy with a tool that size. All the while, he stayed soft, and I was getting harder by the minute. After more talking and just plain flirting, he asked if a cock like his would make me happy. I tried not to appear too ecstatic at the question, so I coolly said, "I'm sure it would." Until this point, I had bottomed only a few times and knew that after the initial hurt, it was great.

It was early evening, around 6:00 pm, right before sunset. He told me to go to the shallower end of the pool, stand up, and bend over the side. My ass was out of the water, but glistening from being wet. He played with my ass and fingered my hole for a few minutes, and then he used his saliva to lube my ass and his monster cock that was easily eight inches of thick meat by now. I put my head down as I felt his cock at my hole, and after playing there for a little while, he slowly began to push it in. Of course, it hurt at first, but after he pulled out and gave my hole a short rest, he slid it in again, and this time it was ecstasy. I moved in and out very slowly, and it was heavenly. All the while, my boss was playing with himself through his jeans while he watched his cousin take good care of my ass.

Well, the session lasted only about five minutes. With the slow, deep thrusts, the cousin moaned and then shot his load deep inside me. I didn't feel his load when he shot it, but when I got out of the pool and went to the bathroom, I pushed out what looked like a cup of thick, white cum. That was my only experience with my boss's cousin or getting naked in front of my boss. I would have welcomed other opportunities, but the offer never came. I think my boss was concerned about playing like that with an employee, and, as I said, he never touched me during the pool fun. A few years later, our facility closed, and we all went our separate ways. I ran into the two of them a few times around town, but never went skinny dipping again.

His shirt was off the first time I saw him, with tats circling the neck on his collar bone. The top of his head was shaved as smooth as his rounded pecs and thick belly. Big, clear, brown eyes, and a full thick beard.

Married, Divorced

Wearing just flip flops and sagging camouflage shorts with strategic rips around the crotch, he stared at me as I stepped on to the patio outside the bar. The afternoon sun was giving his brown Latin skin a sweaty shine. Without a word, he opened a beer and handed it to me as I sat down. This gay bar was the perfect place. With an outside patio, and some semi-private fenced "booths" beyond in the backyard, men— especially married men like me—could slip away from work and gather in the afternoon for anonymous play. Two or sometimes more men can gather around on the picnic tables, sucking and fucking. Some totally naked and enjoying every bit of attention, some with just their dick out, watching around nervously. A wonderful place.

"My name is Carlos." His wide eyes softened, and he smiled. We clinked our beer bottles and talked and talked. When I left my office at lunchtime, I hadn't expected to spend the rest of the afternoon and another bucket of beers becoming friends with a guy that would become my friend and lover for years. Looks can be deceiving; Carlos was a mixed bag. He had traveled all over the world, told stories and jokes that made me laugh out loud. Not what I expected. I found myself not just aroused but drawn to be close to him. He would gently touch my arm or my cheek as I talked about myself, really private stuff. It felt like we'd known each other forever.

I began to feel more like I wanted an intimate friendship instead of the simple blowjob that I had come to the bar looking for hours earlier. My wife was out of town, and I wanted to continue with Carlos. He held my hand when he asked me to join him at his house for dinner. We ate on the deck, and it was more romantic than sexual. Light kisses, and the quick, gentle touches heightened every sense, and our kisses became more passionate. He slipped off one of his flip flops and put his bare foot in my lap under the table. I hardened as he began to rub my crotch. I slid from my seat to one knee and began to kiss and suck his toes. His gasp let me know I was on the right track. His calves were hairless, thick and muscular as I ran my tongue up and down his leg. My hand reached for his groin and slipped into one of the tears in his shorts. He was hard already, and I felt smooth, hairless, loose balls. He was completely shaved.

"Come with me," he said, and he turned and walked across the deck to his bedroom. I followed. The room was both masculine and elegant with a tall four-poster bed in the center. Everything about Carlos was an enigma, smart and sweet, but still rugged, even rough in a testosterone-soaked way. Short with thick muscles, but silky smooth from head to toe except for the full coarse beard. Oh, I wanted to feel that scratchy thick Brillo pad all over me

Married, Divorced

in my most sensitive tender places. He leaned against the bed. I was mesmerized by his penis, short really, but crazy thick. And I was mesmerized by the precum that was dripping from the tip. His smooth balls were hanging low, and I knew I was about to taste the sweat behind those heavy cum-filled globes of manliness. I wanted to dive in between his legs and smell his hairless, smooth ass hole. I knew it would have the distinctive odor of a man because we had been sitting outside most of the day. I wanted everything to do with this erudite man, dripping in masculinity.

I started to drop to my knees in front of him. "Not yet," he whispered, and he began to kiss me, deep into my mouth. He licked and kissed behind my ears, and his beard scratched my shoulders. He nibbled my nipples, and the scratchiness continued down my stomach. He turned and lifted me up on the bed and went to his knees, taking my erection deep into his throat. He held me there, sucking and squeezing my cock with the muscles in his throat. More of that amazing scratchiness on my balls and then on my tender inner thighs as he began to poke his tongue in my hole. He worked for some time, and my tight muscle ring relaxed. I was ready for the tough-ass Mexican man I had just met to push his manhood deep into my most private space. The precum and his spit helped some, but honestly, it hurt as he pushed himself into me. He leaned forward and kissed me again. He grabbed the poppers bottle from the sheets and gave me a couple of deep hits, kissed me again, a long hit for himself, then me. Tossing the bottle, he pulled back to get a full thrust in me.

I love being fucked. I've always loved a rough, bad boy manhandling me, forcing me; the overflowing masculinity of a hard fuck makes me sweaty for sure, but it makes me feel like a man. Don't get me wrong, I'm not a submissive pussy. I'm a submissive man, powering back just as hard with the top pounding me. Carlos was no exception. Possibly the thickest man I've ever been with, he rammed me as hard as he could, repeatedly. His force and his stamina melted me. This was so much more than I was looking for when I showed up for a quick anonymous suck-and-fuck in the backyard of the bar just a few hours ago. He pulled out and shot a huge load of creamy cum across me. The force and intensity of his eyes shifted as he flipped me over on top of him, found my cock, and guided me into his hole. I eased the whole shaft in, and it was my turn to serve the Rush. I sniffed first and smiled as I felt him squeeze my penis with his ass muscles. As he hit hard three or four times, his eyes shifted to a warmth and satisfaction coming from having our bodies tangled in the most personal and intimate way possible. I began to rock my hips to a rhythm, both of us moaning from the intensity we were feeling, heightened by the poppers. When it was my time, I withdrew, I wanted for him to see the strong shot of my juice he had worked for that was now shooting across his belly. My thick, white juice looked amazing sprayed across his tats.

Our eyes caught again, and we leaned in to seal our intimate moment. I paused over his chest just long enough to scoop up a tongue full of my cum on my way to his mouth where our lips met, moistened by the cum as we kissed, with our tongues twirling and swirling over each other. Our mouths separated from each other, and we started licking and cleaning the cum that was all over both of us. We lazily kissed and tongued our way over each other. Sleepy, we cuddled. I'd never stayed in another man's bed all night. But with my wife out of town, there was no reason not to be where I wanted to be—in Carlos's arms, listening to his heart beat.

Some have shared their first experiences. Heck, I had many encounters as a young boy playing with other boys, none of which ended in a climax but were very enjoyable. Next were my high school and college days, playing with other horny boys, which usually ended with jacking off. Sometimes I would lay on top of another guy, usually younger than me, where I climaxed while rubbing against him. The pressure between our bodies made me think I was fucking him. Then at twenty-one, I married my high school sweetheart like everyone did in that rural community. That's when I went into what I call my dry period. I had sex with her regularly, but I was usually fantasizing I was doing it with a man. Her puritan upbringing kept her from ever saying she enjoyed what we were doing.

Occasionally, I could sneak away to a town where they had an adult theater. I remember a fat older guy approached me the first time, but I bolted and left the theater. Luckily, they added video booths. It was there I first allowed guys to suck me off through the glory holes. Some booths even had gay movies where I saw guys fucking others. Wow, that looked hot. Those made me anxious to try fucking another guy in the ass.

A few years later, our marriage was facing some difficulties. I actually returned home early from a conference when in grad school and caught my wife and best friend in bed together. I think I was more jealous than mad, since I secretly would dream I was with him when fucking her. He was totally straight, and we had never touched in any suggestive way. After that, my wife and I slept in separate bedrooms and rarely had sex again.

Married, Divorced

A year later, I was convinced we would end in divorce. I had the evidence on her but did not want to smear her name in our community. I had a four-day convention which was held a long way from my home office. The first two days, I shared a room with a cute guy from our firm. He was single and probably interested in M2M, but I think he was uncertain if I was interested or maybe afraid to make the moves on a married man. He had to leave early. The last night was my only night with the room alone. I had already visited the adult arcade just blocks from the hotel and had seen the advertisement for a local gay bar. That night after the big banquet, I got in my car and drove to that bar. I figured it was safe since I was hundreds of miles from home. I never looked around. I just went up to the bar and sat down next to a man that looked about my age, thirty. We started talking. He was a married, local man with wife and two kids at home. I shared that my dream was to fuck a man in the ass. Turns out he loves getting fucked but had not had that happen much. I said I had a hotel room and convinced him to come with me. We had to stop at a store for Vaseline, and then at a bookstore for something called poppers to help him relax. Then to my room.

It was my first time ever in another man's ass. First time doing poppers. I doubt I was a tremendous fucker since I was totally inexperienced. Feeling the wonderful sensations of dick on tight anal tissues and muscles for the first time ever was so much more exciting than pussy. I entered him doggy style at first, after applying lots of Vaseline. The poppers made everything unbelievably wild. Somewhere in our lovemaking, I lost the cover for the poppers when it rolled onto the floor. I never did find it. I believe he climaxed into the sheets while I was fucking him, laying on top of him face down in the sheets. After we both climaxed, he cleaned up and went home. From that moment on, I knew where my sexual future lay—men, not a cold wife who was afraid to enjoy sex.

I got a call from her the following morning that her uncle had died. She asked if I could drive home early so we could drive to attend the funeral back in our home community the next day. I went back to the final half day of the conference, leaving early with the excuse of the funeral. Funny, in the two hours I was there, I got hit on by three different conference attendees. They had each also gone to the gay bar and had apparently seen me talking to the married man. I was so far into the closet that I freaked at their offers to share rooms at future conferences.

I knew from that point there was no turning back. Within six months, we were separated and then divorced. I changed jobs, moved 700 miles away and started slowly coming out of the closet.

Married, Divorced

I have had many rewarding sexual encounters over the years. That time might not be a story to get you physically turned on. Yet, perhaps the most important sexual experience for me might have been that day when I knew I was going to play and fuck with men. From then on, I knew where I belonged in this sexual world. I soon learned also to suck dick. Now I love eating ass, sucking dick, and I am sure I am a much better top than on that first night. And yes, I am very happy knowing who I am.

I can only relate the experiences of a closeted, happily married, bisexual motorcyclist, because that's what I am. I am not gay. I am not conflicted. I just enjoy the occasional sexual playtime with another man. Women are wonderful, and the woman who attends to my satisfaction will keep me forever, I'm sure, just so long as I attend to hers. After many years of togetherness and frequent marital heterosex, it never gets boring. Over 11,000 times and counting. So it's not lack of sex that drives me to men, it's the desire of variety. It's touching, holding, stroking, cupping, kneading, and sucking on a man's entire body and on his manhood. It's getting to experience what my woman does to me. I want to know what she knows when her man is climbing that delicious crest-of-no-return and surrenders to biology.

Why motorcyclist? Because it provides a very convenient solution for the need to separate home life from man-to-man playtime. Ride all day, and then share a private room with a willing man, far from home, with comfort, time, and privacy—that was the plan. Everything is there for a night of relaxed sexual exploration with a happy ending. Discretion was also a necessity. I found no need to upset my wonderful wife by telling her I wanted something she could not provide. So a riding friend with benefits on overnight trips was the goal. Search and you will find. It took a lot of searching. Silverdaddies and Craigslist were targets of my main search efforts, using 'motorcycle' as the search word. Eventually, a connection was made with another married, bisexual motorcyclist, and a five-state road trip was planned.

He sent a picture of himself, bare from the waist up, standing by his ride. We live in different states with a third state between us. Our first face-to-face meeting was at a Dollar General parking lot in that third state. I knew what to expect, what he looked like, and what bike he was riding. We communicated well over emails, so I expected our personalities to mesh. What I did not expect was how tall he was, a good twelve to fourteen inches taller than me. He was a big man, and he was not overweight. He told me to call him Chris.

We rode the rest of the day, gradually getting to know each other. All was good, no personality glitches. Despite his imposing stature and the high-powered crotch rocket he was riding, he always wanted me to ride point. He only wanted to follow, never lead. I was beginning to think that contrary to appearances he had a submissive core. This could be a fun week. We found a motel in the early evening. Because of his size, he requested a king bed and that was the only bed in the room. We used the shower to get physically acquainted. We washed each other's backs; we soaped each other's cocks. I honestly cannot remember any more of that evening. You would think that after all the effort, all the planning, the anticipation of discovering another man's body, and the privacy, we'd have a memorable first cumming together. Maybe what happened during the night shouldered aside any memory of our shower activity.

I woke sometime in the middle of night. I had a good, stiff hard-on. Coming to wakefulness, I see Chris on the far side of the bed, on his side with his back to me. I scooted within arms length and started petting his back. He moved but made no noise. "So that's what you want!" he said. It was a quick, clear statement. Chris rolled off his side and had me physically pinned down within seconds. He was holding my legs down with his weight and holding my chest down with his hands. His mouth was over my hard cock, now pointing straight up in the air.

He looked up at me, found my nipples with his fingers, and literally engulfed my cock in one warm and wet stroke. His tongue was huge, wrapping around the whole bottom of my shaft and curling around both sides. I'd say he deep-throated me, but I'm not that long. The size of his mouth matched the rest of him. Then it started. What hardness I'd lost in being pinned down returned with ready stiffness. His broad tongue found a lapping rhythm, like a big cat at water. Exactly like a big cat at water. He must have also sucked his cheeks in on me. My cock was in a warm home. Chris stuck his fingers in my mouth and told me to get them wet, and then back they went to working my nips.

I'm old enough to have mature ejaculation, not premature. But that tongue! A feeling I've never had before, constant lapping, base to tip, feeling like my cock was being milked by something hungry. It was encouraging, warm, enthusiastic and welcoming—wide, firm strokes with a base level of wanting. The quickest I've ever cum from a blowjob. There's that little bump of permission when you know your orgasm is wanted. I could feel the build-up and it quickly came to the point where nothing could stop the orgasm. The lapping continued as I had the first contractions. Chris made triumphal murmurs as he changed from lapping to gently sucking as I filled his mouth. He stayed on me until I softened, rolled back over, and went to sleep. This should be an interesting week.

I had some fun with a neighbor whom I met at one of the adult bookstores. He loved my uncut cock, just as I loved his uncut cock. After several meet ups at the bookstore, he gave me his address and phone number and asked me to check with him on Saturday mornings.

I would usually go to the university to do research and work on lesson plans on Saturdays. I would be in a lab without a phone, so my wife could not checkup on me. I would go to his house in the late morning. He was always in his third-floor area with his computer and some couches. He used some program—remember that this was almost twenty years ago—that I think was called CuCMe that allowed him to look in on a lot of live sex activity but also allowed his using a camera to send our sex to the site. It was mostly his sucking my rather large, uncut cock. No faces were ever seen.

Many times, over a two-year period, he would have other guys at his place. This is when we would play around with each other. He usually fucked this one married hunk that had close to a nine inch hard dick, while I would suck off the huge dick. I would frequently get underneath to lick the fucker's dick and the asshole of the fuckee. What a time I had. Unfortunately, this fun ended when he moved to Arizona.

MILITARY

I did a stint in the Navy because I knew the military would pay for my college tuition. Learned a lot during those years but the biggest learning lesson was I had a talented mouth for cocks and a tight ass that was good for being fucked. On ship I serviced other shipmates, petty officers, and military officers. The later two helped me get special perks that served me almost daily. I was always first off the ship when we docked at ports. I never did a night watch, only when I requested it. I cleaned the officers' quarters for an extended amount of time, longer then the usual four weeks.

During that time, I of course cleaned the bunks, but I also sucked and got fucked by nearly ALL of the officers. One particular officer was also from So. Cal. So we related. One morning I was cleaning his room and bathroom—depending on their officer status they usually only had two per room. His bunk mate was on duty, so we were alone. I was washing down his shower, and he mentioned how clean it would be on his next use. I finished, and he mentioned he wanted to use it right away. I said I would leave and return later to finish the room. He told me to stay. It wouldn't bother him, if it didn't bother me. He told me that I didn't need to mention this to anyone, and I agreed.

He then stripped naked, while I pretended to be cleaning the room. Awesome young guy, tight body, nice squared shoulders, well developed arms. He had a firm, round butt, perfect for rimming. As he walked to the shower, his beautiful cock, long and thick, swung back and forth. Two round, cum-filled balls to finish the package, topped with a furry, thick bush of dishwater blond pubes. He left the door open, and I heard the shower start. As I pretended to clean, I walked past the door; the shower curtain was open, and he was washing/stroking his now hard, long cock! I walked in the bathroom, "Excuse me, Sir, I forgot some of my supplies!" (LIE!). He turned towards me, cock and balls soapy, cock hard. He said, "I wonder if you can help me?" He rinsed off his jewels and walked towards me; I dropped to my knees.

I swallowed his long, hard cock, cupped and massaged his balls. Caressed and rubbed his perfect ass. Within minutes, he was about to cum. He stiffened, moaned, and grabbed my head. He drove his cock in my mouth as far as it would go. His shaft was all the way in my mouth, and I felt his pubes against my nose. Then I felt his warm, creamy cum shooting in my mouth. He filled my mouth; I swallowed. He filled my mouth again, and I again swallowed. He was sensitive, so I gently tongued his shaft, drinking in his last cum droplets.

Again, he mentioned NOT to tell anyone, which I didn't. It turned out he was married, but when we were out at sea, he considered being sucked and fucking another guy wasn't cheating. Many of my shipmates had that same way of thinking. Kept me busy at sea. Needless to say, that officer and myself had many, many sexual encounters after that. Those years on ship were a very busy time for me!

After being in the military closet for twenty fuckin' years, I'm now a totally out and a proud, gay man.

After tech school, I wound up at Kelly AFB in 1971. I was eighteen with a nice hard body and would show it off as much as I could, without having any questions raised. We were two to a room and an open shower. Two weeks after I got there, another airman arrived and moved next door. We became fast friends and would take showers and eat together, go to movies, and, since I had a car, we would go into town when we could. After a couple weeks of this, he told me he was having wet dreams, which led to a discussion of how many times we both were jacking off.

On a payday Friday night on a three-day weekend, we came back to the barracks around midnight after working out at the gym. The barracks were empty. We met in the showers and started talking about his wet dreams. I turned around and showed him that his talking about wet dreams made my cock hard, but not his. I figured since I was this bold, I'd press further, and started to stroke mine. He did the same. I didn't say a word; I just walked over to him, played with his right nipple, put my right arm around him, and kissed him right there. I knew he was interested when he opened his mouth for my tongue and his arm went around me. We stood there, under the running water making out for a few minutes, and I told him I wanted to suck him off in my room.

We left the showers, and when we got to my room, we put our shaving kits down and started kissing again. I pushed him down on the bed and started my way down, licking his ears, chowing down on his pits and nipples, and licking my way down to his balls. Then I spread his legs and lifted them so I could lick his hole. I started sucking his eight inch cock. He was moaning pretty good, and I felt his cockhead growing. He grabbed my head. I had a huge load of his cum in my mouth. He looked at me, I opened my mouth to show him, and then swallowed it all so he could watch.

After a couple of minutes, he caught his breath and told me he'd had a guy just suck his dick, but he'd jack off to cum. He'd never had his pits or asshole licked nor had his balls sucked on, and never had blown a load into a mouth before. I then told him queers know how to suck a dick. During our talk, I was flicking his nipple, and his dick was half-hard. He told me he would have to jack off again since I was working on him. I asked him how long it would take him to cum again and he told me he jacks it for at least five minutes for a second load. I crawled on top of him, and we started kissing, which made him harder than ever. I whispered in his ear that I wanted him to fuck me. He told me he was a virgin!

While I was coating his cock with some hand lotion, I looked at him, and the look on his face told me he wanted my ass. We got on our knees, and he guided his cock to my hole. I jumped when the head got in and just eased the rest of his cock in until his balls were on my ass. After I got used to him, he fucked me doggy style, and I was fucking him back. Took awhile, but he dumped another good load deep in me. He fucked me three more times that night. I wanted him to wear out my hole.

When we woke up, he had another hard-on and was also waking up. He asked if he could fuck me again before we showered! Of course! We went back to the showers, where we kissed, massaged, and washed each other. He told me he wanted to spend the day in bed with me, and wanted to learn how to suck cock. We did just that. He is a quick learner and swallowed on the first blowjob he gave me, but he wasn't too sure about my nearly ten inch, thick cock in his ass.

I lay back on the bed and positioned his ass over my mouth and rimmed his hole for a long time. He had the cutest bubble butt I'd ever seen, and I wanted to enjoy it. I rimmed his hole long enough, and he started begging me to fuck him. He started crawling away as soon as the big head of my cock popped in, but then eased back on me, moaning all the time. After I came in him, I rolled over and pulled his ass over so he could sit on my face. I started rimming him again and was lapping my cum out of his ass, when he turned around and fed me his dick. I swallowed one of the biggest loads he had ever produced. He said it was the most incredible feeling he'd ever had. We sucked and fucked each other the entire three-day weekend.

On Tuesday, he got permission and moved in. Almost everyday from then until we were transferred, I had some dick. I would get home first, and when he got there, he would fuck me before we went down to eat. As time went on, we met other gay Air Force guys, and we would eventually tell them about our daily thing. There were about twelve of us, and we all went to a motel in Austin for a party.

That is another story. So is the Philippines and three guys, one was black and we had a fun three-day weekend. I was a bottom for a well-built black man for four years in the Washington area and did the oreo when his cousin came into town, getting fisted after double penetration, black balled by eight guys. Memories is all I have left now since mobility issues set in, and sex is too painful with four decompressed discs, arthritis, legs full of scar tissue, and now neuropathy.

I was looking at some pics, and I started to remember my exploits in the Navy. I knew this one guy in Boot Camp we all called Dillon. Small guy but tight, a body that wouldn't quit and a set of cock and balls that would even make a straight man gay. During our weeks of training, I found out he had hustled for a bit on the streets of LA. Said he turned tricks because his mom and stepfather had thrown him out because he was gay. He had NOTHING to worry about, but luckily he had enlisted to better himself.

During our talks, I had told him I liked to suck cock and get fucked. Even though his previous profession had HIM sucking cocks and being fucked, he was relieved that I would do him for a change. During our night patrols together, we would go into a bathroom stall, and I would suck his tasty cock. Many times he would fuck me afterward. Being in our twenties, we could do many orgasms. To this day, I remember sucking his hard cock, holding his tight, firm ass cheeks, licking his round cum-filled balls. How he would grab my head, as he EXPLODED in my mouth, a flow of warm, creamy cum. For a little guy, he had a lot of cum; I remember I had to swallow two or three times to keep up. That was the start of my cock sucking career in the Navy, I realized then and there, that these men needed my warm mouth!

Just a quick note. Over the years I have had the pleasure of seeing some AWESOME tattoos on guys' cocks. A dragon, Pinocchio's nose, an elephant trunk. When I was in the Navy, my Petty Officer had a barber's pole on his cock. I had the extreme pleasure of seeing it grow before my very eyes. He wasn't much to look at, but he more then made up for it in the cock department. Plus, he loved to get sucked and to fuck my ass. He was the one that introduced me to the "society" on board the carrier I was on. They were always looking for fresh meat on board.

Military

I was about thirty years old and, not unlike today, loved to frequent adult bookstores in search of hot cocks needing a good thorough sucking. By this time, I was especially fond of married men and the cock they had between their legs. I also had and continue to have a deep sexual attraction for men in uniform, especially cops and military men. I have always found myself checking out men's crotches and penises, especially when in a men's room when they whip it out to take a piss. If the men were ever in uniform, I would almost drop to my knees right then and there.

This one night started out like most other nights. I went to the local adult bookstore in North East Philly. Although I live in NJ, NE Philly is just about ten minutes away for me. I arrived at the bookstore, anticipating sucking cock and getting my mouth filled with some creamy man seed. I pulled into the parking lot adjacent to the bookstore and looked around. Since the parking lot could only hold about six cars, many guys parked on the street, and several of those didn't even venture into the store unless they saw someone who interested them. I guess I was not as particular and would always go in, in search of some cock to satisfy.

This one night, I was looking around at the various cars before I was heading inside and noticed this one Ford SUV. There was a man in the SUV, and he was looking back at me. I stared for a moment and saw him motioning to me. Curious as I was, I took a few steps in his direction, and although I could not see him clearly through the windows, I noticed his license plate had an FOP designation for the Philadelphia Police. I was both hesitant and intrigued by this and proceeded with caution. I knew merely going to an adult bookstore was not illegal, and I didn't want to get in his vehicle if he was there as part of some sting operation.

Remember guys, I was still quite horny, wanting to find cock to satisfy. So I approached the vehicle and saw a gray-haired man in jeans and a sweatshirt, asking if I wanted to get into his SUV. He seemed friendly enough, and I couldn't resist the sight of his full package bulging in his jeans. I got in. I asked him about the license-plate FOP emblem, and he said the vehicle was his brother-in-law's car. I accepted his reply but told him that I had hoped it was his vehicle and that perhaps he had an affiliation with the police department.

As I recall, we chatted for quite a while, not really having much sexual contact other than conversation. He ultimately admitted that he was a cop. When he admitted it, I almost shot in my pants. By this time, it was getting late and other than getting a quick glimpse of his huge beefy cock, he told me he had to leave to get home so his wife wouldn't be too suspicious. I couldn't let this opportunity go without the prospect of seeing him again, so I told him I lived just over the bridge. I could have a guy back at my place and loved a man in uniform. I asked if he would take my phone number. Remember, this was the time before smart phones, but fortunately not long after most everyone had a flip phone. So he took my phone number, and I just prayed he would have the urge to call me.

Several weeks went by, and I almost gave up hope, when out of the blue, he called and said he had just finished his shift in the city and had some time to come over. I could hardly contain myself. He arrived about twenty minutes later and was still wearing most of his uniform. He walked in and said he locked his gun in the car for safety reasons, but brought his night stick, a city issued one as well.

I couldn't wait to get on my knees in front of him, dressed in his uniform, and slowly undress him and lick every inch of his manly body. He told me how his wife didn't appreciate his penis or body. Despite feeling he was telling me this in order to help him get over his issues, I didn't care. He also told me he had been in the Marines years before, as if being a cop wasn't enough. I felt like I was in leather heaven.

I wrapped my lips around his cock and didn't want to let go. I took as much as I could down my throat and listened to him say how good it was. I felt his strong hands pushing my head deeper on his shaft. He tried to tell me to slow down, but I was relentless and just sucked and sucked, until he finally told me he was about to shoot if I didn't stop. I didn't stop. He filled my mouth with his hot, married cop cum and I swallowed as fast as he filled my mouth. When he finished filling my mouth, I still didn't want to stop sucking his cock but reluctantly withdrew. I then just started to fondle it gently, licking up any bits of cum that were still oozing from his manly penis.

We sat for a while. I still wasn't ready to give up on his cock and balls. I got down once again and proceeded to suck his fully hard cock again. He doubted whether he could cum again, but I persisted. Low and behold, soon I was swallowing another load of his semen. Unfortunately, I never heard from him again, but at least I have the memory of those two very special evenings that I will never forget.

Military

I guess I lost what little modesty I had in the Navy. On land you have to eat, sleep, shower, change—do all of your bodily functions with, I think, thirty-six other guys. Then when you hit your ship, it continues. Of course, I took the route of sucking and being fucked by thousands of guys. During those four years, I pretty much experienced most of my fantasies, what I liked and disliked. I realized that I loved a hard cock up my ass. I have tried "water sports" a couple of times, not really my thing.

However, the most memorable piss was when I was off ship. After I got drunk at a local bar, this one guy came on to me for some fucking at a bathhouse. We paid the clerk like $20.00 to let us both go up the stairs. After I sucked this guy, he poured a huge load in my tight ass, and then we hit the showers. There, we came across numerous guys who were sucking and fucking in the common shower room. I sucked plenty of cocks and got fucked again by most of the cocks on hand—nothing like your hole all lubed up with cum, to welcome a new set of cocks! After I was done servicing the room, the guys decided to unload their piss on me. That was my first time being drenched in warm piss, naked, from head to toe. Must admit I got a raging hard-on and ended up sucking and being fucked by the guys AGAIN.

When I'm really bored, I go to a local bookstore that is notorious for gay action. Straight guys come in, looking for a guy to suck their cocks and/or fuck a tight ass. Then they start to play that "selective shopper" game, which I do not play! That game turns me off immediately. I let them play their games, let the twinks struggle over each other to get the prize. I stand back, let them realize that I will suck their cocks, but they need to come to me. Sometimes I win, sometimes I lose—all is fair in the "sucking cock" world. Maybe I'm just too old to play their games, or maybe I just don't care who they wrap around their cocks. I just know I'm the best cock sucker around, so if you want the best, I'm here!

Been thinking about a boy I introduced to the world of cocksucking in the mid-70s at my base in Italy. I am amazed I got so brazen with this kid at his age. But he was so willing, so inquisitive, so anxious for anything to do with sex, and wanted to experience what I could teach him. Oh, yeah, he got off many times too.

His name was Steve. He lived next door to us in our last few months at our base where we lived in base housing for about five months before I left. I remember his name because he was the son of the base commander. His dad was a great guy, so was his wife, and we got along really well. On base we had a yard, and the grass needed to be mowed. I would borrow the mower of my neighbor on the other side of us, which was the base legal office, and mow ours and their lawns. One day, as I was finishing and getting ready to sit down with a coke or something, Steve came out and joined me.

We chatted about all sorts of things as we always did. He was a great kid and anxious to grow into a man, like all of us were at that age. He asked tons of questions on all sorts of topics, and I just answered the ones I knew about and was honest to say "I don't know" on the ones I didn't. He naturally talked about girls and the frustrations he had with them. They were nice to dance with but they would not allow him to get to second base. Very frustrating for a guy heading off to college soon. I mentioned that at that age "Rosy Palm" had been a good friend to me, and he picked up on that. "Yeah, for me too. But I sure would like to try a real pussy for a change." There, right there, that was my opening, so I said, "Well, there are ways to mimic a pussy that may surprise you." After that, he got me to admit that I'd had blowjobs that were just as good as pussy, and that they can be administered by a guy. I said that men knew best how to suck a cock and make a happy man out of a frustrated man.

Well, it was no time at all before he asked if I'd suck him. At the same time, he wanted assurances that I'd never tell his folks—or anyone else for that matter. I said absolutely, and the same assurances were essential from him. He agreed.

Talk about taking chances! He led me to his room, and I sat him down on the bed after pulling his gym shorts down. He had a nice boy cock of about five inches, a blazing hard, and I took it in my hand kneeling down. "Now, close your eyes, Steve, and imagine your girl is letting you fuck her. That's exactly how this will feel." He did, and I gently sucked that boy's cock.

He took to it like a duck to water. He was, he thought, happy to masturbate and get off that way. But he knew there was more to it and that no doubt it would feel better than Rosy Palm could provide. And that played out that afternoon. In about fifteen minutes, he could not hold it any longer and came in my mouth. Nice, creamy, hot boy cum, and lots of it. "Shit, that is totally awesome," he remarked. "I have never cum that much before! It felt so good!"

Well, one thing led to another, and he asked me to suck his cock several more times. He began to ask questions of other guys about homosexuality and began to understand that gays fucked each other as well as sucked each other. And he asked me about that. "Oh yes, that happens. Is that something you'd like to try, son?"

He said he did, and so I let him fuck me. Again in his room, just me, bending over and letting him get to my asshole. He was used to getting off now, thanks to me, and this was a logical next step. He stroked in and out too fast like kids do, and it diminished my pleasure. But he sure enjoyed that ride. And he came in my ass twice that afternoon. Eventually, I asked him if he'd like to try being penetrated. I told him the first feeling might be a little painful, but after that nirvana. So I fucked him and did it face to face so he could see me all the while.

He said he loved it, and he jacked all the while. We came about the same time. He was a good kid, and I enjoyed helping him. Now here's the kicker. Turns out he moved here when his dad retired, and still lives here. In the 90s, I interviewed with him for a job. By 1998 he was working as a manager of an IBM service agency. It took a while for us to recognize each other, but once we did, we shook hands again. What a surprise. By then he was married with two kids.

Back in the early 80s after naval schooling, I was stationed on the Enterprise CVN 61. The ship had a big gay subculture because it was all men, and it was the "Don't tell days." When I arrived, I was soon included in their gay subculture, and was introduced by another fellow seaman that I had developed a sexual relationship with. At the time, the ship was in dry dock, so our hook-ups were less then at sea. After the second week when at sea, they were begging to get sucked and/or fuck a warm ass.

David had been on the ship about four months before me. He was from Boston, with a big barrel chest, light dish-water fur, a hard chiseled beard. And, as I later found out, a tasty batch of pubic hairs, topping a decent, thick cock, with two beautiful, round, cum-filled balls. We knew each other but didn't hang out together. I was told to meet a hot guy in one of our secret closets. We never knew their names unless they wanted us to know. I arrived early, ass douched and mouth ready, waiting and wanting a cock to penetrate me. Heard the hatch unlock. I turned and there was David! We immediately recognized each other, kinda smiled, chit-chatted nervously. I was up front and told him we didn't have to complete the deal. He smiled, "Oh Hell no! I paid for a suck and fuck. Trust me, I need it!"

Military

I got on my knees, unbelted and unzipped his Navy blues. As I pulled down his underwear, I was mesmerized by that beautiful, cut, ginger cock meat. I took him in my mouth as he grabbed my head and moaned. He was soon hard and pumping my mouth with his low-hanging balls slapping my chin. I licked his balls, sucked his cock for about twenty minutes, then he lifted me to my feet and said, "I need to fuck you." We quickly undressed. I lubed his stiff cock and my cock's hungry hole. We didn't use condoms much because, first of all, it was the early 80s and AIDS wasn't well known then. Secondly, condoms couldn't be left behind. If you did use one, it had to be taken out with you. I leaned against the bulkhead as he slowly drove his cock shaft home. We both welcomed the fact when his cock sunk to the base, embedded in my tight hole. We both moaned. Soon he was pumping my hole with uncontrollable manly desire. I could feel his balls slap my ass cheeks as he drove his shaft home.

I expected he would cum soon, but I was not prepared by his intensity. That was one of the few times I actually felt cum shooting into my ass. That was also the first time the guy had so much cum that it filled and spilled out of my hole as he fucked me. Both of us stood there with his cock still in me, panting, out of breath from our awesome fuck. Finally, he got soft and his cock slipped out. I used my underwear to mop up the extra cum on his cock, on my stretched hole, and down my legs. I wanted to savor his sticky nectar.

We agreed that we wanted to fuck again, and we did. From then on, we did hang out. He was with me on many of my Navy adventures, and when we fucked at sea, he was always charged.

Speaking of sucking cock, I remember sucking a fellow military man in a tent near Camp Humphries when I was stationed in the USAF in South Korea. We were supporting Ulchi Focus Lens, a joint force exercise. This man was not AF but Army. It just was the luck of the draw as to who bunked with whom, based on when you arrived.

Anyway, he was pleasant enough and after pleasantries he admitted about needing a blowjob to bring our busy days to a close and how good that would be. But we did not act on it right then. I put him on my to-do list. I had long meetings that first night. What greeted me when I got back to our tent—he was buck naked and fast asleep. It was summer and very warm and humid so it was understandable that he'd sleep naked.

Remembering our conversation, I made a plan to suck his dick until he came. It would probably mimic a wet dream for him. So I undressed and got down on my knees right next to his bunk, and I sucked his penis right into my mouth. He was in deep sleep, having long breaths which I did not seem to interrupt at all. I carefully sucked the length of his cock and crown without touching his abdomen with my face. Not easy to do when you are a cocksucker like me and want to get your full face into the action. But hey, I did not specifically have his permission and so treaded lightly. Pretty soon he got hard, and I could tell his body really liked the sexual attention he was getting. Then he changed position and got onto his back. His knee pushed me away, so I had to change my position and got between his legs.

His cock was rigid. I kept on sucking, knowing he was getting ready to spill. You know how in a wet dream it seems so real and so wonderful that you never want it to stop? And when it happens and you ejaculate you want it all to flow. That's why we get such a big mess in our beds or in our jimmies, because the ejaculations are so intense and complete. Anyway, I was hoping I'd get a big load from this Army guy.

Pretty soon he went kinda limp and moaned, and his stiff cock let loose with a torrent of semen into my mouth. Rip after rip of cum streamed out of him, and I figured he'd wake up thinking he'd made a mess. But he snoozed on. When he was done shooting cum, I let his cock subside and shrink. I hoped he'd be OK with what I did for him and not be mad. Couldn't think why he would be, but you sometimes don't know what an outcome will be.

I cleaned up a few spilled drops and let him sleep. I crawled into my bed on the adjacent cot and figured I'd get some needed sleep. But my suck buddy woke up and realized he'd had a wet dream. "Shit," he said, "where's the mess? I just had a wet dream." "Friend, there's no mess this time. It's in me," I replied. "Man, oh man, I have not cum like that in a long time. Thank you! Can I return the favor?" He was a red head and you know I like red headed cocksuckers.

So began two weeks of great evening fun for the both of us when our shifts allowed. Amazingly, no one ever walked in on us. There's no way to lock a tent.

Another story, this time it was after my enlistment in the Navy. It was the early 80s, I had moved to Huntington Beach with a buddy, two blocks from the beach. We were there for about eighteen months, long enough to enjoy two summers. It actually was a good rental, four units, and they had large rooms. Two bedrooms with two bathrooms—nice.

We lived upstairs, in back. First summer, a couple of Marines took the front unit, down stairs. There were six of them, but since they had different shifts, they were never all there at the same time. Of course, we introduced ourselves. My roommate was straight, but I was totally checking them out. All from back East and some of them had never seen an ocean. We partied at the beach and at the apartment. They were fun.

One evening, my roommate was gone. I was drinking, so I ventured to the apartment up front to offer them a beer. Surprise! There was one guy there and he was drinking. I don't remember his name, but does it really matter? Cute, young, hung, with a tight body, and from South Carolina. We sat at the kitchen table, talked about living there, the beach, the girls; I lied. He mentioned how horny he was and how he had jacked off in the shower, but it hadn't really helped. I mentioned, well, I could blow him, if he didn't tell anyone? Would you really? Sure! Our secret!

We moved to the couch. He dropped his swimsuit, exposing two beautiful cum- filled balls and a semi-hard, long, relatively thick cock, topped with a curly patch of dirty-blond pubes. This was before man-scraping, so his pubes were naturally curly. I bent down and took his cock in my mouth. He quickly became hard, so I slid my mouth up and down. I kinda worried if he could cum, since he had previously cum in the shower. But he was young, hung, and a Marine! I licked his balls, his shaft, his delicious cockhead. He soon grabbed my head and drove his cock all the way in. He was about to cum!

I could feel him squirting his delicious, warm, creamy cum in my mouth. Squirt, after squirt, I swallowed. Ran my tongue up his shaft, the slit of his cockhead, and swallowed his cock to its base. He was impressed, said it was one of the best. He asked if we could do it again; I said OK!

We did have sex again, four times, and he fucked me three times. Truth is, I had all six of those Marines. If they only knew.

We have a cruising place near where I live that is pretty good most of the time and not bothered by the police. I live at the far end of the county. It is patrolled by the county, and they don't get out this way much, since we don't have much going on. Well, the Navy base is out here, but it is now used mostly by older personnel after the re-organization of the base. That turned out to be a good thing for me at least, since there are a whole lot of men on the down low in uniform there. Anyway, I always take a book with me so if anyone does come by I can tell them I am sitting in my car reading. This one day I was sitting there reading in my shorts and a tank top and had been for quite a while when the sheriff drove by and stopped and started to talk. He was a damn good-looking guy also, with dark hair and eyes, built like a tank. He had me get out of the car so he could look at my license and just talk bull shit for a bit. I knew it was the start of his shift since it was late in the day, and he was probably the only one in this end of the county. I found out that he was new to the area, having moved here from the west coast the year before. I had moved here from the same area quite a few years earlier also, so that was all that was needed for him to really start talking.

He stayed and talked for over an hour, which I didn't mind at all until he finally said that he needed to go back and sign off. He asked if I would still be here later, and I said I probably would. He told me he would swing by. I couldn't believe it, and I immediately got a hard-on which he noticed since I was wearing no underwear. He smiled, and as he passed by I felt his hand brush my cock. I couldn't wait to get my cock out and didn't even wait for his car to leave. I got back in my car and started to jack off. He just smiled at me and left. I couldn't believe my luck. His package was huge, and he wasn't even hard.

There was another car not far from us that started to move right after the sheriff left. He came over to me and started to talk about the sheriff. This guy was blond, hairy as an ape, and had no shirt on, just a pair of jeans that were left unbuttoned at the top. I couldn't believe my luck with two beautiful men in one day. I started to run my fingers over his hairy chest and told him my name was Richard. He said his name was Rick. He grabbed my cock, kissed me deep, and started to play with my ass with his other hand. I moaned to let him know I wanted him bad. He asked if I thought the cop would want a threesome. I thought he would, so and Rick said that we would wait and see.

Sure enough, about a half hour later, a car came by and stopped. The sheriff got out, looked at us, and asked who my friend was. I told him Rick's name and mine. He laughed and told us his name was Dana. This time he was dressed in jeans and a polo. He took off his shirt, revealing a hairy chest, and said that he might as well join us. He slid his hand down the back of my cut-offs. I unbuttoned them and let them slide down. I stood naked in front of them, hard and proud, and ready to be used. I told them I was theirs for the taking. Dana looked around, pointed to the woods, and said let's go up there. I pulled up my shorts and we started to walk, our hands never leaving each other. After we got out of view of the road and anyone who might drive by, I dropped my shorts, and they dropped their jeans. My mouth started exploring their bodies. I tongued and sucked their nipples and ear lobes and kissed them. They did the same to me as we jacked off, and they explored my hole with their fingers.

I finally dropped to my knees and took their cocks in my mouth. Rick had at least ten inches, and Dana had a little more. I wanted them in my ass so bad I couldn't stand it. I could hear them kissing and moaning as I sucked their cocks and balls and fingered their holes. I finally began to move my head around so I could eat their asses, and they almost went wild when I did. I could hear Dana say that he had never had that done; I couldn't believe it. Rick had dropped to his knees and was sucking my cock like a wild man at this point, Dana pulled up my legs to expose my hole, and Rick went in with his tongue. I lost it. I fished out poppers from my shorts and went crazy like I always do, telling them to fuck me like a whore. Just keep me poppered up and I was theirs!

I lived a couple of months at the beach in south California. During that time, we had six Marines that lived for a time in the front unit. I had all six. One of them was Roger, the most outspoken one of the bunch. He was cute, blond, tight body from North Carolina. One day, we had spent the day at the beach, came home, and enjoyed a couple of beers as the night came upon us. We partied at my apartment, then his, a couple of beer runs—one of the typical summer nights at the beach. The night got late, we were drunk, the guys were in his apartment, but my roommate had gone for the evening.

Like I said, we were drunk, a day at the beach, and we hadn't showered yet. I told him he could use my shower if he wanted; he wanted! We went into the bathroom. I was going to leave, but he stripped, jumped in the shower like nothing, so I stayed, took a pee, enjoying the site through the frosted shower glass. Then he said he needed me to wash his back. I could jump in if I wanted. Well, that was the only invitation I needed. I soaped his back, and then he soaped mine. He turned, and I soaped his chest and abs. I avoided his cock, only because I wasn't sure where this was going.

He soaped my chest and my stomach, and then he progressed to my cock. I quickly got hard. I reached and soaped his beautiful cock. I cupped his cum-filled balls. He turned and rinsed but then turned to have his throbbing cock face me, so I dropped to my knees. He took in a mouthful of cock, even though he had a very defined, big cockhead. I was very impressed. I swallowed his cock, even though his big cockhead filled my mouth. I sucked him for a good ten minutes, and then I stood up while he soaped my cock-hungry hole. I told him to be gentle, my hole is tight, he made a crack about how the Subic Bay whores he had were anything but tight. "You're going to love my tight hole then," I thought.

He pushed his mushroom head against my hole; it slipped in. Then the shaft, then I could feel his pubes and balls touch my ass cheeks. We got a rhythm going as he pounded my hole! He grabbed my tits, twisted, and pinched. He wrapped his arms around me while he drove his cock to its limits. He pounded for a while, though I didn't mind. His stiff rod was being pumped and buried in my ass. When he was cumming, he held my hips and drove his cock deep inside me. I could feel his base ram my ass cheeks. He drove his cock in me one final time, held my hips as his cock, deep inside, pulsed as it unloaded his white, creamy nectar.

We stood frozen as his cock pulsed. He licked my ear and my neck. He pulled out, and said, "That was HOT!" I told him we could fuck again, let me know. I asked him, "You won't tell anyone?" "Of course not! he answered. "That's cool, because I wouldn't want the guys to find out I like fucking guys' asses?" Little did he know that the rest of the guys liked my blowjobs and tight ass!

Roger and the guys were fun, a bit clueless but maybe that's just the East Coast and the Marine guys I was dealing with. Either way, I was fucked and cum-filled by those guys!

When I was in The Navy, my ship was dry docked in Bremerton, Washington. We were getting loopy on ship, so we took over an apartment that some buddies had, and we were there for about three months. There were four of us in that apartment, but with different shifts we were never there at the same time. With only one bed and one room it was small, but when you're in the service, being naked around each other was no big deal. During that time, I saw lots of different cocks—light, dark, long, short, thick, skinny, average, and OMG!

Military

During this time, one of the guys was Randy, from Michigan. He is an OMG! One evening, I went to the apartment, thinking I was going to be alone, so I stopped for some groceries. Walked in and Randy was there watching TV. Went to the fridge as we talked, and told him I thought I would be alone. Had enough food for two, so he offered to go out and get some beer. I made dinner, we watched TV, ate, and then proceeded to attack the twelve pack he had brought back. As we sat on the couch, I mentioned that I was going to actually take a bath in the tub, even though we had showers. He said that sounded good. I said that when I was done that he could bathe. I filled the tub, got naked, and climbed in the tub. Maybe fifteen minutes later, Randy walked in the bathroom, naked and with his big cock just swinging.

It was a big lion claw tub, room for two but there would be touching. He asked, "Can't we bathe together?" I was drunk, and he was drunk, so I said, "OK!" He sat on the other side of the tub, putting his legs and feet on the outer side of my hips. My legs and feet were in the middle, up against his thick cock. My foot was touching his cock and balls, so I kept saying, "Sorry, sorry." He said, "You can touch my cock; I don't mind." I soon noticed his cock was getting bigger, harder! I just came out and asked, "So how big is your cock?" "He answered, "I don't know; never measured it." I told him, "Looks huge!" He then said, "You want to touch it, with your hand not your foot!"

Still sitting, I reached over and rapped my fingers around his shaft. He immediately got rock hard. He stood up, so his monster cock was at face level. I took him in my mouth, cupped his balls, and attempted to deep-throat him. I sucked; he moaned. Soon he was squirting thick, warm, creamy cum in my mouth. I swallowed. We didn't fuck that night, but we did sleep naked, spooning all night, and I did suck him off one more time.

He asked me if I was in that "secret society" of Navy cocksuckers. When I admitted that I was, he said he had never tried it. I told him if he wanted, just ask me and I would never charge him for services rendered. The least I could do.

STUDENT

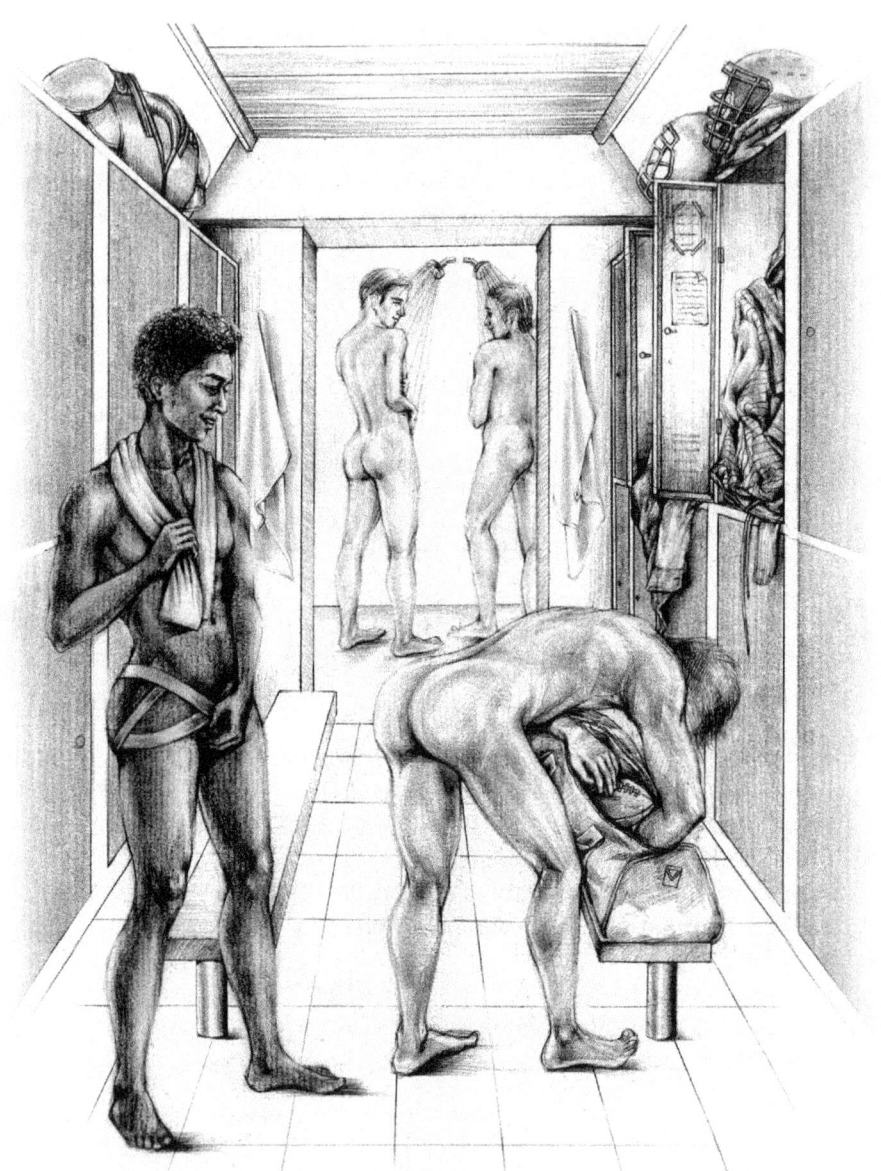

I had been living in New Orleans for five years during college and hadn't had sex with either a man or a woman. I knew I was interested in cock. I didn't think I was gay. However, I knew I wanted a blowjob.

Student

I went to the French Quarter, looking to find someone, probably for pay. In New Orleans you can get drinks anywhere. I went into a straight porn theater, a really small place in the first floor of a building, watched for a while, got hard and got up the courage to ask the bartender if he knew where I could get a blowjob. He asked if I was looking for a man or a woman. He didn't look gay. I assumed that he'd send me where the ladies congregated, so I told him a mouth was a mouth. I was young and not too bad looking. He told me to come behind the bar and motioned toward the back storage room. He leaned me against the wall, touched my body, and opened my zipper. I panicked and asked what would happen if someone needed a drink. He said that the guy at the box office was his cover.

By that time, my cock was doing all the thinking. He pulled my pants down and put his lips on the head of my cock. I remember that moment like it was twenty seconds ago. God was it good. He sucked for a bit. I asked him if he would switch places with me. He looked surprised, and asked if I were gay. I told him I didn't think so but wanted to see what a cock felt like in my mouth. Unfortunately, he wasn't hard. It was a big piece of sausage with foreskin. A couple of swipes were all that I needed. We reversed positions, and I let him have my load. That was the beginning of my having sex in movie houses, which I continued at the Metropole on 14th St. in NYC. What great cruising. It took a few years before I appreciated having a soft cock in my mouth and feeling it grow.

When I was a youngster in high-school, I knew guys turned me on, and one of the only things that I liked about gym class was showering and getting changed after gym class. I got to see thirty naked, young guys with all sorts of dicks and balls. I learned very quickly how not to throw a boner. One of the guys had an eight inch, uncut dick with the smoothest, silkiest looking skin. A couple of other guys were cut and had nice mushroom heads.

Then there was the tall, slim, black guy, who was a year or so older and played on the basketball team. I saw him a couple of times in the changing room. He had a scrot that hung down at least six inches and had two of the nicest smooth, chocolate eggs you'd ever want to see. As soon as I got home from school, I'd jack off—I was doing that at least three times a day.

Learning how to JO was another story. Some of my buddies talked about it, but I was a bit slow. I had wet dreams but never jacked off. I asked one of my friends how to do it, and he said to just hold your dick between two fingers and pull up and down. Well, that didn't work for me. I got so frustrated that finally I did that until I shot my first JO load. WOW! I did, however, have a bruise on my dick for a few days. I also discovered that for me, a fist worked much better than two fingers. Once I got started, I was addicted. I JO'd at least three times a day even when I was in my late teens.

Many years ago when I was in college, I picked up a trick at our local gay bar. He was a hot college guy who was sharing an apartment with a friend. When we got back to his apartment, much to my surprise, his roommate also had a trick. The two roommates' beds were shoved together like a huge, king-size play area. My trick and I started playing around, and the next thing I knew the other two guys were joining us.

My trick's roommate had a huge cock and wanted to fuck the rest of us with his man hood. He fucked his trick and shot his load up his ass, and then he moved on to my trick and proceeded to fuck him. Luckily, for the sake of my ass, he was spent by the time he got to me, so I ended up fucking him while the other two watched. It was one of the most memorable sexual nights I have ever had. Just wish more of them would come along nowadays!

My first summer off from college I went back home and ran around with a few friends from high school who had just graduated or who were visiting from their schools. My ex-girlfriend from high school was one of the people I hung out with occasionally, and she introduced me to a new friend of hers, "Matt." He was a few inches shorter than my 6'2", with spiked, dark brown hair with tips, a nose piercing, and a tattoo from his shoulder across his back almost to his spine. This was, after all, the 1990s.

After we'd hung out in a group a few times, Matt and I got to know each other a bit, and he introduced me to his boyfriend, Craig, with his long, straight, boy-band blond hair. He could only be described as that perfect bubble-butt-shaking twink. By August, the three of us were good friends, and decided to camp out in some woods nearby.

It was one of those perfect August summer nights that teenagers are made for, and we'd spent the time walking into the woods far enough to be almost totally guaranteed privacy, even if we slept in well past noon the next day.

We set up our tent in a small clearing by a stream as the sun went down. Since they were both city boys and it was a warm night, I decided not to bother with building a fire. When it was dark and we were treated to a beautiful sky of stars, I suggested to them that we all hang out naked since we were men alone in the woods at night.

Almost immediately, Craig claimed to be cold, which I suspect was a lie. Since body heat was all I had to offer, I brushed that off. Matt and I snuggled up on either side of him on a sleeping bag we'd opened and lay on the grass in the clearing. For most of the rest of the night, the three of us took turns in nearly every position, mostly with Craig taking it in both ends like a champ. By the time the horizon was starting to pale, all three of us were covered in sweat, and Craig's ass was quite a bit looser and oozier than when the sun had gone down. I reminded him that he'd been cold at the start of this, that we'd gotten no sleep, and he had suggested we all crawl into the tent, cram both our dicks into Nick's ass, and try to get some sleep. So that's what we did, except we didn't actually end up sleeping. Testosterone never sleeps.

Years ago, when I was in college, I knew two guys that were gay and in the closet. I guess we all were; none of us were out, though we skinny dipped, changed in front of each other, and had our track team showers together.

We had planned a trip to Hawaii for two weeks. We did all the tourists' stuff, of course. We were invited to stay at my cousin's, but since my cousin and his roommates were gone for about four days, we had the place to ourselves! One night we got drunk, crossed the street to skinny dip in the ocean, and later went back and drank some more. Jim passed out, but Rick and I stayed up and drank more. Again, we crossed the street to skinny dip in the ocean.

We swam for a bit, then returned to our towels and lay there naked. We discussed sex, getting laid and how often. He had a girlfriend; I did not. We both got hard cocks, and I asked if he had ever tasted cock? He said he hadn't, but I confessed that I had. I lied and said that I had tasted cock, sucked cock and swallowed cum. I told him I would lick his cock, and we would tell no one.

He lay down, and I swallowed his cock to the base! Licked his balls, his crotch, even his pubes. After about ten minutes of this, I came up for air and asked Rick if he had ever fucked a guy? Of course he said he hadn't. I lay on my towel, raised my ass cheeks and spread them, waiting for his entry.

He lay on top of me, with his hard cock between us. I guided his cockhead to my hole, told him to go slow because we had no lube, only spit. He entered me and moaned from satisfaction. He started pumping and nipping my ear. I could feel his balls, slapping my ass cheeks and his shaft, pleasing my hole. Soon he increased his strokes; he was going to cum.

He grabbed my hips and drove his cock as deep as he could go. His breathing got heavy, and he was sucking my ears. He came so much, his cum spilled out of my hole. Warm, fresh, creamy cum.

We lay there, his cock deep in my hole. He confessed that I had given him the best blowjob and fuck he had ever had. I said, "You're welcome, and I would love to do again, any time!" Though we never did.

I was a very naive college freshman, attending a very conservative, church-related college. I had played a little while in high school but only JO with other guys. I needed a suit, so I went down to the only men's clothing store and this mid-twenties guy waited on me. Of course, he had to measure my inseam a couple of times and bumped against my package in the process, but I didn't think much about it. When we were done, he asked me if I would like to go to a musical the college was presenting the next night. I agreed to go.

The next evening, he picked me up at the dorm, and we enjoyed the musical together. When it was over, he asked me to go to a local club with him. I thought why not, although I had never drunk any alcohol or been to a club. When we got there, we joined several of his friends at a large round table. He ordered me a wine cooler, which I finally was able to get down. After visiting awhile with the others, we left, and he drove out of town to a very remote dirt, back road. The car mysteriously quit. This was in northern Iowa in the middle of January. He suggested that we take off our shoes, put our legs up on the seat facing each other, and cover them with a blanket. This meant that our legs were parallel to each other with one foot in each other's crouch. I began to feel his toes rub my crouch, so I did the same to him. Soon we were both hard. We pulled our pants down and started playing with each other. He had the biggest cock I had ever seen, and haven't seen many bigger since then.

He asked me to lean over the seat so he could play with my butt—I had never even heard of anal sex at the time. He played with my ass a little, and soon I felt him pushing his dick against my ass hole. I was shocked but didn't say a thing. This was before the AIDS outbreak, and he didn't have any lube. There was no way he could enter me, so he suggested we swap places. I was able to fuck him. It was the best feeling I had ever experienced. I could have fucked him all night!

But soon I saw a vehicle coming up the road, and we quickly got dressed. Turns out it was a tow truck driven by one of the guys from the club. He got the car started, and we drove back to town. He dropped me off at the dorm, and I never saw him again. I also went on to get married and divorced two times. Finally, came out when I retired and am enjoying topping whenever I get the chance.

A man replied to my post, asking me if I cared how old he was. Even being horny as fuck and wanting sex, I did not say, "Yes," readily, but instead asked how young he was. After all, the age of consent here in Ohio is eighteen—or one could be thrown in the slammer if the police found out. He answered, "Fourteen." I knew as a school teacher, I was putting my career and reputation in jeopardy—but again, being hornier than fuck I finally said, "Yes, I will meet you." He lived about ten miles south of me. He was going to meet me at the post office. He and his parents had divorced. His father had no idea what he was doing. Even though he lived with his mother, she was clueless.

Upon arriving at the post office, I saw this young, hung man. Wow, I had hit the jackpot. That first night we went to the local park where we sucked, and he lost his virginity. Many times people would walk around us, and we had to cover ourselves up. He really sucked like a pro, even though he told me it was his first time—must have watched a lot of porn. You know, porn is nothing but an educational piece, and I love to be educated. Oh, how could I ever forget that his monster cock was fucking the daylights out of me but was certainly satisfying as well.

Consequently, we decided we would meet again. We found a wide open space out in the middle of a corn field where no one could see us. And luck would have it that most of the time the moon was shining. Wow, could he suck and fuck; I loved every minute of sucking this fourteen-year-old young man, going down on him all the way to the pubes, and his fucking my mouth all the way to the back of my tonsils. While I was rubbing his big endowment, he told me he would be sitting in school paying no attention to the teacher but knowing that night we would be meeting for some hot M2M sex. And, believe you me, we did every night. I love hot M2M sex, and I think I got him hooked too. We had a lot of hot sucking and fucking sessions.

However, he met online a forty-year-old man who lived at least three hours from him. Of course, our rendezvous did not end. We continued to enjoy hot fucking and sucking sessions for a while when the other guy was not in the picture, because, as I told, you he was hooked. He would drive all that way for the weekend, and they would spend the time together in a motel. I told you his mother had no idea what he was doing. It even got to the point that when he had a week or so break from school, the father-figure of his would come and spend that entire time in a motel with him. I asked him once if he had told him he was not a virgin. And he said, "Yes." During one of the days we met, he told me that when he turned sixteen, his daddy was going to adopt him and move the three hours away from where he lived. We conversed with one another on a chat site, but then he told me his daddy would be adopting him, so we would not be meeting.

I never heard from that stud again; I guess it was some consolation to me that I did not lose my teaching certification or job, since he had moved to another state. Of course, I do not think that mattered at all. He was just thrilled that he found a sexy man who wanted to have sex with a young stud like him—did I not say I had him hooked? Fortunately or unfortunately, that is the last young man that I ever had hot M2M sex with. Sometimes I wonder, "Are he and has daddy still together?" I spent the summer up where he lived with daddy, but needless to say, I did not try to track them down.

I was pretty much a slut in those days, always looking for a cock to suck and to fill my tight hole. I was on the college track team, and a buddy of mine was on the shot put team. Needless to say, he was very muscular. Danny was his name. Most muscular guys are a bit tiny in the cock department, but not Danny. A dishwater blond, with light fur on his chest and a thick, uncut cock and round beautiful orbs, filled with tasty cum.

This is probably when I developed a fascination with gingers! After practice, I always enjoyed showering with the team, lots of cocks swinging freely. Occasionally, the other teams would shower at the same time. That's when I saw Danny in all his naked glory. It seemed that he would always shower next to me, slowly and erotically soaping his cock and balls.

The first time we were together, when the teams had finished showering, Danny and I seemed to be the last ones around, alone in the showers. He soaped his cock and rolled his balls in his soapy hand. We both got hard. He stroked his cock, making his cockhead peek out of his foreskin. I wanted to get on my knees for him, but we could hear voices in the locker room.

He moaned slightly and began to cum on my leg. Stroke after stroke, releasing squirt after squirt of his warm, fresh, creamy cum. It was highly erotic, even though we had no real physical contact besides our wanting eyes. We did suck and fuck each other, but that was later and a different story.

I started out sucking cock when I was ten and swallowed precum and cum as soon as they were old enough to shoot. Then my friend's brother took my cherry on my fourteenth birthday. The first time it hurt a bit, but I wanted it the next day. The third time was when I was working to get him hard so I could ride him. I was fisted at nineteen, double penetrated at twenty-four, and double fisted the same day. I was more interested in getting the other guy off than myself and still am! I wish there was a cure for all my mobility issues.

My best friend and I met in Jr. High. We were both only children, but we became like real brothers. Due to that, we managed to stay away from jacking off with each other. But in high school, we got drunk one night, and he stayed over at my house. My parents were away. We just somehow got naked together. I was amazed at his gorgeous, huge cock. It was incredible—large head, long shaft, huge low-hangers. Dripping cum already. I took it into my hand, and then instinctively bent down and curled my tongue to catch the clear drop that was about to fall from his cockhead. I got it, then put my mouth on the cockhead and started to suck. I thought, "This is better than ice cream." I was addicted to ice cream and had to have it daily.

He pulled my head forward brutally, and I took as much of him in as I could. He was eight-plus inches, and it was beautiful trying to get him all down my throat. I damn near did because his penis curved just right to go down my throat. I sucked furiously and thought he would cum.

He suddenly pulled away, pushed me on the bed, and grabbed my cock. He jerked it furiously, and then sucked me deep; the feeling was incredible. Before I realized what happened, using my precum, he lubed his cockhead, turned me around on the end of the bed, and put his cock in my asshole. He shoved the head in. I screamed in pain, but he slowly went forward into me.

Deep. Deeper. I felt like I would cum any second, and the pain vanished. He stroked my prostate with his huge cock, slowly at first, but then he fucked me with a fury that was shocking to my whole body. I loved it. In just a few seconds, he said, "I'm gonna cum!" I felt splashes of the hot, thick fluid hitting my insides, and when it did, I was shocked to see myself spurting my own cum high into the air without even touching myself. It was glorious. We sucked each other clean. We rested, talked, and then went at it again. Everything had changed. We were closer than ever. And we enjoyed each other's cocks and balls and muscles and asses more than anything else. Even ice cream.

It was eleventh grade PE, and I was sitting out the 600 yard run because I had a huge headache. Coach came over and asked what my problem was, and I told him. Now, coach was what you'd call swarthy. He was about 6'2" and around 200 pounds. His dark hair was cut very short and his arms and legs were covered with the same dark hair. He was very well built with huge arms and thighs. One damn fine looking man in his white PE gear.

He asked me if I would mind his trying to help me get over my headache, and I answered, saying I'd appreciate anything to get rid of this hanging headache. Kneeling in back of me, he put his hands on the side of my head and started rubbing and pressing my skull. It felt fantastic, I have to tell you. After a bit, he let up on the pressure a little and touched my ears with the palms of his hands. I don't know why, but I sprung an erection almost immediately after he did this. I put my hands in my lap, hoping he wouldn't notice. He kept this up for a while until it was time for everyone to hit the showers. Since this was the last period of the day, I thanked him for his excellent help and decided to sit for a while longer. The locker room was nearly empty when I came in, and I was the last one in the showers. I took a long hot shower since it seemed to help the headache recede even more after coach's ministrations.

When I came out of the shower and wrapped a towel around my waist, I realized that the locker room had cleared out totally. Well, that is except for coach seated in a swivel chair in his office. As I walked by, he asked me about my headache, and if it was getting any better. I replied that it was getting better, but still hurt. He asked if I wanted him to work on it some more. Without hesitation, I told him I'd appreciate it a great deal. As I entered his office, he rolled himself out from behind the desk and faced me with his legs spread apart. When I sat down on the floor between his legs, my towel came loose from around my waist and totally exposed me. I didn't care because he'd seen us all naked in the showers, and this wasn't so far from that. Right away he started to massage my head, which felt fantastic. It wasn't long before he touched my ears again, and I popped another hard-on which he couldn't miss. He continued gently stroking my head and ears. Still not knowing what possessed me, I scooted around so I was facing him. We looked each other in the eye as I reached up, unsnapped his shorts, and started pulling his zipper down. We continued looking at each other as I fished around in his jock for his very hard cock. Coach raised his hips a little, and I pulled his shorts and jock down around his ankles. His cock was beautiful. It was about average compared to the guys I'd seen in the showers. I leaned over, kissed the top of his cockhead, and began licking all over his hot cock. He started moaning.

Not long after I started licking his cock, I rose up and put the head in my mouth, sucking on his hard helmet. Carrying on, I continued taking more and more of his throbbing cock into my mouth, all the time sucking like I had a piece of hard candy. Only once did I choke before I had engulfed all of his fine meat and rested my chin in his dark bush. His moaning got louder while I was sucking on him, and after a little bit he started pumping his swollen cock into my mouth. He was fucking my mouth. This was so erotic that I had to start jerking off my own hard cock that was leaking precum. After a few minutes of his fucking my sucking mouth, he grew even larger and harder, or so it seemed. His moans changed into very heavy breathing, and he was saying something I couldn't understand. However, I did understand him when he started saying he was going to cum.

He pumped faster, and I sucked harder as all of a sudden I felt shot after shot of hot liquid hitting the back of my throat. My sucking turned to swallowing. He had grabbed the back of my head and pounded his exploding cock into my mouth. This was too much for me to hold back any longer, and I shot a load of cum with fantastic force all over my face and chest.

After we came, we just sat there for a moment with his cock in my mouth until it started deflating, and I finally stopped sucking. When he pulled his cock out of my mouth, he leaned over, took my head in his hands again, and started licking all the cum from my face. Then he kissed me. I'd never felt a kiss like this one. He got up, pulled his jock and shorts up, and pushed the chair behind his desk. I got up and went back to the showers to get the cum out of the hair on my chest.
 We never said a word about this, nor did it ever happen again. Only two things changed. One was the way we looked at each other when we passed by, sharing a secret. The other was that I knew that I love men, and always will.

I had my first taste of dick when I was about thirteen. It was my fifteen-year-old cousin's big, fat, uncut cock. We were in bed one night, sleeping over at our grandmother's, and I "accidentally" backed my ass crack against his rock-hard cock while he slept. I wanted it real bad, and I think he did too. Over the course of the night, his arm ended up around me, eventually settling on my already hard meat. Electricity went through my body. His hand slipped down my pajama pants and began stroking my cock—even at that age I was precumming a river and about to blow when he stopped and whispered for me to roll over on my back and face him. After doing so, he pulled the waistband of his pj's down and a thick, six inch, uncut cock smacked up into his stomach. It was almost the size of a can of soda, even at his age.

He proceeded to slide that loose foreskin of his up and down, inch by inch, revealing his huge mushroom head, moaning about how good it felt, and asking if I jacked off. If not, he'd be happy to show me how. I was pretty well-versed in getting my rocks off by that time, and I suggested we beat off together, anything so he wouldn't stop working that dick of his. After a while, he said he admired my technique and if I wouldn't mind showing him my strokes on his dick. I was more than happy to oblige! He was squirming in no time and leaking precum like a faucet. He remarked on how good it felt, asking me to slow down, speed up, grip tighter, use both hands, cup his balls, and work his giant cock-head.

After a while he asked what I thought of his dick, saying, "This is what a real man looks like." I told him that his cock was fantastic, and I couldn't wait to see it cum. He said that if I kept up with what I was doing, I'd see fireworks soon enough! He then asked if I would sniff and lick the tip, if I wanted to. I didn't need anymore coaxing! He was moaning and asked if I could lick the head, get it wet, and suck on it "to get used to it." It felt like I had a plum in my mouth, warming his fat dick-head in my mouth, covered in spit. Then without warning, he pushed my head down to his crotch, making me gag on dick for my first time, all the way down the shaft, the fat fucker filling my throat and stretching it wide. But that didn't stop me. Coming up for air, I bobbed my head right back down, opening my mouth wider, sucking his fat cock harder, faster, breathing through my nose, and eyes watering.

About a minute later, his body stiffened, and he held my head down firm in his lap, growling, "shit, shit, shit," over and over, in time with the hot hard jets of cum that flooded my mouth. There was so much, so fast, oozing out of my mouth, into his hairy crotch, streaking down his balls, cock throbbing slowly, until there was no cum left. I rolled off his softening but still huge cock and beat out the biggest load and most intense orgasm I had ever had up to that point in my life. Needless to say, we got together for sleepovers as often as we could after that! He's married with kids now, of course.

Just thought I'd share a quick story. I was fourteen or so and my cousin who was also a great friend was sixteen. He was half a head taller than me and weighed about thirty pounds more than me. We did all kinds of fun activities together. One evening both sets of parents went out to dinner, leaving us alone. We had something to eat and were watching a wrestling show.

All of a sudden my cousin says, "Why don't we wrestle?" I thought it would be great fun. We stripped down to our briefs and began. We wrestled for about half an hour to forty-five minutes, and I was getting tired. So we agreed one more time and, of course, he pinned me with his upper body across my chest and one of my legs between his. I struggled, but he wouldn't let me up. He began to lightly caress my tummy, and soon I started getting hard. He reached down and played with my erection through my briefs. I struggled, but he wouldn't let me up. Soon he pushed my briefs down and began to gently stroke my cock. I struggled and fought, but he just laughed and kept playing with my cock. Sometimes, he lightly caressed my balls and other times stroked my cock. This went on for some time. Since I had been masturbating for several years, I knew what the eventual outcome was going to be. He kept playing with me, and soon the pleasure took over and I just relaxed. He was really good, teasing me, but then he went to end it and stroked me. I closed my eyes, and soon I hit the point of no return. That instant I felt the exquisite pleasure, and I came. My legs lifted up off the floor, the pleasure was so intense.

He got off me and then said, "Your turn." He pulled his briefs down, and I saw that beautiful erection. I gently reached out and began to stroke him. I did what he had done, and soon he was moaning. Then he came. It was such fun and so erotic to know that I had given him so much pleasure. I watched the pearly colored cum squirt out of his cock, and I thought it was just amazingly beautiful. We both giggled when done, and from that time on for the next six years we wrestled every chance we had. Our wrestling moved beyond hand jobs, and it was always thrilling.

I have lived in the great cornfields of the mid-west all of my life. I started playing around with other guys at a very young age and quickly became addicted to cock. One thing about cornfields—they provided an immense, private playground for guys like us who found so much pleasure in our cocks. Being country boys, we had access to the fields, barns, and plenty of surrounding forest area, not to mention the nearby creek and farm ponds that gave us lots of opportunities for skinny dipping. Skinny dipping was always fun because you could be naked with other guys, and the only way anyone would see your hard-on was if they were under water. That way, if a local farmer happened by, our throbbing dicks could easily be hidden under water until they went soft—although that was sometimes a challenge.

Rich's grandparents were our neighbors. Rich came out to visit his grandparents a lot, and since he and I were the same age, we hung out whenever he was around. He started telling me tales of his adventures involving guys he went to school with in the city. Just listening to him talk about groups of guys having sleep-overs and their taking turns sucking each other's cocks all night long certainly caught my interest! Even as a young kid, I knew I was attracted to other guys. I was infatuated with some of the girls, thinking I actually had a crush on them. But the stirrings inside when I was around another guy were completely different. It was like nothing else I had ever experienced, and certainly did not compare with feelings I had for the girl crushes back then.

Rich was the first guy with whom I experimented. We hugged, we kissed, we ground our cocks together through our pants. That didn't last long, though, before the clothes came off. Always within five minutes of his arrival at his grandparents', we were off somewhere naked together—kissing, rubbing naked bodies together, sucking—and Rich loved to rub his cock against the crack of my ass. He never mentioned, and I never thought, that it would be anything sexually exciting for either of us to slide our cocks into each other's ass. We both knew it felt good around the outside. But we were both still quite young and neither really knew anything of sex except for what we found while experimenting. In retrospect, I sure do wish one of us had heard about fucking. It was just something that had not entered either of our minds.

We would play around as soon as he arrived, then we would play around again as soon as one of us rebounded enough to cum again. At that young age, we each pretty much had a perpetual hard-on, so it was never an issue about the number of times we could both cum together. It was not unusual for us to have some pretty intense play three or four times during his visit. We knew we had to be very careful and be visible if anyone came looking for us. We knew we could not hole-up somewhere for long, because there were always others around. If we disappeared together, too often for too long, it might arouse suspicions. We were young, but we knew that what we were doing could spell disaster if the wrong person caught us.

Playing with Rich got me wondering if any of my other hot buds would be interested in this sort of play. It usually never took much more than having a conversation about sex to get both me and the guy I was talking with to pop wood. We would start talking about masturbating and different methods of jacking our cocks. One thing would always lead to another until we would be jacking together. I was probably the source of many of my buds' first blowjobs. Pity the poor woman who had to follow my blowjob, because—as several of buddies have told me since—no woman could suck a dick like I could! We used to have group campouts where we would pair up, sharing one sleeping bag. There was always lots of hot moaning around the campfire! Sometimes we'd swap sleeping bag mates in the middle of the night. We camped out enough that we all got to sleep with each other numerous times. This continued on a very regular basis until I graduated from high school and left for college.

Student

I always love to hear about other guys' introductions to M2M sex.

While I have written a couple of stories of things that are pretty much true about things that have happened to me, this one is what happened to me with my first love in high school. I grew up in a military family with an extremely harsh and abusive father from the south as well as a mother who worked a great deal to make up for the things he didn't provide for. We lived in a place outside of San Diego that was originally designed as an upper-class, senior citizens' town with a great deal of Hollywood elite get-away homes. Middle class and children were definitely not welcomed there. During the 70s, gays were clearly not wanted, and being in the family I was in with five children I was terrified to be found out. So I pretended and played the game of being straight, although I never had sex with the few girls I dated until I was nineteen, and then only twice. Even then thinking to myself, "What is the big deal?"

I always knew I was attracted to men, got hard very easily around them, was terrified about having to be in gym, and was overjoyed when I found out that I was allergic to grass and couldn't take gym. I was forced to attend the special class for gym, which meant that I didn't have to shower with everyone else. The only things we did were things like archery, bowling, or things where you didn't sweat at all. But I still got hard looking at the hard bodies in their shorts and with their shirts off. I was overweight as a defense mechanism to keep the girls away, but still got hit on by older men. So I went out for the clubs that used my mind, like business clubs and classes, and did very well in them.

In my junior year, I was eighteen and decided to lose weight and run for a state office in the business club I was in. Well, I didn't get the office. On Saturday night after the banquet at a hotel in Santa Barbara, I went for a walk on the beach to have a cigarette. I changed into shorts, took off my shoes, and was walking when an older man in a bikini asked me for cigarette. He was actually about thirty-five and had been drinking. I gave him one, and he fell into me as he took it. Being as naive as I was I didn't realize what he was doing. I told him he might need some help and he said probably, and asked if I would help. I agreed, so he put his arm around my waist, and I put my arm around his. We started to walk again, and he asked me why I was there. Suddenly, I felt his hand moving up and down my side as he said what a nice night it was, and how nice it would be to swim in the ocean naked. I then got the hint. I had been hard for quite a while already since I had never been this close to a man before, and he was very good-looking. He was dark and hairy and in a bikini, and since he was talking that way and feeling me I started to feel him, and I dared and put my fingers in his suit.

He suggested we sit on the beach for a while, so we did. We sat close, and he put his hand on my leg. We talked about the warm wind, and he said I needed to take off my shirt and feel the breeze. So I did. He told me I had a real nice body and ran his hands over it, paying real close attention to my nipples. I couldn't help letting out a small moan as he did so. He asked if it felt good and I said yes, and he said it was supposed to. He pinched them. I really moaned as he sucked them, and then he started to undo my shorts. I just lay back on the beach and let him take my shorts off as well as my underwear. He took off his bikini, and he kissed me. His hands were all over me. He lay on top of me as he spread my legs and began to work his way down. He sucked me and swallowed my cock and my cum, and then began to fuck my ass. He took my virginity on the beach. He then got up and left.

Not long after that, my best friend, Rick, and I were out drinking in his father's orange grove one night. We were pretty drunk. I stood by the side of the car, and as he opened the door he asked me who it was that I had fucked on the beach in Santa Barbara. I almost choked right then and there. As I climbed into the car, he said someone saw me, but that I was so far away they couldn't see if it was a man or a woman. Now, Rick was the all-American kid, blond, blue-eyed, quarterback of the football team and going with a girl I had set him up with. It shocked me that anyone had seen me. He was originally a friend of my brother's, but they had a falling out while we had stayed friends. Well, we kept drinking and really got drunk. He kept talking about it, and the later it got the more intense it got. I got out of the car to take a piss, and all of a sudden he was standing there beside me, which was strange as guys never did this. It was a "queer" thing to do, but all of a sudden here was the quarterback standing next to me as I pissed, and he was holding his cock also, watching me piss. He finished before I did, but didn't put his cock away. He said, "You have a nice dick," and reached over for it. I just stood there, looking at him in shock for a few seconds, when he asked me if I wanted to touch him. I took his cock, and both of us were hard in an instant. He said he knew I was gay and had hoped I was, which is why he wanted me to set him up with the girl he was with. It meant he could be closer to me. He was bi.

He had a blanket in the trunk, so we took off our clothes, and I saw that beautiful hard, hard body I had wanted for three years. I held him as we kissed. He ran his hands over me. I touched him, felt his cock and ass, and he probed mine. We sucked each other, licked each other's balls, sucked nipples, rimmed, and he fucked me three times that night. We fell asleep in the back seat of the car and awoke at dawn in each other's arms. We had sex again before we went home. We were lovers for three years. Often times, he would leave a date and come to me so we could have a second date to fulfill our secret desires.

It took an older man to open my mind to a world of the pleasures of gay sex and secret and forbidden love that fulfilled me at the beginning of my life.

My cousin and I were only a month apart in age. We had a good time growing up together. We played cowboys, army, and Robin Hood outside when the weather was good and when not so good we played those same things down in the basement. There was an old, converted couch down in the basement, which meant that the back could be lowered and turned into a bed. We were about twelve years of age when one day we had the couch open, and we started wrestling. We were pretty evenly matched with his pinning me sometimes and my pinning him other times.

One day, everything changed for us. He pinned me on my back, but instead of letting me up so we could resume he began to rub the front of my pants. Immediately, I got hard. I began to struggle for him to let me up. Then he unzipped my pants, unsnapped my jeans, and pulled my pants down to my knees. I struggled but just couldn't get him off me. I didn't want to yell for help because I did not want us to get in trouble from parents or aunt and uncle. As I struggled, he started to stroke me. I struggled, but he had me pinned down. Soon his stroking felt simply amazing.

Now, I had masturbated many times before, but it was intensely different with him doing it. Soon he was having his way with me. He let me go, but I didn't move as he stroked my erection and played with my balls. It felt so good, so soothing. He kept it up until I squirted a large load of cum all over my chest. I cleaned myself up, and then we began round two. This time, I won and proceeded to remove his pants. His cock was hard and bigger than mine. I began to stroke and lightly caress it. I played with his balls and stroked his cock. Soon he shot his load all over himself. He lay there, like I had before, almost motionless. After a while, he cleaned himself up, and we went back to playing cowboys and Indians. That was only the beginning, and every time after that, when we got together we wrestled to our hearts' content, sometimes having four or more bouts in the same afternoon. I look back on those times with a smile on my face and a hard-on in my pants. As time passed, we went on to other explorations which also were intense.

This is one of many stories of how I got into M2M. My freshman year at college, I had to live in an all-male dorm, which was fine by me! It was hot, humid, and August in the South. I quickly learned that the roof was the place to be. Guys were going up there to sunbathe nude. So I had to check it out. I didn't have a class till 11:00 am, so I grabbed a towel and took a chance. There were four guys, all naked, one on his back with his fat, limp cock lying across his leg. The other three were on their stomachs. All had great asses, but one in particular had his legs spread, and you could almost see his hole thru his sparse hair.

I oiled up a little and lay down. Soon three of them had to shower before class. I was left alone with the guy with the fat cock. We chatted a little, and he asked if I could rub some oil on his back. Of course I could! I rubbed him down and asked how far he wanted me to rub. He said he would tell me when to stop. I got to his hard muscled orbs and he opened his legs. He had not said to stop so I began to rub his tight butt. He moaned as I kept kneading his cheeks. I could see his pink hole thru his hair. I began to rub his crack as he moaned louder and arched his back. I gently rubbed his hole, and then put a finger in that tight manhole. I was hard and dripping by this time. He rolled onto his back to show me his hard cock. Six inches but very thick, with precum glistening on the cut head. He asked if I liked cock, and without answering, I took him in my mouth. I was working his greasy hole with two fingers as I sucked him and tasted his sweet precum. Before he could shoot me a load, we heard some guys coming up the stairs. We both lay on our bellies to hide our stiff dicks. We didn't get to finish our playtime that day, but we had many good times after that. But that is another story for another time.

My best friend from middle school showed me how to cum. When I did cum that first time I thought something was terribly wrong, that I was going to explode with piss all over my bed. He taught me to keep jacking and just let that feeling happen. He was so right, and he even put his mouth over my cock crown to lap up my thirteen-year-old cum.

Student

This began a relationship between us that lasted for many years. He and I had paper routes in Seattle; this was in the 60s. After each delivery was done we'd go to his house or mine, shut the bedroom door and have sex. We started out mostly oral, but graduated to hugging and kissing, 69, and then anal. Blessed anal sex. I love being fucked well. But we were young, so getting off was the goal then. But over time we learned to take our time so as to have really good orgasms and ejaculations. Edging was a learned tactic to really enjoy sex.

This lasted into high school and by then we were steady boyfriends. Not out in any sense, but friends with benefits. We had sex at least once a day and sometimes more. We experimented with different lubes to help things along. We even had sex while hiking in the mountains and snowshoeing. It was great to have sex in the outdoors with full sun. It was a thrill. We were quite unafraid and probably reckless. But we had good and quite great sex.

In high school, we began to find other partners. We'd compare notes on different guys, and then increase our efforts together for more perfect sex. We even traded guys if we found someone who was particularly good. Many of these guys were frustrated—like we had been trying to get into a girl's panties. We just opted for guys because they are easier to bed. Way easier.

In college (1970-74), I was amazed at how many guys were open to M2M sex. I mean they were everywhere. By the time I started as a freshman, I'd probably had had at least 150 guys; that number easily doubled in my four years on the college campus. Heck, sex was always on a guy's mind; erections were steel hard and easy, and guys had holes that they wanted fucked. I was a top back then. I am mostly a bottom now, though way less active—way less. Married with grown kids has changed my priorities. Spent many years in the USAF and found the same thing. Many guys open to M2M action. Again, I was surprised at the number. I think there are many more cocksuckers out there than any of the studies show.

The first time I tasted cum was when I was nine. He was thirty and asleep. We were sharing the same sleeping bag. I woke up with his hard cock in my hand. I had never felt a cock before, let alone a hard cock. I slowly got down into the sleeping bag and pulled his cock out of his pj's. It was like an instinct. I just started sucking his cock, and then I felt a huge rush of sperm gushing into my mouth which made me swallow and swallow.

I didn't know what to do next when I heard him say that was good. That was the beginning of a ten-year cocksucking fulfillment until I when away to college.

My sex story is pretty amazing. I was in college and during frat week one of the upperclassmen came by my dorm room and told me he liked what I had to offer the fraternity. I, of course, told him I was happy to be considered. He said there was a sure-fire way for me to get brotherhood. He reached down, opened up his jeans, and showed me his cock. He told me it was simple. Get on my knees, open my mouth, suck him off, and then take his big love of creamy spunk in my mouth. Well, I agreed since I am bi, and down I went. He had a great cock but more than that, tons of precum. He face fucked me, and then dropped a thick load of sperm in my mouth. He smiled, kissed me, and told me to swallow or be kicked out of contention. Needless to say, I was in the fraternity, and we met several times after that. To this day we are still friends.

When I was a junior in high school, a fellow classmate kept bragging that he could get a group of us into a friend's house during lunch to watch porn videos. Every day he would brag about this. One day, I told him I didn't believe him. He said that he would check with the owner of the house and see if a group of us could go there during our lunch period.

The next day, everyone else had chickened out and didn't show up at his locker. I was the only one that went. We got in this car, and he drove to the house. He found the key under the mat where the owner told him he'd place it, and we went in.

We went upstairs to the owner's bedroom, and my classmate turned on the television and the VCR. On the screen flashed some straight porn. I wasn't into the woman but was very interested in watching the guys. As my friend was rubbing his cock through his pants, he asked me if I'd every jacked off with another guy. I told him I hadn't. He slowly unzipped his pants and dug out the biggest cock I'd ever seen. It was huge and dripping. He walked over to me and told me to jack it.

I grabbed hold of his cock and gave it a few jerks. He then unzipped my pants and pushed them down around my ankles. He then started to give me a blowjob. He slowly sucked my cock deep into his mouth. When my cock was wet, he pushed me on my back onto the bed. He crawled up and sat on my cock. I didn't even know that guys did that with each other. How did that go up his ass, I wondered? He rode my cock until he shot his load all over my chest. As he climbed off my cock, I shot my load. He bent down and licked it.

As we were cleaning up, he said, "Tomorrow it's your turn. I'm going to bust your cherry butt." I wondered how in hell I would ever take his cock up my ass. I was nervous and scared all at the same time. The next day, he delivered on his promise. I've been craving cock since that day.

Carson V. was exceptional in every way. He was the very personification of ethereal. Handsome, wealthy, intelligent, kind, and generous, he was adored by everyone at the small midwestern college I attended as a young man. Carson—great name, huh? Carson had the face of an angel, lantern jawed, soft brown eyes, perfect nose, full rich mouth—all framed by blond, curling hair. His father was the dean of students, from a well-connected East coast family that found itself now ensconced in Iowa, of all places. He was, to my surprise, always kind and solicitous to me, always acknowledged me when he was with his buddies, and never failed to make me feel good about myself.

In the winter of 1971, I was placed in charge of a group of students who were studying art, music, history, and science for a semester in Europe. We had a professor who accompanied us, who was fond of a wide array of bars in London, Paris, Antwerp, Rome, and Amsterdam. He thus left the mechanics of the tour to me. As the head student, I was granted my own room in each hotel, a luxury I appreciated very much. Carson had to share rooms with four other boys, jostling for the best bed and time in the cramped, out-of-date bathrooms.

Amsterdam was exciting, naughty, and icy cold. The very sheets on the bed seemed to hold the damp and frigid temperatures. We constantly snuggled up against the cold, inside and out. That was why one evening, after dinner, I was shocked to see Carson at my door, dressed in a tight pair of cloth shorts. He seemed oblivious to the weather. I saw him for the first time without a shirt or long pants—fine-cut chest, amazing abs, exceptional legs, wonderful forearms and biceps. Even his toes were perfect. He had shoulders for days. Occupied with journaling the day's events, I was irritated at the disturbance, wondering why he didn't join the other students with the professor to bar hop in the wild city of canals.

After exchanging a few preliminaries, he moved into the room from the hall, and then closed the door. He moved over behind me and put his hands on my shoulders while he asked, "Do you never relax? Why are you always working?"

"Why aren't you with the others?" I asked in return, not really answering him. He patted my shoulders, then moved over to my bed.

"May I?" he said, gesturing to it.

I nodded and watched as he sat upright with my pillows at his back, legs spread. He talked of nothing in particular, but my attention was soon riveted to the obvious bulge of his left testicle, which was bursting from the short leg of his cut-offs. With every movement, more and more of that luscious, egg-sized bit of him came into view, big, thick and meaty. I tried to be cool and not stare, but my gaze centered on that incredible nut sack.

"Like what you see?" His comment came out of the blue, without warning. I was caught staring at his crotch, my growing hard-on getting difficult to conceal. Quickly, I looked away and tried to mutter an apology. Carson merely smiled and adjusting the leg of his shorts once again, drew out both testicles, magnificent and hanging down between his legs like two avocados in a silken sack. My mouth fell open at the sight.

"Word is on campus you've got a big dick for a little guy," he said. Let's compare." With that, he unbuttoned and unzipped his shorts and pulled them off. His erection was solid and thick, a good average circumcised cock rising above two magnificent, oversized balls. He got up, walked over to me and gently pulled me from my chair. He smelled of fresh soap and just a hint of cologne mixed with his own scent. Somehow it made me drop all of my defenses, as he slowly drew close, brought me into his arms and embraced me. I could feel that hard, gorgeous body against my own.

"Wow, you *are* big!" he commented, grabbing my own hard cock through my clothes. He began to kiss me as he undressed me. He seemed expert at what to do. The geek and the stud, I kept telling myself. Why on earth would this god condescend to even look at me let alone have sex with me or even think of me in that way. I had no words, but merely let him lead the proceedings until I felt confident enough to respond in kind.

He wanted to be fucked. Luckily, I knew what to do and did it well, having learned the previous summer at construction work exactly what to do. He got off three times, soaking my sheets each time with his thick, white cum, the loads diminishing in size with each volley. I enjoyed fondling his balls, which turned him on more than cock or ass play. To this day a good pair of nuts is a definite turn-on for me.

"I so envy your balls!" I said between encounters. Their size was so big I could scarcely get one in my mouth.

"I envy your big cock. It looks so big because you are so small in body," he commented. "If you only knew what you have to offer," he smiled. "You need to let people get to know you better. You don't always need to hide."

Carson and I became good but discreet friends. After graduation, we parted and never saw one another again. But the memories are clear and sweet. I carry him still in my "Journal of Personal Encounters," a catalogue of sexual experiences that remind me that we all have something to offer, even a geek to a god—and vice versa.

My cousin's name was Freddy. He was a very sweet, gentle, and handsome guy. I guess we were both about twelve or thirteen years old in the early 60s. I fell in love with him back then, and I was always so very happy when his parents visited my parents, usually once a month or more. Well, at first, neither one of our parents discovered us lying, hugging, touching, kissing, and arousing together on the couch in my parent's house. These were very strong emotions, lots of romance in my mind, so definitely an emotional and a physical relationship. He knew more about kissing men, etc., and I learned from him. He was the more active partner, and I loved being excited by him. I felt a very strong bond.

But sadly, after we were discovered, his parents never again brought Freddy to visit. I really missed him, and I did not know what to do about my erotic lusts and attraction for men. So I guess that put me in the closet for high school. Then I married a woman I loved, and still love to this day. Later, she initiated a divorce for other reasons.

But the attraction and desire for a male partner and gay sex was always a part of me that I thought I had under control, but a few times I did lose that control. Memories of hot, pleasurable, and loving times with Freddy were pushed back but never forgotten. Finally, in the early 1980s when I got divorced, I decided I needed to check out my gay yearnings. I wanted to be sure of my sexuality before committing myself to a new relationship.

Well, I did not see Freddy again until about thirty years after we had been separated from our boyhood relationship. Freddy was still so sweet and beautiful. I introduced him to my first gay partner in the early 1990s. Sadly, Freddy got infected with HIV by his former partner, and he died from AIDS about two years later. At that time, the HIV drugs were not very good and sometimes were toxic as well. His friends told me after his funeral that he was so glad I was his cousin and proud of my accomplishments. He was Mister Sweetness. I still miss him, and always will.

For the rest of the day I couldn't think of anything but my time with this really hot buddy of mine. He sure was fucking hot that morning, so the debate in my mind was, "Should I go back to his place later that night or not?" Here I was, an eighteen-year-old kid, (I'm sixty-nine now) and knew very little about sex, whether with a woman or a man. At the time, I believed it wasn't right for two men to have sex, but it sure felt good. I drove home, showered, ate, and then told my folks that I was going out to a club for a while. I drove back to the man's condo. I got to his place and sat in the lot for fifteen minutes, deciding whether to go in or not. I finally decided to go in.

He greeted me at the door and said he didn't know if I would ever come back, but he was happy I did. We talked for a while, and he told he was bi and enjoyed both me and women. That was very reassuring to me because I did like women. After talking for a while he invited me to his bedroom. I was already hard. I helped him turn down the bed; we both undressed, and got in. We chatted for a bit, lightly caressing each other, and then he kissed me. Unlike earlier when I felt awkward, this really felt right. We both got into it, and the kiss lasted for a long time, our tongues darting in and out of each other's mouths.

He began to kiss my face, ear, neck, and shoulders. As he kissed his way down, he licked my nipples. You start on my nipples and I'm yours. He began to stroke my cock and play with my balls. Then he came back up and kissed me, and I returned the favor. I kissed him, licked his nipples, and stroked his cock. It was such fun to watch him react and to see his cock jump as I pleased him. It made me feel good to know that I could make him feel that good. I came back up, and we kissed and caressed. It was very hot. Then he kissed his way down my body between my legs and began to please me orally. He ran his tongue up and down my cock from base to tip. He would squeeze it, and when a drop of precum would appear, he licked it. As he sucked and licked, he began to play with my balls. I'm not sure where or when he did it, but he got some lube on his finger and as he sucked me he pressed his finger into my asshole. At first, I tensed up, but the more he sucked and the more he applied gentle pressure, I felt good with it.

He sucked and fucked my asshole with his finger. It felt so good, and then he looked up and said, "You are doing great. You have two fingers in you now." I was shocked. I didn't know when he slipped the second finger in, but it felt good. He went on licking, sucking, and fucking. He could sense when I was cumming, and then he would back off and then start again, only to back off. I discovered years later that this was called edging. Well, he was a master at it. He then looked up and said, "I'd like to fuck you. But I don't want to force you." He kept sliding his fingers in and out of me as we talked. He told me he would be gentle, and if it hurt he would stop. He did tell me it would feel uncomfortable at the beginning but that it would feel better. I finally said, "Ok, let's try." This was long before HIV so he rode me bareback.

He lubed up his cock; thankfully, he wasn't hung. Then he lubed my asshole again. He told me to pull my legs up and rest them on his shoulders. I did. I felt his cockhead press into me. He was very gentle with me and did not want to hurt me. Little by little, until he was all the way in. Once in, I rest my feet on his shoulders, and he didn't move. He just wanted me to get accustomed to his cock. He was right; it did feel a bit uncomfortable, kind of like a burn, but soon that went away. He then began to move in and out. Very slowly, and it began to feel good, very good. I just never knew what I had been missing.

He fucked me long and deep, and then he began to speed up. Finally, he yelled, "Fuck," and he came. He stopped thrusting and pulled out. He lay down between my legs and began to fuck my ass with his fingers as he sucked me. It felt totally and completely amazing. I was so hot that it took only a little while and I came. It felt like an out of body experience. It was simply awesome. He lay down next to me, and we just lay in each other's arms. I met with him several more times until I went back to college. He was a great guy, and I appreciated him.

Student

I got married several years later, but always had the yen to be with a guy again. About forty years later, I had my chance.

TRAVEL

In Louvain, Belgium, there is a Roman Catholic seminary, which operated under the auspices of the United States Conference of Catholic Bishops. Much against the will of my parents, I determined upon a vocation as a Roman Catholic priest with a career in the Diplomatic Corps because of my interest in languages. I entered as a novice at the school in Louvain, Belgium. Since my French was perfect, I advanced quickly in the curriculum and was a star pupil in the classroom.

Poverty and Obedience were relatively easy for me. But chastity in all things—thought, word, and deed—that was another matter. My body could not lie nor fool anyone. My erection seemed to be permanent. There was no time or opportunity to jerk off. In short, I was horny as hell but equally trying to suppress my sexual nature. "Keep busy and pray hard," I was admonished from the confessional.

The extreme conditions were to mold us into beings whose sexual responses needed to be constantly suppressed and forgotten. The only other novice who seemed to suffer from a similar lack of focus was a young man from Germany, Klaus. In the showers, I couldn't help but notice his average but very thick erection and amazing low hangers. His penis was so thick he couldn't possibly wrap his fist around it and close the fingers together. It was incredibly hot. We would steal glances at one another but were never allowed to speak.

Because of my excellent marks and strong work ethic, I was rewarded in November—after four months of enforced chastity—to a weekend in Bruxelles (Brussels). A further plus was to learn that my companion in scholarly success was none other than Klaus. At last we would get to meet and talk. We were given a room together in an annex of the Bishop's Palace, and, of course, one of the priests from the school as a chaperon. We would dine with the Bishop on Saturday and attend a performance of Wagner's *Siegfried* that same evening. Evening clothes were rented for us for both the dinner and the opera.

We returned to our rooms, the chaperon still with us. But shortly after midnight, he quietly left to attend services, closing the door silently behind him and assuming we were both fast asleep. Seconds later, Klaus was in my bed, flicking on the night-light and pulling off his pajamas. I quickly followed his lead. We knew we had a little less than an hour, so we went straight to play, fondling, stroking, jerking, licking, and kissing every part of each other's bodies. His cockhead was so thick and so mushroom-like that I could not take it all in my mouth. He quivered as I licked his shaft and those massive balls. The more I squeezed and fondled them, the more passionate he grew. He told me he loved my long thick dick—not as thick as his, however. His body was beautiful, firm, and well proportioned.

He delighted in the fact that I could suck my own cock. He beat his meat loudly, the balls bouncing against his hand, as I threw my legs up near my head and took my dick head into my mouth. He was kneeling before my ass, taking in the view of hole, balls, and cock in my mouth as he wanked his thick, pulsating member. I could almost see the veins pop as he approached his orgasm.

He spent in several thick ropes of cum, trying hard not to make too much noise as he climaxed. Big pools of his spooge splashed on my ass, my hands, and my legs. It seemed to dance around us as it fell here and there. I could feel my own orgasm building to an incredible level. Sucking wildly on my own dick, I pulled it out to watch the bursts of cum. The first splashed onto my face, causing Klaus to howl softly in delight. I brought my legs back down as I continued to shoot, most of the blasts going completely over my head and hitting the wall behind the bed. It felt as though I would never stop; I think there were about fourteen or fifteen, each one slightly diminishing after the other.

Klaus collapsed on top of me, laughing softly. We drifted off into a calm and relaxing sleep, enfolded in each other's arms and forgetting everything in the aftermath of our pleasure. That is how our chaperon found us a few hours later. We were expelled on the spot and had to find our own way home.

Knowing what I know now, I still think I would have made a good priest. I often wonder if Klaus recovered; it took me awhile to fall back into a layman's life myself. We gave each other a delightful last night in the seminary to remember for years to come.

After an intensive week touring Israel with a group, I broke and went on my own to Egypt, and, among other things, wandered the back streets of Cairo and Luxor. It is a land of beautiful olive skin, dark hair, slim men. On a number of occasions, one of these men approached me and asked where I was from, was I married, did I have a girlfriend, and then did I have a boyfriend? After saying yes they would say let's talk, have tea. After talking about life issues there and in the US, it would turn to sex. That led us to a place on a boat, my hotel, or a very dark corner of a park where I would suck them off.

The best was when a really hot guy took me to the roof of a hotel where he worked. He made sure I knew that he was not gay and that this was against his religion before taking off his shirt and opening his pants, revealing a beautiful and long cock. At one point while sucking him, he asked to see my cock. He felt it, and then, not really sucking, put his mouth on it. I went back to sucking him and soon received one of the biggest loads of cum ever, after which I shot all over the floor. The experience was really hot itself, but the feel of being in this exotic and clandestine location heightened it beyond amazing.

My story is a bit of an old one. When I was a student in London, I went to the movies as often as I could. During one particularly long film, I was getting restless in my seat, shifting weight from side to side wasn't really helping. The seat next to me was vacant, so I swung my legs over the armrest and sat that way for a bit, quite comfortably actually. About five minutes later, I was horrified when something moved under my legs. The moviegoer one seat over had already done the same and now my legs were on top of his. Jeez, I started to think quickly. Why didn't he say something right away, or move, or give some sign that he was already there. There was only one answer—he liked it. Wow, that was quite something to imagine.

A few minutes later, I swung my legs back in front of me, and he took that opportunity to shift seats to be next to me. We let our hands wander around in the darkness until the movie was over, and then we went outside so that I could get a good look at him. Damn, he was about my age—twenty—and really hot. There seemed to be only one thing to do, take him home and fuck like bunnies. It was also the early 80s so both of us ended up well seeded that night! Never saw him again, but I do think about it and, of course, it hasn't been repeated in the hundreds of films I must have seen since!

One of the hottest weeks of my life was several years ago when I decided to go to a clothing-optional gay week at an all-inclusive resort in the Dominican Republic. The resort was absolute paradise! And having 120 men romping around naked on the beaches, well it doesn't get any better than that! Most of the time the resort functioned as a straight swingers' sex club. But this was gay week so it was all cock—no pussies allowed. I also went to this resort to take part in a "Celebrating the Body Erotic" workshop presented by The Body Electric School that took place during the first two days of the gay outing. The Body Electric workshop experience was mind-blowing and life changing!

The very first day of the workshop, I was immediately attracted to a cute guy from New York. The feeling was mutual, and we kept checking each other out and flirting throughout the workshop. He was a wild, crazy blond with a beautiful thick cock and nice hanging balls. He was smaller framed—about my size—so his impressive bulging package really stood out. I'm sure my eyes kept drifting down to his crotch every time we talked during the breaks. I couldn't keep my eyes off his gorgeous tool! As soon as the first day of the workshop ended, we were all over each other, and we started fooling around in the swimming pool, kissing passionately and sucking and rimming each other. It was so hot and intense! Being naked together in such a beautiful paradise resort just fueled the fire!

The next day after the workshop was over, we headed to the beach for more fun, and we discovered several beautiful four-poster beds with draperies blowing in the breezes. It was sheer fantasy! We quickly claimed the last bed on the beach, and this became our playpen for the next few days. I loved sucking his big thick cock and we 69ed for hours, exploring each other's bodies and cocks and asses. We kept edging each other and not cumming for long periods of time so we could make it last. All concept of time seemed to disappear. At one point during our playtime, things took an interesting turn. I'm not sure how it happened, but he suddenly started taking charge and playing a dominant role. His voice changed as he took full command of me.

He started slapping me with his hard cock and rubbing it in my face. I was so turned on; I was leaking lots of precum, which he would take with his fingers and force feed to me. He started slapping my hard cock and my ass, and pinching and twisting my nipples. I had not done any role playing before but, surprisingly, I was not scared and found myself naturally falling into the sub role. It was an incredibly erotic feeling that surged through my entire body as he manhandled me. At one point, he told me to lie still, and he grabbed some of the draperies from the four-poster bed and tied my hands to the upper bedposts. He then proceeded to tie each of my legs to the bottom two posts. I was totally and completely naked and vulnerable to his wants and needs and commands—and I was hard as a rock! One of the most erotic experiences of my life!

At one point, he forced me to lower my head over the end of the bed, and he started jamming his huge meat down my throat. It was then that I discovered we had an audience! We were so into playing out this hot Dom/Sub fantasy that neither of us noticed there were about six other naked guys discreetly watching us and stroking their cocks as they watched. That only made the fantasy hotter of course! We ended up sleeping most of the night naked together on our beach bed in each other's arms. This was many years ago, but I still have vivid memories like it was yesterday. I've only role played a few times since then, and I've discovered that I like both the Dom and the Sub roles. Life's an adventure…and this was one of my hottest ones!

I travel for business. This time I arrived in Puerto Rico and from the shuttle I noticed a good-looking, white, skinny man with curly black hair—my age or so. When I checked in, he was behind me in line. We made small talk, and he told me he was there for a few days of RandR. I told him I was there for a little business and would have every afternoon free. So he said, "Maybe we will be beer buddies." I smiled and said maybe we would.

That evening I went to the bar to have dinner, and he was there. He had just had a salad, and we shared a few beers. We watched Sunday Night Football. Around 10:00 pm and four beers later, I said I was tired and that I'd watch the fourth quarter in my room. He said he'd do this as well. I did not realize that he meant he would watch it in my room instead of his own.

We took the elevator, and we both exited on the same floor; I did not make anything of it. I walked to my room, and he followed me. I asked if he was on the same floor, and he said he was on a different floor. We both laughed, and he quickly asked if there were two beds in my room and if I would mind if he watched the game there too. I said no problem, come in. He came in, and we each took one bed. We made small talk, and when I said the flight had me stressed out, he offered me a back rub. I am a sucker for back rubs.

He started and quickly asked if I had body lotion. I did, so he asked me to remove my shirt. One thing led to another. We were naked and having sex. We heard the final score of the game with heavy breathing and his coming on my chest. We spent every single evening and night together after that first one. We joked that one of us should have cancelled his room. On top of everything, we both had the same flight back to Miami. You better believe I saw him a few more times in Miami.

Travel

I've written before about exploits when I am in Brazil for work. So this happened yesterday, and it turned out it was a blond, blue-eyed Dutch man rather than my usual favorite—tall, dark, and handsome.

I had an off day, and decided to read and sleep by the resort pool. Winter in the US but warm, and sunny in Brazil! Not crowded as it was on a weekday. I smiled and gave a nod to the young, blond guy (Jon) standing in the pool. He gave a little wave as he ruffled the water out of his hair. He had a slight build, tight muscles, and beautiful, big, pink nipples. As he walked up the steps out of the water, I couldn't tell dick size because he had on baggy board shorts. He had a beautiful treasure trail of dark blond hair on his belly and his back, leading to his waistband above his perky muscular ass. His lips were full and pouty, and he had a beautiful, bright smile when he walked by, heading to his lounge chair, and said, "Bom Tarde!"

We both read and napped, checking each other out every so often. Horny and curious about what was in those board shorts—and since nobody was around—I opted for bold. I walked over, sat down next to him, and we made small talk about visiting and working in Brazil. He had not tried the national drink of Brazil, a capirina. I headed to the bar and returned with two drinks, both doubles. Hell, yes, I wanted us both tipsy. We drank and talked and laughed. He didn't pull away when I would rest my hand on his, or squeezed his shoulder.

He liked the drink, and I suggested we go to the concierge lounge on the top floor. He readily agreed, and the bartender there plied us with more drinks. I think the bartender understood what I was up to and heavy-handed his drinks. With soccer on the lounge TV, we decided to go to my room to watch a movie and lie down. The bartender laughed and made us each a drink to take with us. He winked at me as we left. In my suite, I put the TV on and looked for a movie. Not much on, so I suggested an adult selection. He said to go for it. I asked if he had ever watched man-on-man film. He said no, but again said, go for it. Ok.

We watched for a few minutes and finished our drinks. I could tell he was hard in his board shorts. I laughed and told him I had wondered ever since he got out of the pool what he had packed in those shorts. He told me to check it out and untied the string. As I walked toward him, I said, "Whatever you say." His response, "That's exactly what I had in mind." My response, "Yes, sir."

Travel

I knelt before him, put my face in his crotch, inhaled the damp, sweaty aroma, and sighed. I murmured, "Please, sir." He smiled and nodded, "Yes, take me in your mouth." This innocent, young, married guy from Amsterdam was anything but innocent.

He was just over five inches, certainly not six. But it was thick and so hard I could tell he would stay solid for a long time. The head was big and helmet-shaped. He smelled and tasted delicious. With his dick in the back of my throat, I slurped and caressed him with my tongue. I wanted his sweaty balls, low-hangers—that's where his size was! Beautiful big balls. I could get them both in my mouth, but no way his dick and balls. He complemented me for "good tongue work," and told me I did not need to be so delicate. He said that when he has sex with a man, he better damn well know he was with a man.

I let his balls drop from my mouth and began to chew with my teeth on the sweet spot between his legs, behind his low-hangers. I got even harder when I smelled the musk of his ass. As I slid my tongue deep in him, my beard scruff scratched between his cheeks and that tender pink circle. I meant to scratch the hell out of that ass as I ate away. If he wanted to know he was with a man, I couldn't think of a better way than rubbing his sweet white ass with my scruff until it was pink and raw. I think it worked because he never stopped moaning.

When I pulled back and looked between his legs at those deep blue eyes, I didn't know what to expect from him. He grinned for a minute and said, "That's excellent, what else you got, bitch?" Now, I'm usually a bottom, but if his bossy ass wants to know he's with a man then I've got something that only a man can bring. I told him that this bitch has eight inches of cock. (Ok, it's really just over seven but that doesn't sound quite as forceful.) "You want this bitch-man's eight inches banging your sweet wet hole?" He said, "Bang, daddy, hard, fucking hard."

With his ankles on my shoulders, I slid in easily from all my spit and slobber, and soon I was banging him hard. He had to know that he was with a man. He shouted, moaned, cried, and I banged harder and harder. He begged me to finish. I slowed and whispered in his ear, "If you want to be with a man, you will take my dick until I'm done with your man-puss. Do you want to be with a man?" It was his turn to say, "Yes, sir."

I banged him raw and his whining was now begging for more, begging for harder instead of begging me to stop. Sweaty and spent, I shot him full of slippery cum. I collapsed into him and kissed him hard and then gently. We explored with our tongues, and then I dropped to his gorgeous pink nipples. I worked them with my tongue, teeth, and lips. He moaned and squirmed. Seeing how hard he was, I knew his favorite play place. I knew it from the time I saw those wide, pink circles stretching across his tight round pecs. I licked his nips and caressed his balls and dick. Fair to say, his dick was throbbing. He started to slowly jerk off, and I whispered that I wanted his cum on me. On his knees, he jerked off as I twisted his hard nipples and talked nasty, telling him I wanted his cum all over my face. He shot big, and my face was covered, dripping on to my chest.

We hugged and kissed, trading his cum from his tongue to mine and back. By this time it was dark, not late, but definitely night. We both fell asleep. I'm not sure for how long, but it was well deserved because we were truly two men that had worked hard to bring good sex to another man.

We were exhausted after ferocious man-to-man sex and slept soundly until I heard the knock. I grabbed Jon's board shorts off the floor and slid them on. Looking through the peephole, I saw the bartender from the concierge lounge. How long had we been asleep? I opened the door, and he stepped in with a tray that had three drinks and a bottle. He said he was going off shift and thought that I and my friend might like another drink. He set the tray on the table and smiled. I smiled and asked why there were three drinks. At that moment, Jon came through the bedroom door, naked. The bartender looked at him, looked at me, and said he couldn't think of a better place to spend the rest of his evening—that's why he brought the third drink and the bottle.

We toasted each other, and the bartender (Fabiano) leaned in to kiss me. Tonight I was not only to have blond and beautiful, but I was also to have my tall, dark, and handsome too. Clear brown eyes, heavy dark five o'clock shadow, and I knew where I wanted that rough scruff! He kissed me deeply. Jon didn't waste any time coming over. He lowered Fabiano's black pants and unbuttoned his tuxedo shirt. He was hairy, thickly muscled. Awesome thick pecs, awesome thick thighs. Beautiful thick, dark, chest hair and bush. His ass was thick with dark hair. No doubt we were having sex with a Man. And as it turned out Jon and I were both his bitches; he took charge from the start.

He pushed Jon onto his cock and me into his armpit. He was rough, but we did what we were told. Jon looked up from his kneeling position, his face covered with precum and his own slobber. Fabiano called him bitch and dropped a huge gob of spit onto his face. Jon simply went back to sucking that sweet Brazilian cock. I worked hard, cleaning his sweaty pits from a hard day's work. As I caressed his face, I felt the scruff that he had grown as a man does over the day. I knew I wanted what I had given Jon just a few hours before—an ass and hole rubbed pink and raw from a real man's beard, and then covered with the soft cream of his cum.

Dreams do come true. Fabiano ordered me on all fours at the edge of the bed. Expecting to feel some pain from the dry raw thrust of his cock, instead I felt his tongue dancing in my tender hole, then in me. Then what I wanted! He ground his face between my cheeks until truly the skin was raw. Then, instead of the pain of a dry thrust, I felt a big and thick, smooth cock slide deep in me. As the expression goes, more than balls deep.

He put Jon to work, twisting and thumping his nipples while he began to fuck me. Hard. Very hard. Each thrust from those huge thighs pushed me further on to the bed. Jon slid under me, and I had him in my throat. The force from Fabiano's thighs gave me bounce to suck him well. Soon, they both came, filling me with cum above and behind. We all collapsed, sweaty.

The two of them, grateful for my hard work, both began to suck me. My dick, my balls, kissing each other, sucking again, until I shot for the second time that night. We chilled and did shots from the bottle Fabiano had brought, sitting cross-legged in the bed until we fell asleep, or maybe more accurately passed out. The morning would come soon.

I thought I should tell you about a rather naughty scene here in Bangkok, last Sunday evening after dark in Lumpini Park. I had finished my run, wearing short running shorts, with nothing underneath. While cooling down, I prowled around, looking for action. Saw one of my regular tops, a tall and skinny Thai guy with a monster cock who loves to fuck me raw. We stood in the shadows. I got a pounding and an ass full of cum. I put on my shorts and walked away.

Ten minutes later, I saw a group of guys in another dark area, so I went over to take a look. About five guys standing and watching one of them getting a blowjob. I took off my running singlet and shorts and lay down on a bench nearby to watch. One of the guys spoke English, so I told him that if his buddies wanted to piss and cum on me that would be greatly appreciated. One of them started fingering my cummy hole, which turned me on again.

Then a few minutes later, another one gave me a delicious piss shower, mostly over my chest and cock, but some in my mouth, tasty. Watching that was enough to set off two of the others, who promptly shot their loads over me. It wasn't long before I came too.

I rubbed the piss and cum into my chest a bit to savour the different textures, yummy. I let it dry off a bit, then stood up, put on my running singlet and shorts and went home. At home, I smelled the now-stinky shirt to make sure what had happened really had; couldn't help but jerk off again into it. So damn hot.

Guess where I will be this coming Sunday after dark?

I love my adventures in Brazil. I love the dark masculine men, and it's true what they say about dick size—they are bigger there. And they seem to love my blond/blue daddy self with my muscles and my ass.

Staying at a smaller boutique hotel with maybe forty or fifty rooms, you get to see pretty much the same faces at breakfast every morning. I don't know about you, but every man I see, I ask myself, "Would I get naked with him and is that guy likely to get naked with me?" Morning two of a week-long trip I saw a guy, and the answers were, "Yes," and "I'm not sure." I finished my breakfast and hurried to an appointment.

Morning three, I slept a little later and headed to the dining room, wearing loose gym shorts and a tight t-shirt, knowing I had most of the day to myself. He was there—tall, slim, brown, overnight scruff on his face, and dark hair sticking out of the top of his t-shirt. We smiled but didn't speak. We were then together in the elevator, exchanged smiles, and the "look." I stepped off on my floor and took a few steps. I turned, and he was still holding the door open. He smiled and nodded me back in. I smiled and stepped back in. We rode to the top floor to his suite. We didn't speak until we were behind the door in his living room.

He leaned into me and kissed me hard. I responded immediately, wrapping my arm around his neck and pulling him tighter to my mouth. He pushed me to my knees and shoved my face into his crotch still covered with his track pants. He pulled off his shirt, and I saw the hairy chest, the big brown nipples, and his slim waist. As I started to pull his pants down with my teeth, he tipped my head back and slapped me, pretty hard. He stared into my eyes, said he was in charge of me, and would take his time with me. I was shocked, but my cock was also hard.

He pulled me up and took my shirt off. He smiled, kissed me tenderly, nuzzled my neck, and whispered that he wanted to make love to me like only two men can do. He asked if wanted that, if I wanted him. He told me again that he was in charge. I kissed him, softly at first, and then with more passion. I took my tongue out of his mouth long enough to say, "Yes, I wanted him." And I wanted to do whatever to please him. He grinned, said, "I knew it the first morning I saw you." He reached behind him to the desk and grabbed a blindfold and put it on me. I was rock hard.

He pulled his pants down. His cock was straight up. Big. Maybe eight inches. Thick. Way more than the tip of thumb to tip of index finger. He let me begin to lick and suck his helmet head. I nuzzled. I nibbled between his legs and around his balls. He was hairy, very thick bush, very hairy legs. Shaved balls, as I licked the smooth, brown bag with balls that seemed like ping pong balls. He moaned like a son of a bitch. When I tried to take that thick dick in my mouth, he grabbed the back of my head. I knew what was coming, and he forced himself to the back of my throat. Over and over he face-fucked me, as I gagged and tears ran down my cheeks.

He slowed down, and I felt the bottle of poppers he held under my nose. Thankful for the opportunity, I inhaled over and over until I was ready to give his throbbing big dick another ride in and out of my throat. He sat down in the floor beside me and cuddled me with tears on my cheeks. Blindfolded still, I didn't know what to expect. He kissed and stroked my nipples. As I moaned, he realized that the harder the better for me. Kindly, another generous hit of poppers and he worked, twisted, and thumped my nipples until I knew they would still hurt the next day. He stroked my dick through my gym shorts and slid his hand in, caressing my junk, and fingering my ass dry.

He guided me to the bed. Pushed me face down. I thought he was going to fuck me dry, and I braced myself. Instead I felt him caress my ass, he pulled me to my knees with my ass up, and I felt his tongue in my hole. I was in ecstasy. He paused and poppered me. I was expecting his tongue on my ass; I felt the sharp sting of his hand. I cried out, and he stuck a small rubber ball in my mouth, poppered me and began to sting my ass, first with his hand and then with a paddle. It stung, but I was hard again in no time. Then his tongue went deep up my hole. He nibbled the pink circle around my hole, and I felt his fingers begin to stretch my ass. I knew what he would do next.

I was right. He was gentle at first, working his big mushroomy head into the entrance of my hole. He kissed my neck and whispered that I should prepare myself for the fuck of my life. With just spit, he slid in more, and then deeper until he was balls deep. Every nerve in my hole was tingling. I started squeezing my ass muscles. He felt it for sure because he grabbed my face and turned it around, looked at me and grinned. Told me I was a sweet bitch, his sweet bitch. Still deep in me, he poppered me heavy and began to slide way in and out. Each stroke was major, and I was cringing but loving every bit. His speed increased until each long stroke was harder and harder. With abandon and crazy loud moaning, he thrust one last deep plow, and erupted. No doubt you can feel the thick spurts of a big cummer. Over and over he spasmed and emptied his balls in me. He collapsed on top of me, and I squeezed my ass muscles around his thick veiny brown dick. I could picture every squeeze as he moaned, spasmed once more, and shot one last time.

Sweaty and in a pile, we just lay there for a while, and he kissed me. Sliding down my chest, he licked and sucked down to my dick and balls. Then he went back to my ass, my now cum-filled ass. With his face, lips, and tongue covered and his mouth full of his cum, he came back and kissed me hard, smearing his juice all over my face, mouth, and chest. He sucked me, and it wasn't long until he had another load of cum, this time my cum, to share and smear on our bodies.

We fell asleep for hours. Waking up, we made love again. Four more days we were together every moment we weren't working. Never about love, but very definitely about trust and giving ourselves over to each other, and our lust. And at least once, to a room steward that brought us drinks when we called room service and once at a sex club. Those are stories for another day.

I can justly say that I have never shied away from a cock given to me to suck, except for a few guys whose personal hygiene sucked, that is. What a waste not to suck a willing cock and taste that man's seed. There is something we crave in men, the sensation of having their penises in our mouths, feeling them get hard, sucking their crowns, and coaxing out the semen we crave.

Travel

I had a few Japanese men while in Japan, and a few Koreans a few years earlier. A couple of them were as a result of going to the hot baths, especially after a long midnight shift.

I found a couple of beautiful Asian men on Tumblr recently that got my memory juices flowing, and remembered my time in Japan 1985-88. I used to go to the Japanese hot bath (or just "bathhouse") near our base. They were called "onsen" in Japanese, and they are plentiful in the north due to the preponderance of hot springs. We were in Aomori prefecture, in Hachinohe city area, and the town area around the base was Misawa-shi. I wrote all this down just because I happen to remember the names despite the age of the memory. A coup for this old coot.

These places all had their own hot spring to draw on, so the water was hot at about 105º F or even higher. Men and women were separated into their own areas. There were lockers to put your clothes into before stepping nude into the bath area. There was a large warm pool, plus a couple of progressively colder pools, and a very hot pool. But first, you wash. Each man would take a washing station which was a shower area along the wall with a shower head, faucet to control the water into either the shower head or a hose, a place to put your soap, and so forth. Most men brought a small stool to sit on while they washed.

And wash. And wash. The requirement was to be spotless before you got into the main pool to soak. So a few skin washes, hair, fingernails, toenails, penis and balls, and shaving. All that hot water steam made your beard soft, so shaving was easy. There were some who shaved their pubes too. I never did mine in the onsen, but I did shave my balls now and again. And many would clean their ass cracks as part of their regimen. It made for a good show since this activity was fully visible to all the other men in the area.

On a couple of occasions, I was fortunate to hook up with some Japanese men who also enjoyed the attention of men, especially, I suspect, of a white American "round eye," who would suck their cocks. One man saw me eyeing a beautiful fifteen or sixteen-year-old boy as he washed and prepared for the soaking pool. This kid was gorgeous, with a swimmer's build, and a marvelous, uncut cock. I lusted for a taste of his semen. But this man watching me saw my attraction to men and took it to heart. He walked by, tapped me on the shoulder, and motioned that I should follow him. I did.

He led me to a changing room for which he had paid extra—privacy in crowded Japan costs. He pulled the curtain closed and turned to look at me.

Travel

He was forty or so, and built. Very strong arms and legs. Butt cheeks out the ying yang. Probably a fisherman. He asked in halting English, "You suck me?" Oh, and he had a smooth, cut cock of about six inches, a tad more length than me, and thicker than mine. He pointed to his cock which was rising in attention, and it was obvious he wanted to see if I would suck him. I knew very little Japanese, but said what I knew. "Hai dozo," which is, "Yes, thank you," and got down on my knees.

His cock was very clean from his recent washing. I could slightly taste the soap he'd used. As I put his cock into my mouth, he closed his eyes, and his dick got very hard and grew another inch. I worked slowly and deliberately to get his semen into me, but also gave him a very good ride.

He had his hands on my head as he began to cum, and he pressed harder and harder the closer he came to letting go. He came with a vengeance, unleashing a torrent of very hot semen into my mouth. It was all I could do to keep up with it. He exhaled slowly and stood transfixed as he experienced what appeared to be a most intense orgasm and ejaculation.

He took a step back and winked. He bowed—no kidding—and then shook my hand. "Next time, you," he said. And in a few weeks, we were both there again, and he did the same for me. I loved it.

Way back in time I used to travel a significant amount, and one of my trips was to Washington DC. I visited several of the gay bars and other establishments, but this story revolves around a young man, twenty-two years of age, if my memory serves me correctly. I was at an eating establishment, and this young man was there, also alone, and our tables were next to each other. We exchanged greetings and made some small talk about the city and the sites to see. I mentioned by name a museum that I was going to visit the next day.

I got to the Natural History Museum when it opened, and low and be hold Isaac was there, so we toured the place together. We wandered around and had some interesting chat going on. He was on his way to Montreal to visit family, since he had just completed his time in the Israeli military. He was single, not looking for a wife. He was cute as hell. He bought me lunch and about 3:30 pm we parted company. I returned to my hotel and he to friends that he was staying with.

Travel

The next afternoon, I caught a train to NYC and stayed at the YMCA. Again I visited a few of the local bars and gay friendly places. Some very interesting sites and people. I went out to the Statue of Liberty, and on the boat was Isaac! We again had a very good time, and I found out that he was catching a train to Montreal in the morning. It just so happens that I was catching the same train to Vermont. We met at Grand Central Station the next morning and rode the train.

By the time we had left NY, we had discovered that we were both gay, and things picked up from there to a hot and very pleasurable several-hour train excursion. Before we hit the state line, we had visited the restroom. Even though it was a damn small facility, we found out it was possible to have some hot, passionate kissing and oral sex. We returned to our seats, and while he stood behind me, he reached over the seat and massaged my chest and nipples. They are my on and off buttons! He saw the results of his ministrations and suggested we revisit the restroom. So again we are in this tight little space with him still behind me. He unfastened my pants and they hit the floor. I reached behind me and worked on his ever-growing monster in his pants. I was unable to get his pants open or his special tool out, but he was very helpful in that effort. Shortly, we both had our pants down around our ankles. He spit on his hand, lubed his dick and my quivering ass.

I had been fucked before, but I was not much more than a mere novice at getting fucked. He was ever so gentle. and he slipped his circumcised cock into my tight, frightened ass. I was hurting, loving the feeling and the sensation of his dick sliding in and out of my near cherry, tender ass. He knew what he was doing and how to do it. What a lovely experience it was for me to be taken care of by a very kind, friendly, and sexy young man. I was around thirty-seven or thirty-eight, recently out of our military, long before "don't ask, don't tell," so this was a delightful first. I loved the way it felt when he ejaculated, the pulsing of his big, ten-plus inch dick of hot, hard meat exploding in me. If my memory again serves me right, this was probably the first time any man had cum in me. What a feeling when that hot load hit. There was a knock on the door; the conductor was checking tickets. Isaac said he would be right out. We quickly pulled up our pants and exited to a very good-looking and excited conductor. Judging from the bulge in his trousers, we knew he was excited. The conductor was very pleasant and explained that we should go to the car behind because it was empty and was only being transported to be refurbished. We thanked him, and as we left he patted both of us on the ass.

It wasn't long before we, Isaac and I, decided to check out the trailing car. Low and behold, who was sitting alone in the car, the cute conductor. We sat down and talked with him for several minutes before we had other events to take care of. We were fairly secure from intrusion since there was a sign on the door that the car was closed and not in use. I improved my oral skills on the conductor's man meat. He tasted very sweet, and the end explosion was powerful and slightly salty. He then proceeded to take care of me orally, and Isaac, in his best condition and manner again administered his healing touch to my somewhat tender ass. Again, he was gentle, forceful, and in control until I again got his wonderfully hot man seed. Resting for a bit, the conductor wanted to know if I would let him fuck me, and with the oral help from Isaac, the conductor started his exploration of my inner sanctum. He was bigger, that is, longer, bigger around and much more aggressive than Isaac, and I was pretty certain that I was meant to be fucked and fucked good. He pounded me hard for probably fifteen minutes, and with a deep meaningful thrust he unleashed a large load, more than I could hold. It was leaking out of my now well-pounded anus. I went to the restroom and deposited their loads.

The conductor thanked us, and he left the train at the next stop. Isaac and I stayed on for the remainder of the journey and made one more trip to the restroom where he again filled my ass with his glorious cum. I held this in for several hours, and once we got to Vermont I still had about a three-hour car ride. What a great feeling and memories of that trip. As an aside, I also think Isaac was the first circumcised cock that I sucked and had fuck me. We exchanged addresses and phone numbers somewhere along the way, but I can only remember the meat that I took care of and enjoyed. Isaac called me from Israel several months later and invited me to visit. I never made the trip. I look back now, and I think I would have sold a kidney to see him again.

I've continued being naughty in Lumpini Park in Bangkok after running, drinking guys' piss, swallowing their loads, and having cum showers. But that's old news!

This new one is a Work In Progress. Recently met a guy on Tinder—a dating site—who loves worn underwear and cum, preferably together. So for the past four days, I've worn the same pair of black Calvin Klein briefs and have been using them as a cum rag, inside and out, for myself and anyone else who has shot cum over me. The cum stains look just great. It's so hot wearing the same pair of dirty undies under my suit when I go to work—nice on the outside, nasty on the inside. I'll meet him properly in a couple of days. He wants me to barefuck him while I'm still wearing them. I'll have to take them off at some stage because for sure he's going to want them in his mouth. There will be six days of piss drops and cum for him to savour. I hope he likes my handiwork.

Sometimes, I've done the same thing for buddies living overseas, and then mailed the undies to them so they get a nice surprise one day. Thanks and love from me in Bangkok.

I love to winter in Mexico. All the cities are gay friendly, especially Puerto Vallarta. This past visit a gay vendor told us of the semi-bathhouse/hotel just around the corner, afternoons 3:00 pm to 6:00, entry and two drinks for about a dollar. Fucken A!! Crawling with mostly bears, no shirts, guys in the pool and Jacuzzi with bathing suits, all groping. A steamy video room, where I learned some new techniques. Adjacent was a total dark room, wall-to-wall bodies with swinging dicks. Anyway, met this kid, mid-twenties, agreed to come back to our room for 100 pesos ($6), and later asked for another 100 since I took photos—fine with me. Very playful, loved to be fucked.

Returned a few days later. This time joined the orgy room, guessing 15 X 15, totally dark. Had to be thirty guys. A cocksucker's paradise, giving and getting. Also, guys taking it up the ass. Fond memories for when I return to the cold of Iowa.

One of my favorite cities in the world is Bangkok, and I had the opportunity to spend four days there last summer at the end of a business trip. First on my "fun" list was to spend a day at the world-famous, historic, gay spa called Babylon. It's a beautiful gay resort in the middle of the city with a lush outdoor pool, a great restaurant, and hotel—and, of course, the obligatory dark rooms and play areas. I spent the whole day there playing around, lounging by the pool and ogling all the hot eye candy, guys from all over the world from many different ethnic backgrounds. But an unexpected hookup at my hotel actually topped my time at Babylon!
Hotels are very cheap in Bangkok, so I was able to stay in a brand new five-star hotel. I booked a massage at the luxurious spa in the hotel, and a young Thai boy gave me a wonderful therapeutic massage. He was very sweet, and

he looked like he was fourteen years old, but unfortunately no happy ending. This was a five-star hotel after all. The men's locker room in the hotel gym had a nice steam room, so I decided to go there after my massage, just to relax. As I was getting undressed, I noticed a handsome, dark-haired young Thai in the corner of the locker room. A lot of the Thai boys are quite short and small in stature. But this tall, young stud was buff and sexy from head to toe! I have a weakness for guys with thick, jet black hair—and thick, dark cocks for that matter! My first impression was that he was straight. He was busy texting on his cell phone, and I couldn't keep my eyes off him. Then at one point, he looked up, and we made eye contact. Hmmmm? Straight guys don't usually make eye contact in a locker room!

I stripped down, wrapped a towel around me, and headed for the steam room, assuming that the young, twenty-something was just a passing fantasy in my dirty little mind. But moments later the steam room door opened and in walks you know who! I was sitting on my towel completely naked, and he very coyly opened his towel momentarily as he sat down, so I got a nice view of his thick, cut cock before he covered up again. It wasn't huge, but he was hard as a rock! He spoke fluent English so we started to chat. I coyly touched my cock a couple times as we chatted, and he immediately responded, discreetly undoing his towel and exposing his rock-hard boy cock, which was standing straight up against his flat abs. Oh, to be young again, when the cock stands straight up against the belly! He was strikingly handsome, and, for a moment, I wondered if he was a prostitute after money. But as it turns out, he was a local student with a membership to the hotel gym/spa. I moved closer to him, reached over, started lightly touching his nipples, and then I reached down to massage his cock and balls. He started moaning with pleasure. Then he reached out and started stroking me as well, and I suggested he come up to my room. He accepted my invitation without hesitation!

When we got to my room, I slowly undressed him and savored every inch of his hot, young, firm body with my lips and tongue. I threw him on the bed and pressed my naked body against his. There's nothing more heavenly than two naked, male bodies writhing together in passion! And he was intensely horny and passionate! I slowly made my way down to his beautiful young cock and took my time kissing, licking, and sucking him as he continued to moan. I could tell my new Thai playmate was not into kissing, which was disappointing, but when I crawled up the bed and presented him with my hard tool, he quickly devoured it with hunger!

We continued sucking in a 69 position for a while, and he told me he was getting close. He also added, "I have to warn you that I shoot a lot." Hot!! I quickly flipped around and started sucking and stroking him, and then I went deeper down to his balls and taint. This really made him squirm and whimper like a puppy. Bingo! I found one of his G spots! He grabbed his cock and started stroking it hard while I nuzzled and sucked on his taint and balls. I felt his tight body stiffen, and he started shooting long, thick ropes of cum in a perfect straight line up his torso, each one as powerful and thick as the previous. He must have shot seven times! I quickly gathered up some of his hot juices in my hand and started stroking my cock as I knelt over him. I guided his hand to my tight, full nuts and told him to squeeze and pull. That's all it took to make me shoot all over him, and my young Thai mate was a wet mess! He was not in a hurry to leave, so I cleaned him up, and we snuggled and talked a while. One of the sweetest and hottest afternoons I have ever spent to be sure! My only regret is that I did not take a photo of this handsome lad before he left.

Frequent business travel to the same city has the benefit of knowing where I will find man fun without wasting time. This trip was with only one night in São Paulo before moving on to meetings in a new city. I wanted to make it count. I knew my mission, where I wanted to go for lots of action—LeRouge Sauna. And I knew what I wanted—to get nasty, and fucked as many times as possible.

I grabbed the blindfold from the amenity bag on the plane, my cockring, my poppers, and a couple of clothespins and headed to LeRouge which was just a couple of blocks from my hotel. Checked in, I was wearing only a jockstrap and carrying my little purple velvet bag of goodies. I wanted to have a couple of drinks in the bar. My inhibitions were getting loose from the drinks and the room full of towel-wrapped men. Brazilian men are as varied as any other group except they are always brown, and always have beautiful, deep brown eyes. This sauna attracts masculine men, many a little older—or the younger ones that chase us—some muscular, some bears, some Asian mix.

Carrying two drinks, an attractive man wearing only a towel and a nipple ring sat down across from me. Honestly that happens a lot to me there. I'm a nice looking blond, blue-eyed guy, different from the norm there. Tall and fit, and, I will say, a jock strap is a good look on me! He was a muscle bear, probably in his mid-fifties with hair on his chest and on his little bit of a belly, a type I certainly find safe and attractive. Handing me a drink, my new friend, Joao, started a conversation. His English was passable, but he seemed more interested in caressing my pecs and nipples. He saw me hardening in the tight jockstrap. "Is that bag for fun?" he asked motioning toward my Crowne bag. "You bet it is. Meet me upstairs in the cabin rooms. But hurry." I grabbed the bag and headed into the dark maze of black plywood. I knew he was following.

And I knew he would be my first trick. I quickly emptied my bag on the bunk. With clothespins on my nips and poppers on a cord around my neck, I pulled the first-class blindfold over my eyes, blocking the muted, red glow of the bath house, leaving me in the dark. My legs spread and my door open, I expected Joao but didn't really know who would touch me next. Who would force himself into my waiting hole? Who would really be able to do whatever he wanted to me? Yeah, it was risky, but, oh hell, was I turned on in anticipation.

I sensed his presence first, before he touched me. He kissed me, and I could smell the gin and the sweat that I had just tasted in the bar. Joao hardly touched me as he went straight to what he wanted when he handed me that first drink, my tight ass. I really had no idea about his penis; he had kept his towel around his waist downstairs in the bar. He, on the other hand, knew just what a piece of ass he was getting, having had the jock-strap pre-show along with everyone else in the bar. What a lovely fuck! He was big enough to give me pleasure but not so big as to hurt me. He took the poppers, and I could hear him take a long hit. It invigorated him and he pumped away.

I thought he was twisting the clothespins, and my nips were hard as rocks. Then I felt another hard cock shoved into my mouth. This is what I came for, blindfolded I had no idea what this man even looked like who was now face fucking me. Holding my head, he was forcing me to take him all the way to the back of my throat. He paused long enough for somebody to give me a hit of poppers. Joao pulled out, and almost immediately the cock that had been in the back of my throat was now balls deep up my ass. As fast as the guy up my ass thrust and shot his load, someone else slid into me.

He was big. All I knew was that he was a big, thick-dicked man. I didn't know what he looked like, just what he felt like in me. I groaned as he started banging me harder. Poppers? Where were my poppers? Then I felt hands, literally all over me. Pulling my jock aside, stroking my hard manstick, my balls, my face, pinching my nipples. I was sucking one dick, and he pulled out and shot cum across my face. Suddenly, someone fed me a dose of poppers. Fuck, I was buzzed with each hit and each hit made we want more dick. More cum shot on my chest, my face and, of course, in my mouth and ass.

I was positioned on my back, on my knees, on all fours. I was fucked, spanked, sucked, groped. One man lowered himself onto my erection while I was being pounded up my ass; his force hitting me was the force he felt from me up in him. He was one of the loudest as he came and shot cum across my belly. For the record, every man makes noise when he cums, some slow groans, some loud shouts, but all make noise. I think, too, that "fuck, fuck, fuck" is pretty standard for getting close to release, even in Portuguese.

Some men kissed and caressed, some, I think, simply came in and slid into my welcoming hole, left their mark, and then left the room. Sometimes, I think there was just one man, sometimes I expect there were four or five. I was kept well-poppered the whole time and could feel some fatter guys, some smaller, some hairy, some totally smooth. I don't really know how many men used me that evening. There was a lull, and one man sat beside me. He whispered it's time for a break; it was Joao. He pulled my blindfold off and said, "Let's get you cleaned up." I was covered with cum and sweaty. We went to the showers and then to the bar.

Soon there was a line of drinks in front of me, tokens from my anonymous lovers. Joao said he was with me the whole time to make sure nothing bad happened to me. I looked around the bar at the half-naked men, pointing, "Was he there, was he...?" Joao laughed, "Oh, yes," and pointed out some others that smiled at me. "How many," I asked? "I think eighteen," he responded. "I went out a few times with the poppers to attract the best men and bring them back for you." I had to laugh; I wasn't sure if I should think of him as pimping me out, or as my faithful dog chasing hot men to fuck me. Either way, mission accomplished. Le Rouge and as many men as possible!

A few years ago, I was at a straight couple's party on a rooftop deck in Bangkok. We'd all had a few drinks and things were going well, a great mix of people—mostly straight, mixed Asian and Western, with one or two gay guys.

While I was leaning on the balcony railing taking in the view, a ruggedly handsome white guy came up and started talking. I'd seen him before. He was MD of one of the foreign companies so I knew who he was. I'd also met his wife, and I knew that they had two children. We talked about business, expat stuff, the heat, the cultural difference—the usual topics for foreigners. At one point in our conversation, he turned to me and said casually, "What do I have to do to suck your cock?" Well, I was astonished. I couldn't believe my ears. So I replied, "Sorry, I think I've drunk too much and misheard you. What exactly did you say?" He said, "You heard perfectly well." Me, thinking quickly, "Well, you'd better meet me in five minutes in the men's changing room next to the gym on the floor below."

Four minutes later, I was down there, trying to have a pee, but I was so nervous I couldn't. I was starting to get hard thinking about it when he walked in. He motioned to go into the empty sauna room. Once in there, he sunk to his knees, pulled down my trousers and underwear, and starting sucking my cock like there was oxygen coming out of it. After about five minutes of that and being so turned on, there was something a little nicer than oxygen coming out of it. He loved it, wiped his tongue around my cock to clean it up, swallowed it all, and then stood to kiss me. Man, that was so hot. He's rock hard, of course, and I had no problems doing the same for him. Ten minutes later, we wandered back to the party, separately, as if nothing unusual had happened. I picked up my drink where I had left it and thought, "Did that really just happen?"

I saw him again in similar circumstances about a year later, and he did it again. He never really wanted to meet me socially anywhere. I guess the fact that I knew his wife was a bit too close to home for him. That was fine with me. Both of us were getting what we wanted, and I heard that she was pregnant again soon after. She even joked to me one day about how horny and fertile he was. I had to bite my tongue not to agree! Sadly, they moved overseas a bit after that. Sweet memories.

Last Fall my husband and I spent time in Athens as part of a much longer trip. While there, we stayed in the gay Alexander Apartments. It has five floors with the basement, and on the first floor is an amazing sauna. When staying in the apartments, one has free access to the sauna. Were the guys there hotter than at baths in the US? I can't say for sure, but being there and knowing that they were all Greek, and talking in Greek sure made it feel more so. I always expect that as an older guy it is not going to be that easy to connect, but this flowed quite easily. There were quite a good number of sexual contacts but one was a real fantasy lived out. In the basement, it was required that everyone is naked; towels left at the door. That turned out to be my favorite area. The high point was when two hot guys had their not huge but very nice size, uncut cocks in my mouth as I was lying on a sort of ledge. At the same time, another guy was alternating between fingering my ass while sucking my cock and then sucking my ass. What a way to get off!

Baths, Valencia, Spain 2013. My bath house history has been pretty bleak in part because my cruising skills are pretty bleak, but that is a different story. I was on the cusp of starting a 720 mile trek on foot, from Valencia on the Mediterranean to Santiago in NW Spain, almost on the Atlantic. I suspected, correctly it turns out, that opportunities for sex would be limited over the next two months en route to Santiago. So after walking an hour from my hostel to the poorly marked bathhouse, I finally made it. Sunday afternoon. Moderately busy. Older crowd, a few twinks. In minutes, a man slightly younger grabbed my cock, went down on me, and wanted me to fuck him. I rarely top, but I do try to please. Over the course of at least an hour I fucked him at least six times, alternating with sucking each other. Our fucking was spread around the facility, in the theater, in a private room in the maze. Others tried to get in on the action and that would have been more than fine with me, but the guy I was with actively discouraged others. I certainly enjoyed being the exhibitionist and the object of desire. I finally exploded, and the guy was still angling for more, but I was spent. I beat off to the memory of that adventure for the next two months, as step by often painful step I arrived in Santiago. There I found another bathhouse with a man eager to drain me.

Recounting this, I now recall other fond memories of bathhouse adventures in Lima and Quito. In Lima the bathhouse hook-up led to dinner at a nearby restaurant which led to more sex at my hotel. In Quito, again dinner, sex in the hotel afterward. On a date two days later, we spent the day touring the countryside then spent the night at a country house he had access to. During the course of the day, I found out he was a priest.

It was about twenty-five years ago, when flying on an airline was a lot easier and more fun than it is today. I was on an overnight flight from Amsterdam to NYC. While I was waiting to board, I saw a person in uniform I had briefly met at a party, had been attracted to, and who was also boarding the plane. As I passed through first class on my way to my coach seat, our eyes met. He was the chief steward on the flight. As I took my seat in coach, he said that my seat was in first class. What a treat! He was particularly solicitous to my needs, and late that night he walked by my seat, put his finger to his lips, and motioned towards the first-class lavatory. First class wasn't full, and everyone else seemed to be asleep. We both fit in and made out frantically for a few minutes. Then he turned me around, fumbled with my belt, pushed down my pants, spit on his hands, lubed me up as best he could, and plunged balls deep up my ass. We both came quickly, then hurried and cleaned up as best we could. That's how I enjoyed the champagne and first class. And joined the Mile-High Club!

Well, I'm no spring chicken, but for seventy-six I have a pretty active sex life here in Hawaii. I keep myself in excellent shape, hit the gym, and am still working with a demanding schedule, handling the corporate, incentive groups who come to the islands. I keep pace at work with guys a third my age. Others tell me I'm still hot for an older guy. Well endowed. Still have my same college weight and waist. The plumbing still works great, just not like it did when I was nineteen and could easily cum five times a day. I was clearly more sex driven than most of my brothers. Still am. More oral as you'll see, which probably is why I'm still alive today.

One of my favorites is a hot Brazilian surfer dude who loves older guys. We've been playing now for over twenty years. He was just a kid when I met him at a cruisy beach. He was paranoid as hell that any of his straight buds would find out. Huge, uncut cock on him and he comes very easily. Loves to have his cock sucked just slowly and deeply. Huge head on it. Loves to edge for long stretches. His favorite finale is my shooting my big load on his cock, which he then strokes just a couple of times, and then drowns me with his thick cream. He was going to come over Saturday night, and we had it all set up but his girl friend dropped by his house. So I went to bed a bit horny. Woke with the same horns screaming for attention. That restlessness that comes from being horny.

Then another favorite who had been off island texted me early afternoon Sunday, letting me know he was back on the island and horny for a blowjob before going to work where he manages a restaurant. He lives on the other side of the island so the forty-minute drive there would leave us just enough time for fun and games before he had to get to work. An awesome muscled body with a nice cock for sure, but what he does with it while fucking my mouth is simply awesome. As the hurricane said to the palm trees, hang onto your nuts; this ain't going to be no ordinary blowjob. A real trash talker as he edges ever closer and closer. He floods my mouth with a volcanic explosion that leaves both of us exhausted. A truly short and sweet experience.

As I return to my car, I get a text from a straight guy I met about four months ago in a cruisy restroom, wanting to get together on his work break. This meant a fast trip back home. When I first met this hot, tall, muscled stud he wanted a BJ, but then when he came to my place he quickly let me know he wanted a rim job also. His cock is enormous, cut, with huge nuts. Perfect ass with just a small touch of ginger hair—although he sports a thick brown head of hair. I made it back home in time for some real fun. He walks in, immediately pulls his pants down, and bends over, exposing his beautiful puckered hole, his huge nuts and dick swinging down between legs. Tongue fucking is my drug of choice with cock and ball sucking running a close second. I get all three in a super-size dose with this dude. He wants my tongue in there, deep. I tease his ass with my nice cockhead. He loves the tease, but I can tell he's not there yet. Lives with a girl. She's lacking in this kind of kink, which he obviously loves a lot. So he's blown away with our torrid sessions. He can't get enough of my eating his ass. He strokes his cock, balls bouncing as I tongue fuck him deep, finally turning around quickly with a huge spray of hot cum smacking me right in the face, down my chest and all around. He pulls his pants up, "Till next time," he says, as he heads out the door. I'm exhausted and soaked. That just made our fifth encounter. And I'm sure there will be a next time for this guy. Don't even know his name, titled him "Huge" on my phone.

About one hour later, I get a call from my buddy, a construction worker I met in the early 90s. Just out of high school, he was working at that time on the construction of the new Grand Wailea Hotel a few miles to the south. Now he's married with adult kids. Straight, but not much sex life at home. When we first met, he was very limited in what he would do, only wanting to be blown. No reciprocation at all. Now he loves to stroke my big cock, especially as I shoot a big load for him. But his favorite is to be rimmed, which makes a perfect fit. Wants badly to fuck me but that ain't happening. He wants to set up an early encounter Monday morning before work. We've been doing this early morning stuff for years.

Monday. 6:00 am: I have both a straight and a gay movie playing. He comes in, strips, and leans over a bar stool wanting to be rimmed. We soon end up on the floor with his jerking my cock and his ass in my face. It's a struggle to keep him quiet from waking the neighbors in the condo. He's a trash talker and moaner. I notice he is mostly watching the gay flick while we carry on. It doesn't take long until I'm ready to give him a throbbing cum load. He always seems obsessed with hanging on my throbbing cock while I'm shooting. Drives him crazy. I finally have to stop his stroking my now very sensitive dick. He circles around, shoving his cock into my mouth and thrusts away. When he cums, he's lost in ecstasy. Noisy moans! Hope the neighbors didn't hear. Quick rinse off in the shower, and he's off to work. I have to go back to bed for a while. Exhausted. Pleasant dreams, of course.

When I was young, my boyfriend at the time said that a gay man's sex life was pretty much over by thirty-five. Well, that didn't make much sense to me. Nor did that relationship, in the end. The single life is what I'm cut out for. Boyfriends get too jealous of my revolving-door life style. I'm a player. My friend Lee years ago teasingly gave me a t-shirt that said, "You can't be first but you can be next." We all laughed, but it pretty much nailed it. I don't know how much longer I can keep this sort of sex life schedule up. But for those who kiss off sex after fifty or even sixty, it doesn't have to be so. Just so there's plenty of sex in the next life is my hope. At least I don't have to be some obnoxious, prowling, dirty, old man. I practice being a gentleman. Sex pretty much comes to me.

But for the next couple of days I should just chill out. The almost non-stop of the last couple of days takes its toll on this old dude. Recovery takes a bit longer now. Then I'll be ready to rock again. Life is great. And you can take that to the bank.

I made a trip once to Corfu during a three-day break in schedule while stationed in southern Italy. Get on the ship from Brindisi and in a few hours you are in Greece. Corfu is a casino-rich island that was too rich for me. I went to the cheap Europa Hotel in town which, back in 1975 or 1976 you could get a bare room for about $2 a night. No kidding. Very bare, no furnishings, but a sink and a single bunk bed, bare wood floor as I remember. But it was full of tourists from Scandinavia and Germany, men and women, anxious to get to the nude beaches the island was known for.

As I headed out to rent a vespa scooter and got out to the water, a group of guys from Germany talked to me. They were friendly and easy to talk to as they spoke pretty good English. They decided I should join them getting naked on the beach. First, we went to their room and the biggest man, who must have been all of thirty years old, instructed us to get naked and kneel on the bed. "To get us in the mood for the nude beach I want to suck your asses." "Ya," they all said and pulled their cheeks apart to get ready. I was amazed, but I like a good rim like any other man. So I held my cheeks apart too, and awaited my turn.

This guy was very good at licking anuses. All the guys moaned in pleasure, and so did I. Why did it seem so easy to get naked with strangers? The promise of good sex with men who probably knew more than I about it was the main draw for me. Also, it was seemingly rather immediate. And I was always horny back in those days.

The rim job did wonders for me and the other guys. In fact, we were all worked up as a result of it. They all decided to fuck before they took off for the beach and chose me as the first man to fuck. By now, all apprehension was gone for me, and I easily said, "Yes, go ahead," and they lined up behind me. They were all solid fuckers with hard cocks ready to enter me.

Then we went to the beach.

My (then) boyfriend planned a cruise to Mexico. He's strikingly handsome, very friendly, and a bit of an exhibitionist. By the pool, he attracts everyone's attention. Women want him. Gay men want him. And straight men want to be him. He's 6'2", 190 pounds, olive skin, well muscled, big dicked. But it's the wide brown eyes, soft wavy brown eyes, the friendly smile of pearl white teeth, and the confident, friendly attitude that gets people.

He arranged for a private guide to meet us at one port. He met us with a cooler of beer and a bottle of tequila. So the drinking began, and Ricardo drove around showing us the island. Ricardo was a Mexican daddy. Tough, brown, tight muscled, shorter and thicker than us. His tank top showed his strong back and hairy chest. He took us to a secluded place for lunch, really just an open concrete building with the only electricity coming from a generator for the jukebox and the blender. Not a soul there and beautiful views of the deserted beach.

Ricardo pulled up front and told us he'd wait in the jeep. The owner/bartender was a friend, Alex. The name of the bar was Coconuts, but he said guys like us should ask Alex about changing the name to Beach

Balls. Alex came from behind the bar, wearing only board shorts, low on his hips. You could see the small trail from his hard belly crossing the tan/suntan waist line to what looked like a pretty thick cock nestled in that thick bush that you could see the hint of. Dredd locks completed his beach boy, rather beach man, look.

He welcomed us with a hug, Spanglish greetings, and an acknowledgement of his friendship with Ricardo. Then margaritas and best fish tacos ever. Conversation turned to the name of the bar. Coconuts. Alex pulled a photo album off the shelf by the bar—there were several albums. The album was filled with Polaroids of women pulling their tops down and showing off their boobs, er, coconuts. Hilarious, and so many. We asked about the name change to Beach Balls. Alex pulled some albums from beneath the bar, and yes, they were full of polaroids of men dropping their shorts and pics of various angles of their balls. Alex smiled and asked if we wanted to be a part of history. Pretty drunk, and since no faces—hell yes.

We dropped our shorts and were naked. He got the camera from the kitchen and started taking a couple of pictures from different angles between our legs and from behind our butts with balls hanging. We called Fair Play, took the camera, and he pulled his board shorts off. He looked amazing. We took a couple of pics of his hairy balls and ass. With his crooked smile, he said there would be better pics of his balls if his dick is erect. Laughing, we're like, not a problem. I went down on Alex, and boyfriend down on me. We're all hard. Took some pics. Now we start making out. Boyfriend and I both on Alex. Me kissing and licking from the top, boyfriend licking and nibbling from Alex's toes. He's now sprawled on the bar, and we meet in the middle, kissing each other over and around his hard dick, his balls. We flip him and boyfriend eats the beautiful, pink, furry asshole, and I slide around for Alex to suck me hard. It's not long till boyfriend and I switch places, and I slide my seven inches into that juicy wet hole. As I start my sweet slow roll, long slow strokes into Alex, I see boyfriend move towards the door where Ricardo is standing watching.

Boyfriend pulls Ricardo close, whispers in his ear, and nuzzles his neck. Ricardo smiles and pulls off his tank, shorts, and underwear. Boyfriend immediately begins to service a short thick cock, at first almost buried in bush. We're all going at it. Sweat, sweat, precum everywhere. We're all four of us wet and slippery.

We move to the floor, and I wind up sitting on Alex's hard dick. He has an idea. He holds up two fingers and rubs my ass. Ricardo knows what's about to happen. He rolls over and is hard and bigger than I expected. He kisses his fingers and touches my hole. Now I understand and am thrilled with the idea of double penetration, of those two men's hard penises deep in me. Boyfriend smiles and nods. Boyfriend drops another blob or two of spit on my hole, and Ricardo starts to slide in. It's a big helmet head, but he's gentle and slides in deep. I'm caught between them. Impaled, and can't move because they've effectively pinned me between. Ricardo starts to slide in and out. Pumping gets harder, rougher. No doubt Ricardo and Alex have done this together before; their rhythm is amazing for them and for me. Boyfriend shifts to stand in front of me and over them and gags me deep down my throat. All three cum hard, violent spasms in my holes. Alex takes one last hard thrust and hits my prostate, and I shoot as well. We are totally spent, in a pile, covered in sweat and cum. Awesome, so awesome. We just collapsed.

Alex was first to pull away, and we all headed down the stone steps to the beach, going naked into the gentle surf. Arms wrapped around each other, we floated and bobbed and kissed for a long while before we headed back up the steps to our scattered clothes, the jeep, and then the ship.

Boyfriend's friendliness and exhibitionism lands lots of crazy sex stories, including more fun on the rest of the cruise. But this one still warms me with fond memories and a hard dick.

I've been getting my hair cut at the same hotel barbershop in Bangkok for nearly twenty years. In the past few months, I've met a twenty-eight-year-old Thai hottie who works there at the front desk, and we've become fuck buddies. Sometimes when I'm passing through the hotel daytimes for work reasons, I walk by reception and just smile to say hi. He's usually busy with guests and is very discreet; he doesn't want to lose his job.

Last Saturday, I had told him that I was having a haircut and that I would swing by reception to say hi. While I was in the barber's chair, I got a text message from him, saying that he wanted to fuck me in a guest room. Nice idea, I thought, and replied yes. I asked if he had any lube—he didn't, and I don't carry it around with me. I might be a slut but not to that extent! He told me to come to him at reception, ask about availability of suites over Christmas and New Year, and ask to see a room.

After the barber finished, I went to the men's room next to the barbershop, part of the health club/gym there. Of course, they have those miniature bottles of moisturizer and hair gel etc., so I helped myself to the hand and body lotion.

Two minutes later, I'm up at reception doing as I was told. Yes sir, he says, we do have some availability in that period. May I see a room or two please? Of course, sir, please follow me.

We walk into the empty room which is on the pool level, and he closed the patio blinds. We kiss and he is rock hard—so am I. But there is little time for romance; we need action. He's pulling off his uniform—a really nice suit, tie, and shirt—and I'm undoing my jeans. Our trousers and briefs are around our ankles, we suck each other a bit, and then he's lubed up and slides inside me. It takes me a minute or so to get used to it, and then he's pounding me over the arm of the sofa until he starts to say, "I'm going to cum, I'm going to cum." Two minutes later, I can feel his cock enlarge, his breathing speeds up, and he gasps that he's cumming. I let him finish to catch his breath, slide off his cock, and I jerk off quickly. I'm always so turned on when I've been bred; it never takes long.

He had thoughtfully brought some tissues for us to clean up, so we dressed quickly and were out of the room in less then ten minutes. I let him go back to reception, I headed home, as happy as Larry.

I'll give that hotel five stars for service!

It was my first trip to Las Vegas, back in the 90s, before internet was big. I was dating a guy and living with him after my divorce. His mother and father were fond of me and invited him and me to Las Vegas for their yearly visit. We were to go in October, so it would not be too hot out there. We took the red eye out of Syracuse NY and flew to Las Vegas, staying at the Sahara Hotel for a week. Since it was my first time, I budgeted my money so it would last the entire week. My boy friend and I were exploring the first day after check in, walking the strip, and seeing what was around. At this time there were no barriers on the sidewalks, and you could see everything. His parents let us do what we wanted and only asked us to join them for dinner and a couple of shows. This is where I saw my first drag queen.

Travel

Well, long story short, I was out exploring one evening on my own and ended up at a casino, playing slot machines alone. This guy that worked for the casino came up to me and asked if I wanted to have some fun and told me he got off at midnight. I said sure why not, so he said to meet him at this slot machine at midnight, and he would take me to a bar for some entertainment. He was 6' tall, salt and pepper hair, tan, and good looking—nice ass and chest from what I could see thorough his uniform.

So I met him at midnight, and we went to a leather bar. Nothing against leather bars but not my cup of tea. I agreed to go, and when we got there the only thing in the bar that was leather was the bartender's vest. Not what I had seen before on leather nights in Utica, NY, at the Hub Bar. Once inside, he bought me a drink, and we started talking. All of a sudden this younger man shows up and kisses the guy I was with. A long passionate kiss. Ended up it was his live-in lover, and he was a black jack dealer at the Horseshoe Casino in old Las Vegas. Well, after about two hours, they asked me to join them back at their house for drinks and a soak in their hot tub. Beautiful home not far off the strip, gave me a tour and a drink. We went to the patio where they had their hot tub. Both of them stripped naked right in front of me. The older gentleman was slim, nice body, and about a seven inch cock. The younger guy was a little stocky but still a firm body, a nice ass, and an eight inch cock.

Both slipped into the hot tub and told me to strip and join them, so I did. Once in the water with the jets on, they slid closer to me and started to play with my cock and balls. So I returned the favor. I was in all my glory because I had always wanted to try a threesome. My boy friend at the time, however, would not go for it. So one thing led to another. I was sucking the young one's cock as he sat on the side of the hot tub, and the older gentleman was trying to fuck me. Not sure what was wrong, but he never got his cock into my hole at that time. So we moved to the bedroom after a while, and the younger guy forced me to get on top of him, between his legs, and suck his cock, while the older gentleman rimmed my tight hole. This was the first time I had that done to me, and it was pure pleasure. I really did not want to get fucked, especially bareback at the time, so I kept pushing his cock out of my hole. Still sucking his boyfriend's cock, I got him eventually to cum. Then all of a sudden he left the room and said he was going out for last call. The older guy said OK, so I thought it was time for me to leave. This guy had other plans for me. He said, "Now suck my cock like you did for my boyfriend until I cum, and then I will take you back to your hotel." So I sucked on him, and he on me until we both blew.

Travel

He took me back to my hotel. When I arrived, my boyfriend was asleep in the room. Being the horny guy that I was, I washed up and with a raging hard-on went over to him. I started to kiss and lick his entire body to get him nice and hard for me to ride his seven-plus inch cock. I got him good and hard, lubed up my hole and his cock, sat right on top of him, and enjoyed the best fuck I had ever had with him. Of course, there was plenty more with other men, but this was the best with him. So my trip to Vegas was fun, exciting, and the first of many.

FEEDBACK

The authors were asked to comment on sharing their adventures.

Had I been able to access these as a much younger person, what a difference it would have made to know I was not alone in my explorations, fantasies, and desires.

Pretty cool that other men could be getting off on my experience—like having a little audience.

The younger guys never experienced what we went through and I think it's important to let them read about it. For some of us older guys this was an extremely fun and sexually charged time in our lives. The hunt was as sexy as the act.

Writing the stories made the guys I was with more alive in my mind.

Enjoy sharing important moments in my life.

I know we are not alone—thank God.

Videos are staged but these are real life happenings.

I lead a very conservative, married life. We have been together almost 30 years. We have great sex. But these stories do help recharge my batteries and take me into a fantasy world where I had never ventured.

Feedback

Just to get it off my chest. I had never told anyone about the adventures that I wrote about. They seemed too private.

These are real, not some goof just writing down a fantasy that he wishes he tried. Feels good to share my life, do not have many gay friends to talk to about this.

It was exciting to relive the experience. I got hard all over again.

We never tire of new stimulation and each story is another possibility for unzipping and jacking.

Honestly, at age 70, it lets me relive some of my past pleasures and fantasies.

Always taking notes and getting new ideas. Where else can you get good stroke material that's true, and free?

Sometimes while reading the stories my imagination becomes the most realistic kind of porn, "mind-porn," which is often better than digital porn.

Many show the changes in social acceptance and are a glimpse into the struggles of gay/bi men dealing with their sexual inclinations. I love porn. I secretly wanted to be a porn actor. Sharing my stories gave me the feeling I was letting others "watch" and hopefully get turned on.

Most, if not all, of these stories would never be printed by major publishers.

That story has been in my head for a long time and you gave me the chance to let it out.

Feedback

They make me feel young and like I am part of a family, since where I live there isn't much of a gay community.

I hopefully inspired others to write, and perhaps provided some jerkoff material for them.

Men need an outlet to express their deepest and darkest secrets they may have been hiding for decades. It was like going back in time to that special place and re-living the experience. I now live in a red, rural, beach town and ain't nothin goin on here.

Sometimes they are a way to remember being 19 again, full of cum with very hard erections. They can be very therapeutic.

Because of the different way that guys hook up, so easy for some and so difficult for others, like my self. I am 68, and have not been with a man in quite a while, while other men my age are still very active, something I wish I could say.

They sometimes remind me of my own adventures when I was younger, and make me jealous now that I'm older! I write because I am a cheap whore who loves to have sex outdoors—adds a frisson if we might get caught—plus I don't have to make small talk or breakfast!

Hopefully to help those coming out to feel a bit more comfortable with their own stories and to know they are not alone

I love reading stories about other guys' first times! Have always wondered how they got into guys and how it happened.

Wondering what else is out there. More than what's available in my backwards town? Yes, there IS really something out there.

Feedback

To see if there are any other positions I have not tried, or something new that I need to explore.

They're entertainment and most of the time they're the only way I can 'talk' about such stuff.

Makes me feel proud to be one of the group.

Men of different shapes and ages are just as horned, just as sexual, just as daring and, most importantly, just as active. Builds a sense of belonging with other horned pigs, even if we never meet.

Like getting a nice note from a friend expressing joy in sharing his special event.

Like reading good novels, allows me to go places I can't go to & meet guys I could never meet in real life.

It was my first experience and started me on a path that ended with a partner, now husband of 39 years.

They help me feel comfortable and 'normal' about where I am in my life's journey.

Fun to relive & share some of my wildest experiences.

Gay sex is still way too often considered bad or dirty and men who enjoy it can be thought of as over-sexed or 'wrong,' which I totally disagree with.

So that younger men can better understand our shared gay culture and history. For older writers like myself these stories help preserve the memories, not just of sexual encounters but of friends and partners long ago lost to AIDS.

Feedback

Because at 57 I no longer have sex. Mainstream porn is more focused on the very young and hugely hung. These stories offer much more variety.

To share my story with everyone was a kind of release for me. There haven't been many people that I could share that story with—especially without judgment. Hopefully, they found it just as hot as I remember it.

I need relief, or at least confirmation that I can still receive satisfaction, which is most important because I am 77 years old.

Almost like a revisit to the actual sexual experience, a chance to reflect back on some good times.

A value to each that they are not alone in this closet.

I look forward to these stories cause I'm not getting sex at home, and I rely on them to get aroused and stimulated.

I rarely say thank-you but I am now. These stories have come to mean the world to me.

Though I also dated girls in high school I could never deny that I loved watching the guys and the men around me. And when my chance came, I took it, and ran with it, and never looked back.

Feedback

Choke the Chicken

(AKA masturbate, wank. JO, beat off, jerk off, beat your meat, jack off, ejaculate, play with yourself, whack off, fly solo, frigging, pleasure yourself, pound your pud, spank the monkey)

Dear Readers —

In case you're not convinced that this book's an absolute marvel, these last few pages are guaranteed to be the clincher. A few weeks ago under the subject "Major Scientific Survey," I asked my members how often they masturbated per week (no subtlety here). For the record, a variety of studies concede that almost all men do, do often, and do everywhere, though few admit it. Gays, straights, teens, retireds, singles, marrieds, plumbers, priests, especially politicians. But since this is the dirty guarded secret among all males, you would be hard pressed to find a single confession, let alone the dozens that follow here. We just asked that they be candid and truthful.

They were!

Hi Jack, I typically pull my pants down and play with my cock daily, I don't ALWAYS cum when I masturbate. Sometimes I just enjoy the feeling of playing with my erection. I do LOVE to have an audience and often go on cam when I am alone in the mornings for 30-40 min before I have to head to work. Even have had a few guys capture my little masturbation shows on cam and send me a copy! (Isn't digital great!) Sometimes I use my fleshlight.

I used to do it every day but once I got a partner, I usually fuck him daily. He doesn't mind that a bit.

Once a week by myself.

Hey Jack, Sorry been crazy with work & didn't get to respond before now. Long Answer: I always try to edge while slowly scrolling thru your emails daily (now you know why I miss you badly when you are off living life LOL). I especially get super

Feedback

hard looking at the vintage/retro porn that reminds me of my childhood. I always try to shoot a load before lunch, sometimes two. At night, if I get bored I switch over to either Chaturbate or Jmeeting & jack with a fellow jacker. Short answer: 1-3 times daily :)

At least 3 times a week with a fleshlight!

3-4.

I hope this one makes it to you. At 81 I still JO at least a couple times a week.

Usually 7-10 times a week. Sometime twice in one day. Sometimes not at all. Unfortunately all alone.

Once a week.

One to two times a week unless someone does it for me:)))

Prostatectomy (complete removal) five years ago

Can't get an erection, no pills such as Levritra, Viagra or Cialis work. Direct injections nor vacuum pump work

Yet for the past year I awaken twice a week at 3:30-4 am with a full blown erection that last from 1-4 min. I can climax with lots of manual stimulation laying on my left side stroking with my right hand

Anywhere from 10-45 min

I normally do it before going to sleep, 10 pm, and upon awakening at 6 am

Feedback

I once had a complete blow job at the baths. Bless his heart! He sucked a soft cock for 20-30 minutes till I climaxed with no reward.

Once a week.

Once or twice a week depending on what my dick asks for.

Around 10 times per week when I'm alone. I also cum, too, when I can find it - single right now and hoping for better.

Age 55 in Bangkok.

Usually 3-5 times a week. Unfortunately, by myself. Prefer to have some meaty cock in my mouth while doing it, but that is just a treat...like ice cream!

At least 6.

Jack, Every night, don't always cum, but I play with my tackle every night. Thanks.

Once or twice a week.

2 or 3 times a week.

You asked about my regularity of getting off.
I have no special time frame for getting off. Usually it is when I am in the mood which is at least daily. Even in my late 60s I feel the need to get off by the second day. That's when I take measures into my hands and complete the act. Years ago, suggestive magazine stories were my catalyst. Now-a-days if I am without company good internet porn and a hit of poppers leads to that great feeling of relief. Living alone and able to host at

Feedback

home leads to lots of M2M encounters. Most men contact me asking to come over or can I visit them. Most weeks I get at least three opportunities with another person. If I know one is coming up, I will hold off my hand job for the real thing.

I guess my answer would be every other day on average.

Actually I don't jack. I have several Aneros massagers (https://www.aneros.com/) that I ride two or three times a week. I save my spunk for my husband.

5-7 looking at porn using my foreskin as a hand fucker.

Three times a week, in my home office, looking at tumblr.com.

Three to four times a week, unless a partner is available, then less.

Jack, we do have fun. I usually jack about 2 times per week. Now if I could I would suck a man every day, but I don't have that opportunity.

Every night watching porn, unless I have hot man to man sex—horny all the time.

I usually edge for at least a couple of hours, three to four times a week. I usually watch porn videos or read hot stories on Nifty. I always end by shooting into my special "shot" glass and reward myself with drinking a good shot of my warm cum!

Once or twice.

2 to 3 times a week.

Feedback

Although nearly 70, it's an every other day habit. When I was younger, every day. Cumming wasn't a daily thing, however. Even now, I like to save for a week so when I do jerk to cum, the jets are big and jump up to my chest or face. Poppers help the sensation. I use both hands and always massage the balls, which are incredibly sensitive.

3 times per week. Always with porn and vibrators and a cock ring.

Hi Jack, 4-5 times a week I have sex. I'm 64. Try to stay in shape. Very much enjoy and appreciate your emails.

Hmm. That's actually harder to answer than you'd think! So, by myself, I jerk at least once a day and usually at the end of the day when I'm unwinding and reading Jack's stuff or watching porn!!! Add to that that jacking is generally part of play when a fuck buddy visits, usually 2-3 times a week. SO that'll be in the neighborhood of 10 wanks per week. Probably less than the daily activity of some of you studs, but then, I am 62.

Your survey: Not sure if you wanted age...56. No sex in years. Weeknights 1-3 times before bed. Weekends 7-10 each day.

Ok, for your survey: I'll say 0.5 per week, solo. Just a guess.

At least daily.

Every day without fail, and sometimes twice depending on sex with my partner.

Every night, watching porn unless I have hot man to man sex—horny all the time.

About twice a week if all goes well.

Feedback

Hugs Jack. When I am well I get to suck at least two cocks per week. As to jerking off, only when I see a guy to do it. Oh, I always swallow, always.

5/7. used to be 7/7 but hey, I'm getting older. I was married to a woman for eighteen years and have been partnered with a man for twelve. Rate is the same single or partnered. It is not about jackin being a substitute for available sex. It's that there is no substitute for jackin. If I had to choose between sex with someone else and jackin, it's a VERY tough choice.

Two times a week and love doing it to big black cock vids, have become addicted to them.

Hello Jack, Hope you're doing well. For your survey, I jerk off at least 3-4 time s a week, as my boyfriend is a nurse and works nightshifts. Even jerk off with him, and watching him jerk off after I suck him is hot. Best to you.

Five times per month, on average.

ONLY when I can't find a hot ass or mouth to satisfy me though.

Hi Jack, I jerk off about twice a week. My favorite place seems to have become in our sauna while watching porn on my laptop and using some poppers. I like having my nips worked over, so I often have them clamped and use vibrating toothbrushes to use on them before I bring myself off. If I'm certain I have time and that I won't get interrupted, I insert a butt plug and get out my cock pump. I especially like jerking off after having my cock in the pump. I hope this helps your scientific study. :-)

3 times per week....watching porn.

Feedback

Wank daily, sometimes solo, sometimes with bff when he feeds me.

About ten times per week. Every night in bed (usually alone, boo hoo!) and most times after my run in Lumpini Park, normally with a willing hand or mouth.

Six times a week, usually at my desk, and tumblr seems to be the best site for good ole porn.

Hi Jack. After my radical Prostatectomy and radical abdominal Lymphadenectomy surgery for prostate cancer at the age of 60 (I am now 70) I was afraid I would have to say farewell to my beloved lifelong friend—Dick.
 However, I was doing some brain function and neurological plasticity research at the time of my operation, and I discovered that in some cases, and with enough persistence, one can reprogram the circuitry of his brain after a major trauma or surgery.
 Because I enjoyed a strong libido and had masturbated at least once and often two or three times a day since I was twelve years old, I was determined to do my best to continuing enjoying sex for as long as I could.
 Having lost the nerves that are responsible for an erection, I resorted to the use of a vacuum pump which I used several times a day for thirty minutes or more just to keep my penis from shrinking into oblivion. It took weeks and perhaps months of diligent daily practice, but eventually I discovered that if I pumped my cock hard then used a tight ring on my shaft I could enjoy enough of an erection to masturbate and achieve an orgasm.
 I also tried the blue pill to no avail. Penis injections and hormonal urethral suppositories made it feel like I had a plastic

cock wedged between my legs, and at worst were as painful as hell.

Eventually, with my partner's loving help, I was able to regain the ability to get and sustain a natural quasi-hard (sadly not hard enough for penetration) erection that totally delights in being masturbated and all other manner of stimulation. Although I no longer have the ability to ejaculate semen, the good news is that I now leak some pre-cum during masturbation and during orgasm. Speaking of which, my current orgasms are the best and most intense orgasms I have ever experienced in my entire life.

That's not to say I wouldn't be delighted to get my ole buddy Dick back but hey!, an intense toe curler+ orgasm is darnn good for a guy in my situation. My current goal is to live long enough for science to make it possible for me to receive a prostate transplant.

Don't laugh, doctors are routinely doing penis transplants in South Africa, and I'm definitely getting one of those too.

I shared this with you just in case there are some piggies out there that may be dealing with a similar set of conditions. My advice is, never, never, never give up on your best buddy.

And to finally answer your original question, my partner and I masturbate each other about three times a week. I'm guessing another one or two solo wanks each per week just for good measure. Our favorite position is to lay side by side with our heads on opposite ends of the bed and our hands on one another's cocks and balls. In that position, we can tirelessly stroke, stretch ball-sacks, caress, swallow, massage, penetrate and edge each other for extended periods of time (occasionally while watching porn together), and we also vary the type of orgasm we have from individual orgasms to one simultaneous intense orgasm.

We also enjoy giving and receiving oral and anal sex together which may or may not increase the number of orgasms we enjoy in a week.

Feedback

Now that I'm thinking of it, Jack, I sincerely appreciate receiving my daily dose of porn from you. The porn I received from you on a daily basis after my operation was definitely my most valuable tool of recovery, and is to this day my favorite porn to solo-masturbate to. Thank you, thank you.

CPSIA information can be obtained
at www.ICGtesting.com
Printed in the USA
FSHW012000080919
61824FS